Britain in the Age of
Walpole

Britain in the Age of Walpole

EDITED BY
JEREMY BLACK

ST. MARTIN'S PRESS   New York

St. Martin's Press, Inc., 175 Fifth Avenue, New York, NY 10010
Printed in Hong Kong
Published in the United Kingdom by Macmillan Publishers Ltd
First published in the United States of America in 1984

ISBN 0-312-09826-X

Library of Congress Cataloging in Publication Data
Main entry under title:

Britain in the age of Walpole.

Bibliography: p.
Includes index.
1. Great Britain—Politics and government—1714-1760
—Addresses, essays, lectures.   2. Walpole, Robert,
Earl of Orford, 1676-1745—Addresses, essays, lectures.
I. Black, Jeremy.
DA498.B74   1984   941.07   84-15089
ISBN 0-312-09826-X

Contents

Preface

EIGHTEENTH-CENTURY British history has been noted traditionally for the vigour, not to say acrimony, with which
controversies have been conducted. It is therefore a particular
pleasure to record that this volume was produced without any
disagreement. Differing views are presented, as is only healthy,
and the following chapters provide evidence for the very
vigorous nature of current historical scholarship for this period.
Despite considerable effort, it was unfortunately impossible to
fulfil earlier plans for chapters on social and religious developments. I should like to thank the other contributors for their
invaluable advice and assistance, and Sarah Mahaffy and
Vanessa Peerless of Macmillan for their patient help. Finally, I
should like to thank my wife for all her support.

It is an honour to head the list of acknowledgements with the
name of Her Majesty Queen Elizabeth II by whose gracious
permission the Stuart Papers were consulted. Prince Kinsky,
the Duke of Devonshire, the Duke of Richmond, the Marquess
of Cholmondeley, the Earl of Egremont, the Earl of Harrowby,
Earl Waldegrave, Lady Teresa Agnew and Lady Lucas kindly
granted access to their papers.

Thanks are also due to the Huntington Library, the British
Academy, the British Council, the German Academic
Exchange Scheme, the Institut Francophone de Paris, and the
Staff Travel and Research Fund of Durham University.

J.B.

Introduction: an Age of Political Stability?*

JEREMY BLACK

> We enjoy at this Hour an uninterrupted Peace, while all the rest of Europe is either actually engaged in War, or is on the very Brinks of it. Our Trade is at a greater Heighth than ever, while other Countries have scarce any, thro' their own Incapacity, or the Nature of their Government. We are free from Religious Disturbances, which distract almost every other Nation. Our Liberties and our Properties are perfectly secure
>
> *Daily Courant*, 13 June 1734

IT is not necessary to resort to ministerial propaganda, as quoted above, in order to note features of stability in this period. The most dramatic was the longevity of the Walpole government. Walpole dominated British politics for over twenty years, a ministry that contrasted with the preceding and succeeding periods of short governments and a perpetual sense of political instability. To contemporaries this longevity was the most dramatic political feature of the period. Its causes and consequences were much debated, and political assumptions and practices were tested at the time and they have been the subject of historical debate ever since. It is this ministerial longevity that is the most distinctive and widely debated feature of the Walpolean era, and this introduction will not only seek to draw attention to the main reasons for it but will also intimate its limitations.

* I should like to thank Eveline Cruickshanks, Harry Dickinson and Grayson Ditchfield for commenting on an earlier draft of this essay.

I

The early modern period of European history was one in which political legitimacy in monarchical states (the overwhelming majority of countries) was based upon dynasticism. Kingdoms with an elective component in kingship – Poland and to a lesser extent Sweden being the clearest examples – were in a minority, and there had been no attempt in 1688–9 to introduce this as a component of the British constitution. The political coup of 1688 inaugurated a prolonged period of serious dynastic insecurity in British history, a period that was only to be ended by violence. The existence of a rival claimant to the throne, supported by a certain amount of domestic opinion, was a destabilising feature in British politics. It had major implications in international relations, for foreign powers at odds with Britain could always play the Jacobite card. Such a situation was hardly novel: foreign powers attempted to exploit the Catholics in the late sixteenth century and the Royalists in the 1650s. It was serious after 1688 due to the combination of the continuance of the 'British problem' and the rise of Anglo-French rivalry as a major feature of international relations. William III's success in securing England in one brief campaign in 1688, a success that, as Childs has recently shown, was far from certain militarily,[1] had not led to the automatic gain of Scotland and Ireland. The conquest of the latter in particular had been a difficult affair, made more so by the ability of the French to intervene in Irish affairs. Thereafter Scotland and Ireland had to be held down.

The siting of most of the British army in Ireland in the Walpolean period was not simply because this was fiscally expedient – a transfer of the cost of support to the Irish taxpayers – but also because Ireland was a major security risk. Given favourable sailing conditions French warships could reach Irish waters from their major Atlantic base at Brest before the British navy could intervene. The ministry also kept an anxious eye on, and troops in, Scotland. The tone of concern about a potentially explosive situation in State Papers (Scotland) for the 1720s is unmistakable. The security situation was clearly linked to the prospect of foreign intervention. In 1729 General Wade writing from Dalnacardok noted, 'tho' the

Jacobites are more numerous here than in any other part of His Majesty's dominions, by the present disposition of the forces it seems to me impracticable for them to give any disturbance to the government unless supported by troops from abroad'.[2]

Preventing such support was a major feature of Walpolean foreign policy, for this policy was underpinned by a sense of the precarious nature of the security situation. There was no doubt of the ease with which the 'British problem', the difficulties facing English control of Scotland and Ireland, could become serious. The Jacobite rising in 1715 had posed major difficulties. Though the Royal Navy was the strongest in Europe it was not itself sufficient to guarantee the security of the realm.[3] Spanish troops were landed in Scotland in 1719, while the French threatened the control of the Channel in 1744. Thus, the Jacobite threat played a major role in the Anglo-French alliance of 1716–31. The Whig ministry sought to prevent French aid to challenges to British security, just as George I hoped to obtain French assistance for Hanoverian security. The alliance was inherited by the Walpolean ministry and led to political difficulties, particularly in the parliamentary sessions of the late 1720s and 1730 when it served as the basis for serious Opposition attacks that played a role in the 1730 British decision to abandon the alliance. In the late 1710s and 1720s, however, the alliance had played a major role in providing the background for British stability; in the Irish and Scottish case quiescence might be the more appropriate term. In 1725 the French chargé d'affaires in London wrote that one of the major points of government policy was to deny all malcontents, particularly the Jacobites, opportunities to embarrass the government, and that the absence of foreign intervention was crucial.[4]

Had the British ministry maintained good relations with France or at least continued the carefully measured combination of hostility and neutrality of the 1730s it is very probable that the dramatic reopening of the Jacobite and British questions in 1744–6 would not have occurred. Royal and domestic political pressures for intervention against France in the War of the Austrian Succession (1740–8) were too great to make such a policy possible but it is notable that few attempts were made to minimise Anglo-French differences, and thus limit French support for Jacobitism in the war. The French did not want to fight Britain. This had been realised by Walpole, and used by the British ministry during the War of the Polish Succession (1733–5) to limit the extent of French action. During that war, Britain had armed the navy against France, and actively negotiated against her, but no British troops had been sent to Europe. The policy had succeeded. France had not attacked the Austrian Netherlands (Belgium) and had ignored Jacobite requests for assistance. The subtlety of this approach was lost on Lord Carteret who effectively directed foreign policy after Walpole's fall. He destroyed one of the bases of Walpolean political stability, the understanding with France that had survived, albeit in an attenuated form, in the 1730s, and thus precipitated the '45, the greatest crisis that affected the eighteenth-century British state.

J. H. Plumb in his influential work on the growth of political stability from 1675 to 1725 wrote of England, and the factors he referred to were largely restricted to England (and to the Scottish Lowlands to a lesser extent).[5] The wider question of the stability of the British state, more precarious than many historians have allowed for, was closely related to the international situation. Walpole avoided provoking France, the only power capable of seriously intervening; Walpole's successors were fortunate that France put so little effort into helping the Jacobites.[6]

The relationship between Jacobitism and internal English politics is a matter of controversy. In particular, the extent to which the Tories were Jacobite has aroused a lot of recent discussion, with two views being advanced. Dr Cruickshanks has argued that most Tories were Jacobite, whereas Dr Colley has claimed that they were a well-organised party, whose loyalty to the Hanoverian succession was clear, because they had serious prospects of office. Colley thus differs from the view that the Tories were driven to Jacobitism by their proscription from the spoils of power.[7] At least three facts are clear. First, there is no evidence about the attitude of the bulk of the party's rank and file members. Secondly, evidence of widespread, continuous and direct Tory support for Jacobite intrigues is ambiguous, as is only to be expected in the case of conspiracy. Given the systematic ministerial interception of the post, the skill of the government deciphering system,[8] the difficulty of keeping secrets at the factious Jacobite court and the legacy of successful ministerial discovery of Jacobite plots, it is not surprising that serious Jacobite plotters showed a healthy disregard for the written word and the future convenience of historians. The Jacobites claimed widespread Tory support, particularly when seeking foreign assistance; it is difficult to assess how far these claims can be accepted. Thirdly, there is little doubt that Walpole and many of his supporters believed that the Tories were Jacobite. 'Take away the Jacobites and where will you find a Tory', noted Charles Hanbury-Williams in 1739, though he accepted that others disagreed with this view.[9] Walpole frequently told the House of Commons that Jacobite sympathies underlay opposition moves. These claims were not simply designed to taunt the opposition with the charge of treason. Walpole genuinely feared a restoration of the Pretender and believed the Tories were crypto Jacobites.

Dr Colley is particularly strong in her work on the organisation of the Tory party which she shows to have been well led and organised both at Westminster and in the constituencies, and to have enjoyed considerable public support. Her claim that the Tories were loyal, because they knew there was a chance that they would be accepted into a mixed ministry, as a result of George I and George II being prepared to entertain some flexibility in party choice, is more surprising. The failure to produce much evidence for this is understandable, as neither king saw the written word as an obligation for monarchy, and there are few guides, and no sure ones, to their opinions. The evidence Colley cites is weak and will not support her claim that in 1717, 1721, 1725 and 1727 the monarchs went some way towards exploring the practicality of a mixed ministry. The floating of such rumours at times of political crisis is understandable, but royal interest was restricted to recruiting individual Tories of ability, such as Harcourt and Trevor, into the ministry. There was no attempt to create a mixed ministry, nor were those Tories who were recruited able to ensure further recruitment or changes in policy.[10] Neither monarch enjoyed the restrictions to their power resulting from Whig dominance, but both were aware of the incompatibilities between Tory and royal views. The Tories were stridently opposed to Hanoverian influence in British foreign policy, and were keen defenders of their role in the negotiation of the Peace of Utrecht of 1713 when Britain had abandoned her allies, including Hanover. Support for the interests of the Church of England, vital to Tory ideology and essential to their sense of identity confused by the choice between a Hanoverian Lutheran and a Catholic Stuart, clashed with Hanoverian sympathy for nonconformists. George I was concerned to support the interests of oppressed German Protestants and to encourage better relations between Protestant sects, policies alien to Tory ecclesiastical suppositions. The monarchs wanted ministers supporting policies they approved of, and whom they could trust. That they felt the Tories did not fit the bill was noted by foreign envoys in London, ever concerned to discover royal attitudes. The Saxon Le Coq noted George I's total support for the Whigs, the Sardinian Ossorio George II's conviction that the Tories were Jacobites. In 1721 the Duke of Newcastle noted:

> The report of the Tories coming in, having reached the King's ears, he has been so good as to declare to me and many other of his servants the concern he has at the report, and has assured us, that he neither has nor ever had any such thoughts, and is determined to stand by the Whigs, and not take in any one single Tory. He is very sensible the Whig party is the only security he has to depend on.[11]

Possibly the monarchs were wrong; maybe they sought to rationalise the Tory exclusion by persuading themselves of Tory Jacobitism. After 1721 it was clear that Walpole was prepared to accommodate royal wishes. The uneasy relationship between George I and many of his Whig ministers over Baltic policy, that had produced the Whig schism of 1717 and fostered reports of the king turning to the Tories, had been replaced, in an easier international situation, by co-operation, and that remained the case for the rest of the Walpole ministry. Thereafter the Crown had no need to turn to the Tories, and George II's refusal to create a mixed ministry in 1727 was an intelligent response to the political situation. The decision of the Tory parliamentary leadership under Sir William Wyndham to support co-operation with the Opposition Whigs, the so-called Country party, and the stress this alliance placed in the sessions from 1726 until 1732 upon attacking foreign and Hanoverian commitments, such as subsidies to the Landgrave of Hesse–Cassel for troops to protect Hanover, helped to consolidate royal support for the ministry.

It was principally by co-operation between Tories and Opposition Whigs that the ministry was seriously challenged. This method had been attempted by Walpole when in 1717 he went into opposition to the Stanhope–Sunderland ministry. Despite serious parliamentary challenges the ministry survived, and the 1720 reconciliation that brought Walpole and Townshend back into the ministry did not represent the sweeping success they had envisaged in 1717–18. George I's clear determination to support the Stanhope–Sunderland ministry had played a major role in enabling it to maintain its position.

In the early 1720s Opposition Whigs, such as Cowper and Wharton, co-operated with the Tories, but with little success. The period 1722–5 is probably the most obscure and least studied of all eighteenth-century British history. Scanty sources present a particular problem, but these years are of great importance because they witnessed the establishment of the Walpolean 'system'. Walpole displayed his considerable skills to great advantage. His fiscal acumen and connections played a major role in helping the reconstruction of the machinery of public credit after the South Sea Bubble. The South Sea Company survived and credit was restored. Walpole's electoral skills were displayed in the general election of 1722, which witnessed more contests and more Whig gains than the previous one of 1715. Walpole's handling of the Atterbury Plot, a Jacobite conspiracy discovered in 1722 thanks to information supplied by the French ministry, was more intelligent and more successful than the previous Whig attempt to capitalise on the attitudes of a Tory cleric, the Sacheverell trial of 1710.[12] Much of Walpole's success in this period was due to factors outside his control: the continuation of Anglo-French co-operation, and the deaths of his principal Whig opponents – Stanhope and Craggs in 1721, Sunderland in 1722 – and of much of the episcopate. The latter permitted a strengthening of the Whig position in the Lords; the former helped to resolve the political crisis within the Whig party, that had not been settled by the 1720 reconciliation. The 1722 general election, the Atterbury Plot, and Sunderland's attempts to gain Tory support against Walpole, created a sense of peculiar strain and challenge in 1722. Thereafter there was a sense of survival and of a dominant ministerial position, marked by Tory demoralisation, the fairly quiescent sessions of 1724 and 1725 and Walpole's success in removing Sunderland's former supporters – Carteret, Roxburgh, Macclesfield, Cadogan – from influence.

The mid 1720s witnessed a new attempt to create an alliance of Tories and Opposition Whigs. A small group of Opposition Whigs under William Pulteney, who had gone into opposition in 1725 largely out of thwarted ambition, allied with the Tories. Under the influence of Lord Bolingbroke an attempt was made to create a united 'country' political programme for the Opposition. This programme stressed non-party government and violently denounced the supposed corruption of British society and political culture under Walpole.[13] However, it proved impossible to fuse the Tories and the Opposition Whigs. Each remained a separate identifiable element in an Opposition that was therefore handicapped in its attempts to defeat Walpole in Parliament. The failure of the Bolingbroke programme indicated the continued resilience of Whig–Tory differences, particularly over ecclesiastical and foreign policy issues. It also indicated the entrenched nature of Whig and Tory ideologies, and the limited appeal of Bolingbroke's ideas. The ministerial *London Journal* commented in 1730: "'Tis in vain to carry virtue up to a romance, and fly to Harrington's Oceana and schemes of Government which never existed, but in men's heads; nor ever will exist here.'[14]

Ministerial success in surviving attack from the Opposition owed much not only to Opposition weakness and Walpole's political ability, but also to consistent royal support. George II genuinely valued Walpole's abilities; Opposition hopes that he would discard him on his accession (1727), during the ministerial disputes in the winter of 1729–30 and in early 1733 (the excise crisis), or after the death of Walpole's prominent supporter Queen Caroline (1737), proved abortive. During the 1733 political crisis, when George II was under great pressure to remove Walpole, he chose to support him rather than the courtiers to whom he had been closest as Prince of Wales – the Earls of Chesterfield and Scarborough. The importance of royal support is enabling first the Sunderland–Stanhope ministry and then Walpole to weather attacks placed the Opposition in a difficult position. They could hope that the ministry would jeopardise its political position by contentious legislation, as with the Stanhope–Sunderland ministry, and Walpole's excise legislation, or that they would embark upon an over-ambitious foreign policy, as did the Stanhope–Sunderland ministry. However, royal support for the ministry created a major problem. The Opposition had to consider how far they could safely oppose a policy in which the king was interested, and how best to persuade the king to change ministers. Demonstrating that the ministry's control of Parliament or of elections was less than secure was important. In 1722 the Opposition MP Archibald Hutcheson hoped that ministerial failure to win the two Westminster seats in the general election would

> open the King's eye, and give him a different view of things, than that in which sycophants and flatterers, and I may say traitors to him and to their country, have set the same. This might occasion an alteration of some in employments; who, although they deal pretty much with the Devil, would appear to His Majesty not to be such conjurers as they pretend to.[15]

Electoral difficulties were eased by the Septennial Act of 1716, which provided for parliaments of seven years, in place of the former three, and ministerial parliamentary control was helped by the avoidance of contentious legislation. It was not that little legislation was envisaged, prepared or passed; much was, particularly in Walpole's field of expertise, the fiscal sphere. Rather the scope of legislation was limited. This contrasts with the 1710s, a decade which had seen first Tory and then Whig (under the Earl of Sunderland) attempts to use legislation to alter the ecclesiastical and political systems in ways that were both far-reaching and dominated by the drive for party advantage. Those who have suggested that after 1689 the British political establishment was unwilling to consider

political and institutional change need only to look at Sunderland's schemes, particularly his Peerage Bill (which would
have dramatically altered the House of Lords and the nature of
both the British state and aristocratic society), or the major
fiscal changes described by Dr Dickson as a 'financial revolution',[16] to realise that in fact far more than simply the spoils of
office was a stake in the political arena. It was this that played a
large part in producing the highly charged political atmosphere
of the late 1710s and it was against that that Walpole reacted.

Walpole was correctly convinced that Sunderland had
sought to use Whig dominance of the political system in a
manner that was dangerous. Walpole did not intend to
compromise this dominance, but he was determined not to use
it in a way that would increase political tension, by, for
example, legislating benefits for the Dissenters, important
supporters of the Whig interest whose aspirations threatened
many local political structures. Proscription of the Tories was
not to be extended to a wholesale destruction of their influence
in the localities. They were not to be deprived of control of
livings, a control that kept so much of the Church vociferously
Tory. The savage purging of the Commissions of the Peace in
the mid 1710s was not repeated in the Walpolean period.
Walpole was content with the Tories' minority status on the
Commissions. This ensured political control of the localities,
and the desired operation of the local governmental and legal
system. There was no need to extend it to a wholesale purging.
The local political elites were to be disciplined, not destroyed.
Unlike in several European countries there was to be no
attempt to introduce a new level of local government directly
under the control of the national government. Britain was not
an absolutist state, and this was seen most clearly in the small
size of the army (the navy could hardly serve to police
elections), and the absence of an attempt to remodel local
government. Compared with the introduction of new land-
registers (serving as the basis for the reform of the land tax) in
Savoy–Piedmont and Lombardy, the proposal to extend the
excise appears as a paltry instance of supposed absolutist
tendencies.

The Walpole ministry did not seek to use the legislative
process to produce far-ranging social reforms. In Hanover

elementary education had been compulsory for over a century and every major village had a schoolmaster. Professor M. Raeff has recently drawn attention to the comprehensive nature of social, economic, ecclesiastical and administrative legislation in the German states of this period, and coined the term 'the well-ordered police state' to describe them.[17] No such legislative or administrative programme existed in Britain. As with parliamentary legislation much was left to private initiative. This was clearly a source of political stability: any attempt at centrally directed reform would have produced discontent, and it could only be attempted in special circumstances, as in Scotland after the '45, whereas legislation as the result of local initiative gratified those who had pressed for it, and did not direct opposition onto the ministry. However, there was no shortage of schemes for centrally directed reform of just about every aspect of national life, and it cannot be claimed that such a concept was unknown and that there was an unchallenged *laissez-faire* attitude towards the role of the state.[18] Rather the Walpole ministry chose to avoid intervention because it believed it to be neither essential nor politically expedient. Politically the decision was a wise one. The use the opposition made of the excise legislation in 1733, and of the revival of the salt duty the previous year, indicated the dangers of attempting reform; which, as always in early modern Europe, was associated with dubious, if not corrupt, administrative changes. Legislation had to be mediated through an administrative system that was neither meritocratic, nor uncorrupt, nor securely under government control.[19] What were intended as reforms could therefore be honestly viewed as threats to the liberties and property of the subject, and the combative theme of political ideology in this period, the stress, much of it historically derived, on the perpetual struggle between the tyrannical state and the liberties of the subject, encouraged such an interpretation.[20]

II

all my political reasonings proceed upon these two positions; that there is no way to preserve the Church but by preserving the present establishment in the state; and that there is far greater probability that the Tories will be able to destroy our present establishment, in the state, than that the Dissenters will be able to destroy our establishment in the Church.

Bishop Gibson, 1717[21]

There is little sense of stability in religious developments in this period. There was an absence of consensus about the position of the Church and of the Dissenters, and the feeling of a Church under threat, from Catholicism and/or Dissent. Anti-Catholicism was the prime ideological commitment of most Englishmen, a view reiterated endlessly in Parliament, the press, sermons, and the public ceremonials of a society that grounded much of its ritual celebrations and its history on a legacy of struggle with Catholicism.[22] Tension was increased by a belief that Catholicism was growing in Britain[23] and by an awareness of the overt religious struggle in Europe. The age of Walpole falls between two clear threats to the Church of England: the risk of a Stuart succession to Queen Anne and the Jacobite invasion of 1745. Those who under Anne had taken a generally insular view of the ideological and political struggles in which the Church had been engaged, now had to face the unpalatable reality of the accession of a foreign dynasty, not of Anglican provenance, and committed to the support of foreign Protestants, such as those in the Palatinate, engaged in desperate struggles for survival; those who had taken an international view of the religious situation could not but find their assessment of the domestic situation of the Church coloured by deeply rooted Continental fears that the future of Protestantism was menaced by internal decay as well as Catholic aggression. The significance of the age of Walpole in the history of British religion is that it saw the exploration of successive solutions to this dilemma.

The ecclesiastical stance adopted by the Tories was that of support for the Church of England, and this was reciprocated by the support of much of the, particularly parochial, clergy for the Tories. The favoured policy of the Tories, as seen in the legislation of the 1710–14 Tory ministry, was the re-creation of the confessional state, a state in which non-Anglicans could have little role. In April 1721 a parliamentary bill against

'Blasphemy and prophaness' was introduced by Lord Willoughby de Brooke, the High-Church Dean of Windsor, and supported by the Tory Earl of Nottingham. It provided for the imprisonment of those who denied Trinitarian doctrine, and supervision of the dissenting educational system. The bill was defeated in the Lords: the confessional state was unacceptable to the Whigs, who relied on the electoral support of the Dissenters with whom many Whigs sympathised. The arrest the following year of the Tory High-Church Bishop of Rochester, Francis Atterbury, on a charge of high treason, symbolised the fate of the campaign for a confessional state. Faced with an unsympathetic monarch and an entrenched Whig ministry, it was reduced to impotent fulmination or treason. Anger with this situation was an important element in Tory attitudes. Logically this was irreconcilable with any Tory support for the Catholic Stuarts, but many Tories were both Jacobites and fervent supporters of the Church of England, just as in Scotland many of the Episcopalians were Jacobites.[24]

A much smaller group in the Church, led by Wake, Archbishop of Canterbury 1716–37, had taken an international view of religious matters during Anne's reign, and continued to do so, seeking salvation in far-reaching schemes of Church union, which should oppose an international barrier to the threats both of internal decline and external aggression. This scheme failed, partly because of the collapse of Wake's political position at home in the late 1710s when he fell out with the ministry, partly because of his growing unhappiness about the position of Dissent in Britain conflicted with his wider schemes, but still more because international Catholic aggression in Europe was in fact checked in the 1720s, and that states without whose support there would be no Church union had much less interest in pursuing the matter further.[25] Possibly Wake's ideas should be treated like Stanhope's talk of a new international order based on mutual guarantees and Britain as the policeman of Europe: schemes that were not feasible in domestic political terms and whose shelving under Walpole marked a triumph for sobriety.

Walpole's favoured prelate, Edmund Gibson (Bishop of Lincoln 1716–23, London 1723–48), sought to give the Whig ministry (whether Stanhope–Sunderland or Walpole) unequivocal support as a pillar of the Protestant succession, and the backing of a theology much more acceptable and nearer to that of the ordinary clergy than that of the earlier Whig episcopal protagonist, Bishop Hoadly of Bangor. The Whig ministry, bypassing Wake, used Gibson to manage the political activities of the episcopacy.[26] However Gibson found he could neither persuade Whig politicians to surrender their private application of Church patronage in the interests of the political system as a whole, nor could he rely on Walpole's support against the claims of Dissenters. These issues produced a breach between Walpole and Gibson in 1736 and led to the latter being passed over in the succession to Wake.[27]

The relationship between these ecclesiastical quarrels and the level of pastoral care provided by the Church of England is far from clear. In recent work the latter has been praised, and though conditions varied from cleric to cleric, it is clear that standards were far higher than was allowed for by many contemporaries.[28] That the Church, like the Walpole ministry, was condemned as corrupt and fallen is not surprising given the habit of judging institutions and practices in exaggerated language by unrealistically high standards. Stigmatising the Church left one resource: that of salvation by private enterprise, one of the striking aspects of which was the commencement of the evangelistic campaigns of Whitefield and Wesley. Wesley united in his pedigree both the high- and low-church traditions of English life, and combined concern for the Church establishment with first-hand contact with the much-tried Continental Protestants he had encountered in Georgia, Herrnhut and elsewhere.[29]

How far these religious disputes and developments should be regarded as a sign of instability is unclear. In a society where religion was of such fundamental importance for ideological, social, political and cultural reasons, and where norms of conduct and concepts of legitimacy owed so much to religious ideas, it was inevitable that greater attention should be devoted to religious disputes. However, it is important to note that these were not unique to Britain: Methodism was but part of the 'Great Awakening', a widespread movement of Protestant revival, whilst it could be suggested that the tension created by the Dissenters was no worse than that created in France by

Jansenism. It is always tricky to compare developments in various countries. Possibly the most important characteristic of the religious disputes in early eighteenth-century England (the position in Ireland was less favourable) was that they were conducted with little serious violence. Relations in the localities between Anglicans, Dissenters and Catholics were generally good.[30] After the widespread anti-Dissenter riots in the first years of the Hanoverian dynasty, there were few religious disturbances. The Walpole ministry's hesitation about granting Dissenter demands probably played a major role in easing religious tensions. Walpole's jettisoning of a traditional plank of the Whig platform led to Dissenter criticism, and to Walpole claiming that he took care of the Church.[31]

However Walpole's policy was probably a significant factor in maintaining political stability. Had Walpole supported Dissent, a move that would probably not have been discouraged by the Crown, he would have run a serious risk of disrupting peace in the localities and endangering his own parliamentary position. In 1751 his brother Horace wrote:

the late Lord Townshend and my Brother laid it down as a fundamental principle in their management of affairs . . . not to suffer any religious dispute to be canvassed in Parliament or any attempt to be made, if they could prevent it, to alter the laws relating to spiritual concerns being sensible that however reasonable and conciliating any proposition might be to make a stricter union and harmony among all Protestants well affected to the Government, yet the high Church party that is disaffected is so numerous, and warm and ready to lay hold of any occasion to inflame the nation, that any alteration in the form of doctrine of the Church of England would be, although in itself desirable, and right, and perhaps trivial, a dangerous attempt, as productive of greater troubles, than the good expected from it could compensate.[32]

III

The desertion of the men is an intolerable thing. I fear some

of them must be hanged. That would exasperate and provoke
perhaps: but we must govern the mob, or they will govern us,
both at sea and at home, they are got to a great degree of
insolence.

Sir Charles Wager, First Lord of the Admiralty, 1734[33]

One of the most interesting developments in studies of this
period in recent years has been the stress on extra-
parliamentary political action. This is examined in Professor
Dickinson's chapter (Chapter 2), and the role of the press, upon
which a lot of important work has been done in recent years,
receives further consideration in Dr Harris's study (Chapter 8).
It is clear that a widespread interest in politics existed and was
articulated by means of the press in such a way that a national
political consciousness was created. Provincial, Scottish and
Irish newspapers were dominated by national themes,[34] a very
significant and in no way inevitable development, and local
political conflicts tended to match national lines of division,
although the fit was never perfect. However, studies of local
politics do not always reveal the dominance of national
concerns or party configurations, and one must be wary of
extrapolating from the political culture of print, with its starkly
differential partisan positions, to that of the localities.[35]

Most evidence for popular political interest and participation comes from towns. Much good work has lately been done
on eighteenth-century towns, and it is clear that they were of
considerable importance in the definition and creation of
political attitudes.[36] However the extent of their influence over
the rural areas is difficult to evaluate, particularly as most of the
sources are of urban origin. Clearly rural interest and participation in national politics varied greatly, but it is possible that the
stress on urban activities has led to an undervaluation of rural
conservatism, and that historians in concentrating on the
fashionable subject of urban studies have neglected the
interests of the bulk of the British population. This was
certainly true of contemporaries. The electoral system favoured
the urban voter disproportionately and political programmes
were conceived in London, the dominant centre of political
activity.[37] Political attitudes were greatly influenced by urban
norms: the contrast between the respective weight in parlia-

mentary and press discussions attached to 'Trade' and the 'Landed Interest' is most instructive. Trade dominated discussion of the economy, and of ministerial policy towards the economy, in an unbalanced fashion. The interests of trade and agriculture could not be completely separated, but the latter tended to lack the vocal advocates of the former.[38] Thus, Walpole never received the political credit that he deserved for his pro-agrarian policies of the mid 1730s: the attempt in 1732–3 to shift the burden of taxation away from the land tax, and British neutrality in the War of the Polish Succession which permitted a boom in grain exports. The latter produced a benefit for the economy far greater – in terms of specie gained and aid for the rural economy – than the losses suffered when a few British merchantmen in the West Indies were seized by Spain, and yet it was the latter and not the former that received attention.

There is also the danger that in social history disproportionate attention has been devoted to urban developments. Urban culture is of great interest, and many of the schemes for social 'improvement' and/or control – for poor relief, welfare provision, crime control and medical improvement – were urban. The extent to which rural society shared in their benefits is unclear. The countryside was not cut off from the towns; the latter played a major role as markets for the countryside and as centres of and for consumption. Much has recently been made of the development of a consumer society in eighteenth-century Britain. Pedlars from towns brought wares to the countryside; rural readers read newspapers.[39] However, it is too easy to assume that rural society responded rapidly or evenly to urban developments. Hitherto there has been insufficient work on regional variations in social developments. It will only be when work on rural society matches that on urban developments, that it will be possible to discern the extent of popular participation in politics and the social composition of pre-Wilkite radicalism.[40]

IV

Growing interest in extra-parliamentary political activity, the role of the monarch and the Tories, together with an increased awareness of the non-secular nature of society and of the continued political importance of religious disputes, and the developing studies in crime and social disobedience,[41] all suggest that it is possible to re-examine profitably the theme of political stability. Important recent work by Professor Holmes on the 'social context of politics' has drawn attention to social developments, such as the growth in the professions providing outlets for younger sons, that helped to reduce tension. Holmes argues that the root cause of political stability was social stability, and that the latter owed much to a favourable conjunction of economic and social circumstances. This ensured that those outside and below the political nation did not resort to radicalism, whilst the political nation itself enjoyed a sense of common identity stemming from shared interests.[42] A number of scholars have stressed the movement of the Whigs after 1688 from the radical aspects of their traditional ideology. This can be seen as conducive to political stability, but it in no way created it. There was still a rich field of issues to contest in the Walpole period, and foreign policy disputes proved particularly bitter. However much the Whigs may have departed from their principles of the 1680s there were still substantial differences between them and the Tories.[43]

It is difficult to judge the stability of a different society: suppositions about the nature of acceptable disorder alter. Many historians find it difficult to accept that a society can be politically stable and yet also witness periodic violence:

> There was precious little stability in a system in which savage and dangerous rioting was frequent, in which a Prime Minister could stand in danger of his life at the very door of the Commons, as Walpole did in 1733, or another Prime Minister could be forced by ill-informed public pressure from outside parliament to withdraw a modest measure of reform like the Jewish Naturalisation Act of 1753.[44]

Some contemporaries were concerned about popular demonstrations. A ministerial newspaper of 1733 noted, 'the weak part in the Constitution of our Government, is a Tendency to Tumults, Sedition and Rebellion'.[45] Four years later Lord Carteret, then in opposition, stated in the Lords that 'though none of the riots or tumults that have lately happened in this kingdom, seem to have been aimed directly against the government, yet, it must be granted, that no such thing can happen in any country, in which the government is not in some way concerned'.[46] However, the ministerial response to riots varied greatly, depending on the political situation and on the degree to which they thought disturbances might be inspired or exploited for political motives. The authorities in London often reacted with caution to anguished appeals for assistance from local magistrates, particularly in the case of food riots, which rarely lasted long and whose dangerous character was often exaggerated. Encouraging astute action at the local level in the case of food riots and labour disputes was often the best policy, and serious state anxiety about the security implications of food riots appeared infrequently before the 1790s, when it became commonplace. In 1739 the French Ambassador was surprised by the lack of ministerial concern at disturbances by the workers in the Wiltshire cloth industry.[47] It is clear that contemporary commentators often exaggerated the degree of popular discontent, and the consequent likelihood of wide-spread disorders and of the collapse of the ministry. Critics of the ministry and some diplomats were particularly guilty of underestimating British political stability.[48]

Professor Dickinson suggests in his essay that stability and strife were symbiotic, not antithetical. This owed something to the limited nature of effective popular radicalism in this period. Suggestions of a different social order were present, though uncommon. In 1727 *Mist's Weekly Journal*, the leading London Tory newspaper, carried a letter from Melksham referring to the Wiltshire disturbances,

We are at length delivered from the terror of the weavers by their timely suppression. Some odd heterodox notions began to be started by them, like those of Wat Tyler and Jack Straw, of rebellious memory, which brought the country to take arms against them, viz that all laws were illegal, . . . that Adam made no will when he died, and therefore all the goods he left behind him should be equally distributed.[49]

More work is required on early radicalism before the extent of the threat posed to the social order is assessed. The relatively relaxed ministerial response to much disorder suggests that the extent of the threat has been exaggerated. The Black Act of 1723, which introduced the death penalty for many new offences, was inspired by the Jacobite role in disorders in the south of England.[50] Ministerial correspondence was concerned only infrequently with popular disorder and social discontent.

The social stability among the political nation so ably analysed by Professor Holmes is of great importance in the issue of political stability. Significant social strain among the political nation might well have seriously exacerbated political divisions, and led to further attempts to encourage popular participation in politics. However, it would be wrong to assume that social necessarily produces political stability. The most socially stable society can be rent by conflict as a result of religious or political differences. Assessments of stability are a personal matter, and scholars and students alike will adopt differing interpretations each based upon a reasonable assessment of conditions in early eighteenth-century Britain. This author would argue that the growing social stability discussed by Professor Holmes made political peace only more likely, but that it is too easy to underrate the political challenges of the period. The Jacobite rising in 1745–6 is an important commentary on the Walpolean period, and was seen as such by many contemporaries. The nature of the military crisis in 1745 should not be underrated. Though very few were willing to fight for the Jacobites, few were prepared to fight for the Hanoverian succession, which was shown to rest on a very narrow base.[51] Charles Edward's army was small, but Charles XII of Sweden had shown in the 1700s what a small force operating without supply lines could achieve against larger and better-supplied forces.

The political fragility revealed in 1745 vindicates the importance Walpole attached to not rocking the boat. The absence of bold legislative programmes might dismay historians, as much as the corruption of the Walpolean system engendered a moral revulsion that affected many influential contemporaries, ranging from Pope to Wesley. However, it could be suggested that expectations in both spheres were unrealistic. Corruption is a term too easily used to describe habits of political action, obligation and reciprocation that are not appreciated or understood. Walpole probable abused the system but he did not invent it. In February 1722 Charles Whitworth, seeking election to Parliament, wrote 'I am sorry to find corruption prevails so generally in the nation, but since it has, honest men must make use of the same means, to be in a condition of doing good, as ill designing people employ to do harm: It would be very small prudence to be overscrupulous on such occasions.'[52] Much about eighteenth-century society was corrupt by modern standards. The Stanhope–Sunderland ministry had been lavish in their inducements when seeking parliamentary support; Sunderland was notoriously dishonest; many politicians had benefited at the time of the South Sea Bubble from the ambiguous relationship between the ministry and the fiscal system. Corruption is not something that it is easy to measure, but Walpole does not appear to have been more corrupt than Sunderland. Much of the condemnation he received stemmed from the extraordinary longevity of his ministry, which opponents could most conveniently ascribe to his corruption. No doubt corrupt practices, such as the offer of pensions and government posts, played a role in ensuring the parliamentary strength of the ministry. However, it would be a mistake to regard it as the most important factor. Royal support was of great significance, but so too was Walpole's ability. His parliamentary skills are discussed by Dr Cruickshanks. Walpole himself told the Commons in 1739: 'I have lived long enough in the world to know, that the safety of a minister lies in his having the approbation of this House . . . I have always made it my first study to obtain it, and therefore I hope to stand.'[53] An able parliamentary and electoral manager, Walpole was also equal to the very difficult fiscal problems facing the ministry. He possessed an understanding of international affairs and an ability to match foreign policy to national capability that better-informed contemporaries, such as Carteret, lacked. No longer a young man (he was born in 1676) and suffering from a debilitating and painful urinary tract problem that ultimately killed him, Walpole's disinclination for innovation can be explained in personal terms, as well as a matter of policy. As the *Northampton Mercury*, a pro-ministerial newspaper, noted in 1723, 'The first safety of Princes and States lies in avoiding all Councils or Designs of Innovation, in Ancient and established forms and laws, especially those concerning Liberty and Property, and Religion.'[54] It is unfashionable today to ascribe much influence to individuals, but the longevity of the Walpole ministry, and the political stability that this represented and fostered, owed much to Walpole's political skills. The nineteenth century was less hesitant about praising individual statesmen, and, without agreeing with all the eulogy, one may note the opinion of a later prime minister, Sir Robert Peel,

> mainly by his personal exertions contributed to establish and confirm without severity, without bloodshed, a new and unpopular dynasty. . . . Of what public man can it be said with any assurance of certainty, that, placed in the situation of Walpole, he would in the course of an administration of twenty years have committed so few errors, and would have left at the close of it the House of Hanover in equal security, and the finances in equal order? – that he would have secured to England more of the blessings of peace, or would have defeated the machinations of internal enemies with less of vindictive security, or fewer encroachments on the liberty of the subject?'[55]

1. The Political Management of Sir Robert Walpole, 1720–42

EVELINE CRUICKSHANKS

1720 rather than 1721 should be the starting point of Walpole's career as 'the great man', the chief minister, the prime minister. At the reconciliation brought about in 1720 between George I and the Prince of Wales (later George II) and between Sunderland and Walpole and Townshend, Walpole, though nominally only paymaster, was in charge of the Treasury, with John Aislabie the Chancellor of the Exchequer as a mere figurehead. Thus Walpole's appointment as First Lord of the Treasury and Chancellor of the Exchequer in April 1721 merely regularised an existing situation.[1] Sunderland, Walpole's predecessor as prime minister, did not retain control of the secret-service money, as J. H. Plumb believes,[2] since there is evidence that Walpole had the distribution of it at the 1722 election.[3] Pensions to MPs and bribes to electors came out of the secret-service fund which was part of the civil list and not subject to parliamentary control.[4] It was regarded as 'uniquely the private pasture of the political class'[5] and Walpole insisted on having control of it 'knowing the chief power of a minister . . . depends on the distribution of it'. Together with the favour of the Crown and an ability to command a majority in the House of Commons, it made up what contemporaries called 'the plenitude of power'.[6] It was Walpole who completed the process of identification of the Treasury with the premiership, uniting control of Parliament and control of money granted by Parliament in single hands.[7]

Walpole was the first modern prime minister, introducing a new style of premiership, because he chose to stay in the House of Commons. He sat in that House for 41 years, one year longer than John Birch, a recruiter to the Long Parliament who was still sitting in 1690. Walpole had drawn the right conclusions from the failures of his predecessors. In the reign of Queen Anne, Robert Harley had gone to the Lords as Earl of Oxford, while Henry St John had become Viscount Bolingbroke. There had been good reasons for this since the Tory government's position there had been precarious, even after the creation of the dozen peers in 1712. They had left the management of the Commons, however, to second-ranking politicians such as William Bromley, Arthur Moore and others of insufficient stature to carry the House in the last stormy years of the Queen's reign. At the Hanoverian succession, on the other hand, the Whigs had a large in-built majority in the Lords and needed to concentrate on good management of the Commons. Sunderland's choice of managers was poor: first Addison, a Whig hero as a writer, but one who was no speaker and 'knew nothing of business'. Next came James Craggs the younger, who was a good wheeler and dealer, but a man of obscure social origins and of insufficient calibre to lead the Lower House.[8]

The House of Lords was managed by the senior secretary of state, Viscount Townshend and from 1730 onwards by the Duke of Newcastle.[9] They relied on the Whig lords, the 16 Scottish representative peers, the Poor lords[10] and on the 19 or more of the 26 bishops who, in the words of George Heathcote (MP, London), 'all clung together to advance any proposition that had a court air'.[11] Walpole could afford to use the Lords as a long-stop, allowing popular bills such as place and pension bills and bills to prevent bribery at election to pass the Commons unopposed, knowing they would be kicked out upstairs.

In the Commons Walpole was like a fish in water: 'the best House of Commons man we ever had' wrote Philip Yorke, later 2nd Earl of Hardwicke.[12] To George II Walpole was

by so great a superiority the most able man in the kingdom, that he understood the revenue, and knew how to manage that formidable and refractory body, the House of Commons, so much better than any other man, that it was impossible for the business of the crown to be well done without him.[13]

Even political opponents like Chesterfield concurred: 'the best Parliament man, and the ablest manager of Parliament, that I believe ever lived. An artful rather than an eloquent speaker, he saw as if by intuition, the disposition of the House and pressed or receded accordingly'.[14] So great was Walpole's love of the Commons that when going to face the House he dressed as carefully as a lover going to see his mistress.[15] All this contributed considerably to the eclipse of the Upper House by the Lower, a process assisted by the decorum in the conduct of proceedings during the long Speakership of Arthur Onslow from 1728 onwards. Despite his stance of impartiality, Onslow was still a member of the ministerial team, but his immense knowledge of procedure and the respect he earned from MPs helped to establish a recognised standard of parliamentary behaviour.[16]

As a person, Walpole was affable and approachable and well liked in Parliament. He was particularly gracious to new MPs, lying in wait 'in that old spacious court' (the Court of Requests through which Members entered the House), calling each new boy out by name and then offering an invitation to dinner.[17] Without the eloquence of the Elder Pitt, who could speak for four hours holding the House enthralled, Walpole was a clear and powerful orator, speaking with 'warmth and spirit' but 'completely without acrimony'.[18] He and Pulteney, the leader of the Whig opposition, could hurl invective at one another in debates and next be seen talking and laughing together on the benches – a very modern touch.[19]

At the heart of Walpole's political management was his control of patronage, used more systematically and ruthlessly than his predecessors had been able or, in the case of Oxford, willing to use it. Not everyone could be satisfied but, generally speaking, he did not make promises, at least to those that mattered, that he did not keep. Some of the juiciest plums went to his own family. With long years in office and control of the purse-strings Walpole developed a vast spoils system, every office, large or small, being made to serve a political purpose,

down to the appointment of the tidewaiters at Sandwich or
Newcastle, or the landsurveyor to the Port of London.[20] Acting
at first under Bishop Gibson, Walpole had the disposal of
Church patronage, which Queen Anne had reserved for herself.
This comprised not only bishoprics and deaneries, but livings
in the gift of the Crown which were numerous in the Duchies of
Cornwall and of Lancaster. Unlike the Duke of Marlborough
under Queen Anne, he did not have sole disposal of army
patronage, which George I and George II kept for themselves
'as far as the parliamentary interest allowed'.[21] As Plumb has
shown, 90 per cent of Walpole's meetings with the monarch
concerned patronage. It is not surprising, therefore, that he was
dogged not only by 'needy supplicants' but 'by dukes, mar-
quesses, earls, viscounts, barons, knights and gentlemen'.[22] He
came to know not that every man had his price (a misquota-
tion) but that every man in opposition had his price.[23] The
process at times sickened him and he once told Henry Pelham,
his eventual successor, 'when you have the same experience of
mankind as myself you will go near to hate the human
species'.[24] He would therefore treat with special regard those
who could not be bought, like William Shippen, the Jacobite
Tory.

  With the control of patronage went control of Parliament.
There the choice of managers was essential. Walpole was
assisted by men such as Henry Pelham, his deputy leader, and
Philip Yorke, later 1st Earl of Hardwicke, men who were held
in high regard by contemporaries. Two others, on whom
Walpole relied most heavily, were not so esteemed. One was
Thomas Winnington, who was said to be second only to
Walpole in point of ability. A Tory of Jacobite stock who went
over to the Whigs to get into place, 'his jolly way of laughing at
his own want of principles', wrote Hervey, 'had revolted all the
graver sort' in Parliament. Walpole's other henchman, Sir
William Yonge, had an eloquence described as 'astonishing'.
Yonge was so much in tune with his chief that he could open a
debate using Walpole's notes and, later on, Walpole could
come in and take over with no awkwardness. Like Winnington,
Yonge had an unsavoury reputation, though he had done
nothing 'particularly profligate – anything out of the common
track of a ductile courtier and a parliamentary tool – yet his

name was proverbially used to express everything pitiful, corrupt and contemptible'.[25] Like Oxford, Walpole paid particular attention to the elections committee for there the government's majority could be increased by unseating opponents on petition, a process Walpole called 'weeding the House'. Winnington and Yonge were assiduous attenders at the elections committee on Walpole's behalf.[26] On a lower level, the fetching and carrying was done by Thomas Brereton, the son of a Chester innkeeper, who had wrested control of Liverpool from local magnates – such as Lords Derby, Molyneux, Warrington and Barrymore – by using the customs officers as an organised force. Brereton was one of Walpole's 'dunghill worms' as the 1st Lord Egmont called Walpole's lesser tools among MPs.[27]

Walpole was expected not only to manage Parliament but to win the general elections. In modern times, politicians win general elections and then take office, but in the eighteenth century politicians were given office and then won the general election. What prevailed was a system of inverse proportional representation, with 40 English counties with an electorate of about 160,000 voters returning only 80 MPs, whereas 205 boroughs with an electorate of only 101,000 returned 409 MPs. Wales, with an electorate of about 21,000, returned 24 MPs, while Scotland, with an electorate of about 2700, returned 45 MPs.[28] The Opposition as well as the government used corruption in elections with the classic combination of bribes, treats and threats. There was no government monopoly of rotten boroughs: Tories were patrons of Amersham in Buckinghamshire, Newton in Lancashire and Gatton in Surrey, while William Pulteney owned Hedon in Yorkshire. Nevertheless, most of the means of corruption were in the hands of Walpole though government patronage, secret-service money, the Treasury interest and the Admiralty interest in such boroughs as Portsmouth, Plymouth and the Cinque Ports. The government greatly benefited from the munificence of the great Whig magnates such as the Duke of Newcastle with wide interest in Sussex and Nottinghamshire, and the Duke of Devonshire, who dominated Derbyshire elections and had influence in Leicestershire. There were no great political bishops to match Sir Jonathan Trelawny, Bishop of Winchester under Queen Anne, whose impoverished descendants placed four seats at East and West Looe at the disposal of the government in return for an allowance of £500 a year plus £1000 in election years.[29] However, in such constituencies as Exeter, Durham, Winchester and Peterborough the bishops were active on the government's behalf. In garrison towns, such as Carlisle or Berwick, army officers had electoral influence. In winning elections, the government was much assisted by the Septennial Act of 1716 which, by prolonging the length of Parliaments, made elections more expensive because men would pay more for seven years' tenure than for three years and which made boroughs less open and easier to control. In Walpole's time, public opinion did not determine the overall results of general elections. This is not to say that he could afford to disregard public opinion, which in parliamentary terms was generally agreed to be expressed by the counties, especially Yorkshire the largest county, and by large open constituencies such as London, Westminster and Bristol. London's addresses, presented by its sheriffs at the bar of the House of Commons, were regarded at home and abroad, in Walpole's words, as 'the sense of the people'.[30] These prestigious seats tended to go to the Opposition, the counties especially to the Tories.

In the reign of George I the vast majority of the Opposition consisted of Tories, 217 Tories being returned in 1715 as against 341 Whigs, 178 Tories to 379 Whigs in 1722. In the next reign, 130 Tories were elected in 1727 as against 415 ministerial Whigs and 149 to 326 respectively in 1734. Historically the Tory creed was derived from the Cavaliers: belief in hereditary right, non-resistance, defence of the royal prerogative and of Anglican monopoly. Since the Revolution of 1688–9, however, the logic of events had forced the party to modify its stance on all these tenets but the last. Most Tories had been hearty in support of Queen Anne to the exclusion of her half-brother James Francis Edward Stuart, the Old Pretender, who was Charles I's grandson but was a Roman Catholic. On his accession in 1714, however, George I, who hated the Tories for what he regarded as their desertion of Hanover and the Allies at the Peace of Utrecht, proscribed the whole party from office at national and local level. This meant not only that Tories in Parliament could not get places, but that they could not provide for their younger sons in the traditional way nor obtain any kind of favours for their constituents. Obviously, they could not know at first that the proscription would last 45 years and they had hopes that it would be taken off, especially on the accession of George II in 1727. They were disappointed, as George II hated the Tories even more than his father had done. It was the proscription, wrote Bolingbroke, which drove the Tory party to embrace Jacobitism 'universally'. This was the only alternative left and though they disliked 'James III's' religion, they obtained from him guarantees that he would maintain the Church of England, and they lived in hopes that the Stuart princes would be brought up as Anglicans.

The Hanoverian succession had been unpopular with the Tories, but the signs are that they would have accepted it had the first two Georges behaved as kings of the whole nation and not as kings merely of the Whigs. Some historians, however, have asserted that the bulk of the Tories were Hanoverian Tories, seeking to know the feelings of the party better than those who led it in Parliament, who said, on the contrary, that the Tory party had become a Jacobite party.[31] The leading exponent of this view, Dr Linda Colley, in a recent study seeks to prove, largely on the evidence of contemporary pamphlets, that the party defended the Hanoverian prerogative as they had done that of the Stuarts. These anonymous pamphlets purporting to come from or to be addressed to the Tories argued that non-resistance and defence of the royal prerogative were owed to the Hanoverian monarchy. This followed a line of argument used by Addison in 1716 and internal evidence would indicate that they were written by Whigs: indeed in one case where the author is given (George Berkeley) he was a Whig![32] Tory speeches in Parliament, sounder evidence than anonymous pamphlets, show not regard for the prerogative but frequent use of revolution principles (not surprisingly since these were of more use to the Tories than to the Whigs after 1714) and strident anti-Hanoverianism. They also reveal dislike of the Lutheranism of the first two Georges, whom the Tories regarded as Occasional Conformists (a term used for those who took the Anglican sacrament for political conveni-ence). Tories also resented the Hanoverian kings' patronage of low-church Whig bishops. The argument used by Robert

Molesworth, a republican Whig, that Lutheranism had led to absolutism everywhere in Europe was taken up not only by Shippen but by Sir John St Aubyn, an influential MP, who declared 'we now lived under a Prince who being used to arbitrary power in his dominions abroad, was minded to establish it here'.[33] On the other hand, *spontaneous* expressions of loyalty to the sovereign, which are so frequent in private letters and in reported conversations under Queen Anne, are absent on the Tory side after 1714. Indeed, on occasions in Parliament involving the Hanoverian royal family, such as the Princess Royal's marriage portion in 1733, leading Tories such as Shippen, Sir John Hynde Cotton and William Bromley separated themselves from their Whig allies in opposition by speaking against it 'obstinately'. Similarly, when in 1739 William Pulteney the leader of the Whig opposition 'made a long speech professing his zeal for the King and royal family', it was noticed that his words 'visibly gave great uneasiness to his Tory confederates'.[34]

Treating the Tories as beyond the pale obviously suited Walpole, who wanted no multi-party ministries, telling the attorney-general Dudley Ryder that 'he never found any service from Tories'.[35] He delighted in taunting the Tories with being Jacobites and with accusing Whigs in opposition of being the allies of Jacobites, but he was much less cynical than he has sometimes been represented as he believed they *were* Jacobites. He was extremely well informed, through the vast network of Jacobite intelligence he had set up at home and abroad, about disaffection in Britain and about Tory attempts to get military assistance in Europe for a Stuart restoration: 'his fears of invasion and Jacobitism were real, though his enemies affected to say they were state artifices'.[36]

Very shrewdly, Walpole sought not only to prevent European powers from giving assistance to the Tories, but to avoid giving the Tories too great provocation. After using the discovery of the Atterbury plot in 1722–3 both to cow the Tory party and to distract public attention from the discontents caused by the South Sea Bubble, Walpole was conciliatory. There was one particular risk he knew he could not run: to allow the cry of 'the Church in danger' so potent during Dr Sacheverell's trial in 1710 to be raised. Although Dissenters were the mainstay of the Whig interest in many constituencies and George I had appealed in person to London dissenters for support at the 1722 election, Walpole dissuaded Samuel Holden and his dissenting deputies committee from moving for a repeal of the Test Act in 1732. When it was moved by Walter Plumer an opposition Whig in 1736, Walpole opposed it, speaking 'so cautiously with regard to the Church and so affectionately with regard to the Dissenters that neither party had cause to complain of him'. Most of his 'creatures' followed suit 'though in their heart for it', but some placemen voted for it because of 'the obligations they had to the Dissenters in their elections'.[37] When Sir Joseph Jekyll, Master of the Rolls, brought in the mortmain bill to prevent alienation of lands in perpetuity, Walpole persuaded the House of Commons to except the Universities of Oxford and Cambridge from its provisions. Walpole, however, did support the Quakers' tithe bill in the same year designed to prevent the imprisonment of Quakers by ecclesiastical courts for non-payment of tithes, especially as the Quakers were staunch supporters of his in Norfolk elections. When Bishop Gibson contrived to get it thrown out in the Lords, Walpole got rid of him. It is not surprising, therefore, that leading Tories contrasted Walpole's benevolence to the ill-will shown towards them by their Whig allies in opposition.[38]

Walpole also sought to defuse the Jacobite threat abroad by a policy of peace at any price, 'from opinion, from interest and from fear of the Pretender'. He obviously could not go as far as to follow a Tory blue-water policy of relying on the Navy alone for defence and for trade, and agree with Henry Rolle, Tory knight of the shire for Devon, that 'the sure, safe and natural defence of England is the sea'. Nor could he implement the Tory belief that the militia was the only constitutional force allowable in peace-time, given that the army was the pride and joy of George I and George II. He did, however, do all he could to lessen the impact of Hanoverian measures, looking on Hanover as 'a millstone round the neck of British ministers' and longing to be rid 'of all the disagreeable *German* disputes, the Hessian troops, the subsidies, etc.'.[39] He was old enough (having entered Parliament in 1701) to remember that William III had lost control of Parliament in the 1690s over unsuccessful campaigns led by foreign generals and over disputes between British and foreign officers, and was determined to avoid a repetition of this. When taunted by Pulteney with the inglorious part played by Britain in the war of the Polish Succession in the mid 30s, he replied: "twas a comfortable reflexion that 100,000 men had already perished in the war (50,000 of them French) and many millions of money expended, yet not one drop of English blood spilt, or one shilling of English money spent on it'.[40] Most of all, he believed that if war came 'the King's crown would have to be fought for',[41] as it was in 1744–6.

The Whigs in opposition were led by William Pulteney, a former associate of Walpole's but passed over by him in the reconstituted government of 1720. Pulteney was a superb speaker, 'eloquent, entertaining, persuasive, strong and patriotic as occasion required'. His eloquence was his strength for he could personally influence only four MPs, his cousin Daniel Pulteney and his own chief lieutenants Samuel Sandys, Sir John Rushout and Philips Gybbon. The Whig Opposition in the Lords from 1730 was led by Lord Carteret, a former associate of Sunderland, who had been dismissed as secretary of state in 1724. A very able speaker, Carteret had 'few followers besides the Finches', Lord Nottingham's relations. From 1725 onwards the two Pulteneys joined forces with Sir William Wyndham, an able Tory who proclaimed himself a Hanoverian Tory (though an intermittent one), and Wyndham's friend Bolingbroke, calling themselves 'The Patriots' in an attempt to form an organised Whig–Tory Opposition with *The Craftsman* as an organ. The Whig section of this alliance was small at first: 15 in 1727 and 86 in 1734. It was greatly strengthened in 1737 when Frederick, Prince of Wales, went into opposition and placed his household and Duchy of Cornwall patronage at the disposal of opposition Whigs.[42]

In examining the parliamentary Opposition at this time a court–country dichotomy should be discounted, indeed it would not survive a detailed scrutiny of even one session of any parliament. There was indeed a 'country platform' based on reducing the number of placemen and pensioners and curbing electoral corruption,[43] but there was no country party. It is significant that historians who have done detailed work on the period (albeit from differing standpoints) – Romney Sedgwick, myself, B. W. Hill, J. C. D. Clark and Linda Colley – all agree on a Whig–Tory division, not a court–country one.[44] Sandys regarded the popular bills, such as pension and place bills that he himself introduced, as 'the flurries of a day' and was as impatient to come back to court as was Pulteney himself. Even on such a generally agreed 'country' point as opposition to a standing army, the Tories wanted none of any kind while the opposition Whigs would support a small reduction at most. More frequent parliaments was another favourite country theme, but it was with the greatest reluctance that Pulteney could be brought to support the repeal of the Septennial Act in 1734. Time and again, the two wings of the Opposition broke up into its constituent parts and the Tories retained their separate party organisation, clubs and whips.[45]

In the past, historians have very much under-estimated the number of court supporters in Parliament (27 per cent according to J. B. Owen)[46] and very much over-estimated the number of independent Members. Some indication of the working size of the court party may be gauged by the fact that in 1730 150 MPs attended a pre-sessional meeting to hear the contents of the king's speech. This number alone would not have given a parliamentary majority to Walpole, let alone make the House of Commons, as contemporaries acknowledged, so 'submissive to him' that he could get it to do virtually all he wanted.[47] There were besides, a vast army of members of both Houses obligated to the government, not pensioners or placemen themselves but whose sons, brothers, uncles or cousins had places or sought and obtained favours of all kinds for their friends, tenants or constituents. There were few real 'independents' on the Whig side. The first Lord Egmont, whose career is so well documented by his parliamentary diary (the best for the period), prided himself on his independence. Yet his own testimony shows that he could not have maintained his interest at Harwich without Walpole's help and obtained many other favours from him. Sir James Lowther, another self-proclaimed independent, is one of the best examples of this type. Again Lowther could not have supported his interest in Cumberland and Westmorland without help from the ministry by way of places and other favours, as John Beckett has shown.[48] Such people did not always vote with the government but they supported it in crucial divisions.

This stance of independence was helped by the fact that on most issues Walpole had no policy. He was not singular in this for it was only after great national upheavals, the Restoration, the Revolution of 1688–9 and the accession of the House of Hanover in 1714, that circumstances forced a good deal of government-sponsored legislation. Walpole's primary task was to raise the supply for the army, the navy and the Civil List. He did this superbly well. Walpole, said George I to Princess (later Queen) Caroline, 'could turn stones into gold'.[49] He kept himself in power on the accession of George II by obtaining a much-increased Civil List for the king and the largest jointure any queen had had for Queen Caroline and did it because he could command a majority of the Whigs in the Commons, a thing which Spencer Compton, a nonentity who was expected to succeed Walpole, could not do. Walpole was 'so clear in stating the most intricate matters, especially in the finances, that while he was speaking, the most ignorant thought they understood what they really did not'.[50] This was an immense asset. For the rest, most legislation, dealing with trade, roads, rivers and so on, was brought in by private Members, the distinction between public and private bills being one of paying or not paying fees rather than one of contents.[51] To give but one of the more important examples: the Molasses Act of 1733. This was the brainchild of Martin Bladen, a Lord Commissioner of the Board of Trade and a court supporter, whose wife had sugar plantations in the West Indies. Its joint author was Sir William Stapleton, a Tory baronet with West Indian estates, who pushed the molasses bill through and took the chair of the committee on it. The first attempt to tax the North American colonists, it was designed to force them to buy sugar, rum and molasses only from the British West Indies, rather than purchase them more cheaply from the Spanish and French West Indies. In the debate on the bill, the court party was split. Although his brother old Horace spoke for it, Walpole did not and he was said to have been opposed to it, coming so soon after the excise bill: 'I have Old England set against me and do you think I will have New England likewise?' he told Philip Yorke.[52]

Political ideology was not the motivating force of

eighteenth-century legislation and the old cliché was true, Walpole's policy was to let sleeping dogs lie. 'His great maxim in policy', Hervey wrote, 'was to keep everything as undisturbed as he could, to bear with some abuses rather than risk reformations and submit to old inconveniences rather than encourage innovations.'[53] His great departure from this course of action, the excise scheme, proved disastrous. There was, it is true, an element of fairness in the scheme which would have relieved country gentlemen of the too heavy burden of the land tax. Nevertheless, the public at large was convinced he was going to tax every commodity in the land until there was 'not a cobbler but is made to believe that he is to pay an excise before he eats his bread and cheese and drinks his pot of beer'.[54] Another underlying fear was that an army of excise officers would be used in elections in the way customs officers had been and there was even a proposal in Parliament that excisemen should be disenfranchised. In practice, as Professor John Brewer's work on the excise has shown, there would have been little risk of this because of the frequent changes in posting and lack of contact with local communities. As usual the City of London led the dance in opposition to the scheme with a petition so arrogant it was likened to 'the advice of the citizens' rather than a humble petition, and it was followed by a carefully orchestrated campaign of petitions from other corporations throughout the country. The violence of popular agitation was such that even the bishops took fright and began to consider voting against the government. Walpole did manage to defeat, though by only 17 votes, a motion that the London petition be heard by counsel, a move which would have immobilised Parliament for the rest of the session, but he gave up the excise bill itself rather than suffer a humiliating defeat.[55] In parliamentary terms, however, the excise crisis had serious consequences because Walpole, unlike Oxford, believed in disciplining placemen who voted against the court. This led to a series of dismissals. To do away with the Duke of Bolton, who was a fool, or Lord Chesterfield, the wittiest of men but one with little parliamentary following, may not have mattered too much. Lord Cobham, on the other hand, was someone to be reckoned with for his 'cubs', the Elder Pitt, the Grenvilles and the Lytteltons, were the ablest young men on the Whig side, so that gradually the greatest talent came to be lined up against Walpole.

All ministers hate parliamentary inquiries, but Walpole hated them more than most. His attitude of *laissez-faire* regarding some of the worst abuses of the time, even though he was not personally involved, reveals what is to us the unacceptable face of Walpole. One such inquiry, not political as such, was begun by James Edward Oglethorpe, the philanthropist, after the death of one of his friends in a debtors' prison. What the gaols committee (1729–30) found was horrifying. The state of the Fleet prison, where Bambridge the sadistic warden tortured helpless prisoners for his own pleasure, revealed a 'dismal and shocking ... scene of cruelty, barbarity and extortion'. Some prisoners died of bitter cold in the winter, others of 'want of air' in over-crowded conditions in summer. On the women's side healthy prisoners were made to lie with smallpox cases and pay 2s. 10d for the privilege! Monies left for various charities to assist poor prisoners had been embezzled and they were being left to starve. Prisoners with money, on the other hand, were allowed to escape by bribing the gaolers. The inquiry, which led to Bambridge's dismissal and some reforms, met with nothing but 'ill will' from Walpole and his ministers, who opposed, unsuccessfully, an extension of the committee's investigations to the King's Bench. This was not only because, in Walpole's view, such revelations stirred public opinion, but because long sittings forged political links between members of the committee.

Two further inquiries, this time into political scandals involving government supporters, rocked Parliament. Again Walpole himself was not personally involved. The first in 1732, initiated by Lord Gage, an impoverished Roman Catholic who had conformed and became a Whig, concerned the fraudulent sale of the forfeited estates of the Radcliffes, Earls of Derwentwater, after the '15. These, some of the largest estates in the North of England, worth £200,000 and bringing in £7000–8000 a year in rents, not counting the proceeds of their lead mines, had been sold for £1060 by the commissioners for the forfeited estates to one Smith, 'so notorious a jobber and of such infamous character that living by Aldgate he is called Smith of the other gate, meaning Newgate'. The chief beneficiaries were two of the commissioners, Denis Bond and Sergeant Birch, as well as Sir John Eyles, Walpole's manager for the City of London. When all this came out, Walpole 'found such universal displeasure at the foul proceedings of the commissioners and purchasers of this estate, that he saw it was in vain to oppose it and therefore sat silent'. Bond and Birch were expelled from Parliament, but Walpole was able to save Eyles, who got away with a mere reprimand. Lord Gage received the thanks of the Commons conveyed in a most handsome manner from Speaker Onslow. The sale of the Derwentwater estates was declared void and the profits and rents from them were later applied by Act of Parliament to finishing Greenwich Hospital.[56]

The other affair which shook Parliament at that time was that of the Charitable Corporation. This involved leading government supporters. Although the chair of the secret committee of inquiry of 21 men, on which the Opposition prevailed on the ballot, was taken by Samuel Sandys, an opposition Whig, Newcastle rightly suspected that the chief promoter of the investigation was Col. Samuel Robinson, a Jacobite leader of the common council of London. The London-based Charitable Corporation had been founded in 1707 to grant small loans at low rates of interest to the industrious poor. This did not suit Denis Bond, who was reported to have told his fellow directors 'damn the poor, let us go into the City, where we may make some money'. The whole thing became a stockjobbing operation with the directors having 'nothing in view but to enhance the price of their shares'. The authorised capital was raised from £100,000 to £300,000 and then to £600,000, with shares rising sharply each time. When the inquiry began, however, there was only £30,000 left of the capital. Those principally involved apart from Bond were Sir Robert Sutton, a Privy Councillor and ex-ambassador at Paris, and Sir Archibald Grant, who at least employed some of his ill-gotten gains usefully by planting trees in Scotland! John Thompson, the chief warehouse keeper to the corporation, had taken the company's books and papers, with the proof of where the money had gone, to Rome. He appears to have had Jacobite friends and to have enjoyed the friendship of the Pretender. Thompson's going to Rome was no doubt

designed to prevent the government from placing the corporation's books and papers out of the reach of Parliament and the
public as had been done in the case of the South Sea Company
in 1720–1. A letter from the Pretender to the committee of
inquiry offering to make this evidence available was ignored. A
further letter from the Pretender's banker in Rome to the
Speaker, expressing willingness to communicate the corporation's books and papers to Parliament, was ordered to be burnt
by the common hangman as an 'insolent libel'. Throughout the
inquiry Walpole and his friends showed 'tenderness for the
guilty directors of that corporation by endeavouring to alter the
motions in such a manner to bear least hard upon them'. Sir
Robert Sutton was expelled, despite ministerial pleas that he
was guilty of negligence rather than fraud, and Grant was
similarly expelled. Shippen carried a motion of thanks to
members of the committee 'for the pains they have taken, and
for the great skill they have shown, in detecting a dark and
execrable scene of villainy'.[57]

When the government was really threatened, however,
Walpole would turn the tables on his political enemies. His
most skilful parliamentary performance was given in the
debates on Dunkirk in 1730. In the previous session the
coalition so painfully built up by Pulteney and Bolingbroke had
come apart with the Tories separating themselves from the
Whigs in opposition in division after division. Yet early in 1730
Walpole was alarmed to see all the Tories in town acting with
the opposition Whigs. He did not know then, but later found
out, that the Tories had instructions from the Pretender to vote
with those who opposed the government from 'different views
than theirs'.[58] In circumstances of the greatest secrecy, Bolingbroke had sent his friend Sir William Wyndham evidence, with
seamen and merchants as witnesses to back it up, that the
French had been rebuilding the port of Dunkirk contrary to the
provisions of the Peace of Utrecht. Walpole was caught
completely unawares by the charges hurled against him of
negligence and corruption and of having brought his country
into utter dependence on France. He replied that, as it
happened, Colonel Armstrong, an engineer employed to
inspect the port of Dunkirk, was on the spot (he had sent for
him as soon as he heard of the committee of inquiry) and that

Armstrong's evidence would clear up the matter. To gain time, Walpole sent the committee every document about Dunkirk for the last two years, bogging them down in a sea of paper and preventing them from considering Wyndham's evidence on its own. When Armstrong returned, he confirmed everything Wyndham's witnesses had said, so that his evidence could not be examined. In a debate which lasted till three in the morning, Walpole produced his trump card: a personal assurance from Cardinal Fleury, the French chief minister, that any work on the port of Dunkirk would be discontinued forthwith. He then turned on his tormentor: Wyndham was but his master's voice, accompanied with the refrain that Bolingbroke was at the bottom of it all. That name was so discredited on both sides of the House that it was enough to sink the best-laid scheme. With half the House of Lords in the gallery to hear the debate, the motion of censure was lost by 270 votes to 149. Nothing more was heard of Dunkirk![59]

The immense outcry against the excise bill did not lessen Walpole's favour with George II, but the dismissal of Whig placemen who voted for the bill or supported it drove many more Whigs into Opposition, so that after the 1734 election Walpole's majority in the House of Commons was 102 as against 272 in 1727. Walpole still had room for manoeuvre, since Sunderland had regarded 60 as a working majority.[60] But it was a time, unfortunately for him, of a great upsurge of urban radicalism in London and other large centres of population. He had sought to stem popular Toryism in London by the passing of the City Elections Act of 1725 which, whatever its other administrative merits, disqualified about 7000 London voters and by imposing the right of veto by the Court of Aldermen over the addresses of the Court of Common Council threw the corporation of London back to its pre-Civil War state. The government had had a majority on the Court of Aldermen, who were chosen for life. By 1737, however, death had taken its toll of government supporters among the aldermen and the Opposition had gained the upper hand in the whole corporation. This coincided with a popular campaign to extend British trade in Spanish American waters and with smouldering discontent at Spanish efforts to contain that trade and at the employment of Spanish guarda costas to search British vessels on the high seas.[61] In 1738 Micajah Perry, an Opposition Whig merchant, presented a London petition against Spanish depredations and was put in the chair of the committee on the petition, Walpole having failed to get a government supporter as chairman. When Walpole, still determined to avoid war, concluded the Spanish Convention in 1739, the Common Council drew up a petition against it which Sir John Eyles, Walpole's manager, failed to get vetoed in the Court of Aldermen. Seriously alarmed, Walpole told Dudley Ryder that when 'the city of London showed their inclinations against him in this public manner, there was no standing against it and he should think himself bound to yield'. The Convention was approved in the Lords by 95 votes to 74. In the Commons, where Pulteney denounced it as 'scandalous to the British nation', it was debated for ten hours in the fullest House contemporaries could remember. The Convention was approved by 28 votes with 61 abstentions by court supporters, but Walpole had to concede that Spain would not be allowed to search British ships on the high seas. It was, wrote Lord Egmont, 'universally believed that he will not be able to stand his ground next year'.[62] In the summer, Captain (later Admiral) Edward Vernon, a very able seaman who addressed Parliament in the language of Billingsgate, was sent to the West Indies and in October Walpole bowed to the inevitable and grudgingly agreed to a declaration of war against Spain. Walpole was a bad war minister. He had 'no clear fixed plan' and was not cut out by nature 'to carry a truncheon'.[63] He was pessimistic from the start, saying 'they now ring the bells, they will soon wring their hands'. Vernon's capture of Porto Bello made the captain a national hero overnight, but euphoria turned to consternation when the capture proved useless and the expeditionary force was decimated by fever and internecine disputes. Worse still, Admirals Haddock and Norris failed to prevent the French and Spanish fleets from joining up and sailing to the West Indies.[64]

The Opposition scented blood, but moved too early for the kill. On 13 February 1741, the Opposition Whigs without consulting the Tories moved for the dismissal of Walpole from the king's presence and counsels for ever. In the Lords, despite the fact that Carteret made a much better speech in favour than Sandys made in the Commons, the motion was easily defeated.

In the Lower House, Walpole took no chances and 'a guzzling baronet was kept in all night at Sir Robert's house, for fear his faculties should chance to have been so diluted as to make him mistake the lobby for the House'.[65] The motion was defeated by 184 votes, Walpole owing his salvation to the fact that many Tories and some opposition Whigs either withdrew or voted against it. The Tory walkout was led by Humphry Parsons, the Jacobite Lord Mayor of London, while Shippen took himself to Solomon's porch, the passage leading to the Speaker's room, and would vote neither way. The main reason for the Tory withdrawal was political: 'they had too much pride to be the tools of the discontented Whigs, and put their hand under the stirrup to mount them into the saddle' to be afterwards 'swept away with the rest of the rubbish'. The Harleys withdrew, in the words of Edward Harley, because they hated 'even the shadow of bills of pains and penalties' such as had been used against Oxford and his associates in 1715.[66] It has been suggested by Dickinson and by Colley, however, that those who withdrew were Hanoverian Tories who did so out of regard for the royal prerogative.[67] The royal prerogative is not mentioned in any report of this debate, published or unpublished, so far discovered. Two unpublished well-informed accounts deserve special mention because of the light they shed on Tory motives. Sarah, dowager Duchess of Marlborough, writing to Lord Stair about the Tory withdrawal, commented ''tis certain the majority of them are fools and the principles they profess are both foolish and false', adding that they would 'never be satisfied without a Tory to be premier minister'.[68] William Pulteney, commenting on this division, had no doubt as to what had prompted the Tories to act as they did: 'they mean nothing but Jacobitism and most of them plainly own it, so that we are (as it were) ground to pieces between the two millstones of corruption and Jacobitism'.[69]

This episode threw the Opposition into total disarray, but it had regrouped before the 1741 election. In the summer, Chesterfield, apparently acting in collusion with the Duke of Argyll, obtained a letter from the Pretender instructing the Tories to vote with the Whigs in opposition to bring down Walpole. In many constituencies both wings of the Opposition co-operated in elections. In Cornwall, a county with 44 seats, only one less than Scotland, Thomas Pitt, manager for Cornish elections for Frederick, Prince of Wales (who appointed the sheriff of Cornwall), co-operated with prominent Tories, such as the Morices, the Carews and St Aubyn, so that Walpole lost 15 seats. Nevertheless Walpole could have been saved had it not been for the obstinacy of George II. The Duke of Argyll wanted most in the world to be commander-in-chief, and had the king agreed to appoint him, Walpole would not have lost 11 seats in Scotland. Had George II been able to overcome his reluctance to create new peerages, he could have given one to Dodington and Walpole would have got four seats at Weymouth and Melcombe Regis, but the king would not. The result was that Walpole's majority, which stood at 42 at the end of the 1734 Parliament, was only 16 at the meeting of the 1741 Parliament. The Walpoles hoped to increase it after the hearing of election petitions and double returns, young Horace writing cheerfully 'a good majority, like a good sum of money, soon makes itself bigger'. On the Bossiney election petition on 9 and 11 December 1741, however, Walpole had majorities of only six and seven, Horace commenting 'one or two such victories, as Pyrrhus, the member for Macedon said, will be the ruin of us'. On the Westminster election petition, heard at the bar of the House on the 9 December, it came out that the returning officer had been paid £1500 out of secret-service money and that the Guards had been called in to close the poll to prevent the election of Admiral Vernon and a Tory. This was too much even for an eighteen-century House of Commons; many court supporters abstained and the election was declared void.[70]

All now depended on the choice of the chairman of the elections committee. There Walpole's liking for shady men began to tell against him, for he put up Giles Earle who was regarded as 'a very bad character' even on his own side of the House and whose mordant witticisms had antagonised many. The opposition candidate Dr George Lee, on the other hand, was a man of good character and he was chosen instead by four votes. At this late stage, during the Christmas recess, George II tried to rescue Walpole by overcoming his dislike of his eldest son Frederick, Prince of Wales, and offering him 'the other £50,000' of the allowance he himself had had as Prince. Frederick refused on the grounds that Walpole had 'injured' him. On 21 January 1742 Pulteney moved for a secret committee of 21 to inquire into Walpole's administration. Both sides made their utmost effort: 'it was a shocking sight' wrote Horace Walpole, 'to see the sick and dead brought in on both sides'. Some MPs limped in on crutches and Sir William Gordon was taken from his bed and brought in 'with a blister on his head and a flannel hanging from under his wig'. That motion was lost by three votes. Walpole's last stand came at the Chippenham election on 28 January. The rats, headed by the Sackvilles, were fast leaving the sinking ship and the government lost it by one vote.[71] Walpole wrote afterwards to the Duke of Devonshire: 'I must inform you that the panic was so great among what I should call my own friends that *they all* declared my retiring was become absolutely necessary as the only means to carry on the public business.'[72] The next day Walpole resigned. At last and very reluctantly he went to the Lords, as Earl of Orford, as the best way of saving himself from impeachment. Things, however, were never the same again. From now on a successful *prime minister* had to sit in the Commons.

2. Popular Politics in the Age of Walpole

H. T. DICKINSON

BRITISH politics in the age of Walpole has often been described in terms of the dominance of a propertied oligarchy and the securing of stability after more than a generation of political ferment.[1] These two developments, the strengthening of oligarchy and the growth of stability, are seen as being mutually reinforcing. When a narrow Whig oligarchy dominated the court it could exploit Crown patronage in order to win support from a majority of the propertied elite in Parliament and in the country at large. At the same time the reduction in tension over such issues as the succession, religion and foreign policy made it easier for the ruling oligarchy to monopolise places of power and profit without serious opposition from political rivals or social inferiors. The decision of the first two Hanoverians to place their trust in the Whigs and to proscribe the Tories assisted both of these processes, the trend to oligarchy and the growth of stability. So did the political tactics of the Whigs themselves. They blackened the reputation of the Tories by accusing them of harbouring Jacobite sympathies and they weakened the popular appeal of their opponents by keeping the peace, reducing the land tax and seeking to avoid religious controversies. Not content with undermining the political credibility of their parliamentary opponents the Whigs also endeavoured to reduce the influence of the electorate at large. The Septennial Act reduced the frequency of appeals to the voters and, in the process of extending the length of parliaments, also put up the cost of electioneering. This, and the Whig tendency to support a narrow borough franchise whenever possible, enhanced the electoral power of the rich while reducing the independence of the voters. Thus, although the Whigs could never eliminate all political opposition, they were able to reduce the effectiveness of any challenge to their authority.

There is certainly abundant evidence to substantiate this interpretation of political developments in the age of Walpole. None the less, this is a limited perspective on British politics that can only appear convincing if we concentrate exclusively on the narrow confines of court, Parliament and a loose federation of country houses. The political system was certainly not democratic and it did not even fairly represent the interests of all those who possessed some form of property. Yet politics was not simply the preserve of the narrow landed oligarchy that dominated court and Parliament. To understand fully the political system during the years of Walpole's ascendancy it is essential to examine the political actions, culture and ideas of a very much larger proportion of the population than this. The electoral system was undoubtedly influenced by patronage and corruption, but the majority of voters were not simply bought and sold nor were they entirely submissive to the landed elite. Constituencies under the absolute control of a patron remained rare. Many quite small constituencies still needed constant and careful management by those who wished to preserve their electoral interests. In the large, more open constituencies elections were often contested and the voters were never under the complete control of the propertied elite. The majority of voters lived in these larger constituencies and, in the bitterly contested elections of 1734 and 1741, it is possible to argue that, in losing many of these seats, Walpole suffered a popular defeat even though he secured a comfortable majority of the rotten boroughs.

Moreover, it can be shown that it was possible for the electorate, and even for those who did not possess the franchise, to bring their demands before Parliament and to exert pressure upon the people's representatives in the House of Commons. Pressure groups were organised by powerful mercantile interests, mainly in London but also in the larger outports, and by articulate and determined leaders of religious opinion. By the sophisticated lobbying of MPs and the skilful exploitation of printed propaganda such pressure groups could occasionally persuade the ruling oligarchy to take action to promote or defend their sectional interests. Whenever they were sufficiently aroused, the commercial and professional middle classes in London in particular, but in the other large boroughs too, were capable of impressing their views quite forcibly on the political elite. When, as in 1733 and between 1739 and 1742, the urban bourgeoisie were convinced that the government's actions threatened their economic interests, then they displayed a capacity for concerted action that created serious political crises for Walpole's administration. Nationwide petitioning and instruction campaigns, with the lead being given by the commercial middle classes of London, were the highpoints of popular resistance to Walpole's government. Sophisticated extra-parliamentary protests of this kind were always dominated by the urban bourgeoisie, but the lower orders had their own means of influencing the political decisions of the ruling oligarchy. Large crowd demonstrations and violent riots could not be ignored by an elite devoid of an effective professional police force or a large standing army. Plebeian protests of a turbulent and determined nature posed a considerable threat to law and order and either restricted the political options available to the governing elite or forced them into choosing between coercive or conciliatory measures.

Bourgeois petitioning and plebeian crowd activity both stemmed from a conviction that all British subjects were free citizens living in a free state. This concept of British liberties was buttressed and extended by a flourishing political press which often criticised the policies of Walpole's ministry and defended the rights of the ordinary subject. Though it had not yet developed into 'the fourth estate', the press played a crucial role in informing the people 'out-of-doors' about the behaviour of the ruling oligarchy and in acting as the principal medium for the dissemination and articulation of popular protests against the government. The press often acted as the political instructor and as the political agent of those who wished to resist the growth of oligarchy. Its influence was undoubtedly greatest among the middling orders of London, but it was also a significant force among the merchants, shopkeepers, tradesmen and professional men of the other large towns. The concerted protests organised by extra-parliamentary opinion in 1733 and 1739–42 would certainly have been impossible without the aid of the press.

Thus, while a trend towards oligarchy can be detected in the age of Walpole and the people as a whole did not consistently participate in the political process, it is a mistake to ignore extra-parliamentary activity and public opinion. No examination of the political system can be complete if it ignores the political activities of the urban bourgeoisie, the political lead given by London in the major crises, the political dimension of crowd demonstrations and the political influence of the press.

I

While acknowledging that the elite could exercise a very powerful influence in the many small or closed parliamentary constituencies, it is a mistake to conclude from this that the voters in these constituencies were entirely submissive to the will of their social superiors. It is true that in Cornwall a mere 1400 voters elected 42 borough MPs, in Scotland the total electorate fell well short of 3000 voters, and elsewhere there were many boroughs with small electorates such as Banbury with 18 voters, Malmesbury with 15 and Old Sarum with only five.[2] In many of these small constituencies the electors rarely had to vote in a contested election in any case. But evidence of this sort does not prove conclusively that the electoral system was a hollow sham or that the voters had no influence on the composition of the House of Commons. The exploitation of patronage did not always reduce the voters in such small constituencies to the position of servile and submissive dependents of the propertied elite. Most of these voters were certainly deferential to men of wealth, status and power, but they were sufficiently free to render deference not only a voluntary but a political act. Deference precludes inferiors from political leadership, but it does not prevent them from holding an intelligently critical attitude towards the ruling elite. The ideal of deference was not to reduce a man to helpless and imbecilic servility, but to treat him in such a way as to acknowledge his essential independence and self-respect.[3] A large number of voters acted in a manner which both preserved their integrity and showed due regard for the opinions of their social superiors. Deference was given only when it was earned by those who sought it. There was therefore much more to constituency management than the giving of orders by the borough patron and the obeying of them by the voter. It was a political art which called not only for wealth and power, but also for tact and good sense. Most borough patrons lived in the vicinity of their constituency, were personally accessible to the electors, and involved themselves in local affairs by means of patronage, favours, public celebrations and charitable activity. During elections these patrons engaged in the rituals of canvassing and visitations, parades and processions, free treats and entertainments, even when they did not anticipate a contested election. The voters in the small boroughs often took pride in their independence and they were certainly not prepared in all cases to obey the dictates of their superiors. There are numerous examples of small and normally docile constituencies being lost or put in jeopardy by insensitive political management. In Lewes, for example, the election agent warned the Duke of Newcastle in 1733 that his candidate might lose the forthcoming election if he continued to neglect the voters:

It is with the greatest concern I tell your Grace that things grow worse & worse; & if some speedy remedy is not found out the election will be in great danger. If it is lost, the loss of it must be imputed to Mr Pelham's inactivity. . . . He has not been around the Town since he went with your Grace, nor I believe asked a single man for his vote: & I am firmly persuaded that half the voters that have been lost have been lost by this unpardonable negligence: the people are affronted at it; & indeed he has no reason to expect their votes if he does not think them worth asking; when the other side are perpetually courting them.[4]

In the middling boroughs the voters showed an even greater spirit of independence. They expected their representatives to protect their interests and to respect their opinions. No MP could feel confident of retaining his seat in such a constituency if he blatantly flouted the wishes of his constituents. In 1732 Sir Richard Grosvenor almost forfeited his family's electoral interest in Chester because of his opposition to a proposal to widen the River Dee in order to revive the borough's declining trade. The situation was only saved by Grosvenor's death and the new candidate's decision to promote his own River Dee Navigation bill.[5] Before the general election of 1734 Thomas Winford, MP for Hereford, was forced to withdraw from a turnpike trust because it was so unpopular with his constituents, while in Newcastle-under-Lyme Lord Gower was compelled to issue broadsheets to all the borough's voters assuring them that he did not intend supporting the enclosure of town fields or common land.[6]

In the very large and open constituencies the voters enjoyed considerable independence. While such constituencies were in a minority, a high proportion of the voters (in the region of two-thirds) actually resided in them. Furthermore, all the leading politicians recognised that it was in such open constituencies that the will of the electorate was manifested most clearly and most powerfully. The political elite was not preoccupied at election time with the results in the numerous small boroughs, but with the behaviour of the voters in the large counties such as Yorkshire, Middlesex, Surrey, Kent, Norfolk and Essex, and the large boroughs such as London, Westminster, Southwark, Norwich, Bristol and Coventry. General elections were often bitterly contested in these constituencies and it was widely acknowledged that the results could influence the voters elsewhere and that together the decisions in these open constituencies could give a clear verdict on the popularity of the government. Even when these constituencies did not go to the polls in a contested election they had to be very carefully managed. No candidate in the open constituencies was ever in a position to take the electorate for granted. John Scrope, for example, although he was secretary to the Treasury, was defeated at the polls in Bristol in 1734 because he had supported Walpole's Excise Bill, contrary to the instructions sent to him by the city corporation.[7] Support for the Excise Bill also brought about the rejection of MPs in other large constituencies such as Norfolk, Middlesex, Kent, Essex, Coventry and Newcastle. No government candidate even ventured to stand in the city of London in 1734, such was the unpopularity of the ministry in the nation's capital.[8]

In several of the large boroughs the electorate began to reject the leadership of the propertied elite and endeavoured to gain much greater control over the choice of those who would represent them. As early as 1724 there is evidence of independent electors in London meeting at the Half Moon Tavern in Cheapside. By the late 1730s this tavern was the base for a political society co-ordinating the opposition of the London liverymen to the policies of Sir Robert Walpole.[9] The independent electors in Westminster also began to co-ordinate their activities by the late 1730s and in 1741 there emerged a society of independent electors among the middling tradesmen and lawyers of this, the largest urban constituency in the country. A second, more plebeian group met at the Crown and Anchor Tavern. These societies supported Opposition Whig candidates in 1741 and they swept the polls against Walpole's candidates in a very violent election.[10] Even outside the metropolis electors were beginning to establish their own independent political organisations. By the late 1730s Bristol possessed two electoral clubs, the Steadfast Society established by the Tories and the Union Society founded by the Whigs.[11] The former was supported by many smaller, satellite clubs in the poorer parts of Bristol and it exercised considerable influence over the 1741 election. Soon there were similar clubs in Coventry, Colchester, Grantham and even Cirencester.[12] These clubs monitored the parliamentary conduct of MPs and orchestrated popular resistance to aristocratic control in the larger constituencies. Hard-fought contests in such constituencies frequently involved the unenfranchised as well as those qualified to vote. There were violent demonstrations of popular opinion at Hull in 1723, Norwich in 1727, Great Yarmouth in 1734 and Westminster in 1741. The election at Coventry in 1722 had to be declared void because of the severity of the riot. Over 2000 men, on horse and foot, with green twigs and leaves in their hats, colours flying, drums beating and trumpets sounding marched to the polls. They attacked their political opponents, damaged property, and cried out 'Down with the Rump! Down with the King's Head [the Whig headquarters] No Hanoverians! No seven years Parliament!'[13]

II

The casting of votes in elections was neither the most frequent nor the most important way in which the electors or organised opinion 'out-of-doors' could influence the behaviour and the decisions of the ruling oligarchy. When it was effectively organised popular opinion could persuade or pressurise parliament into taking decisions which would be to the advantage of those who united to propose them. Both the ministry and Parliament could be influenced by petitions, by organised extra-parliamentary pressure groups and by nationwide instruction campaigns. All subjects enjoyed the right to petition Crown or Parliament, not simply those men qualified to vote. Although electors were more likely to petition than those who were not enfranchised, borough petitions in particular were frequently signed by non-voters. Indeed, some petitions came from urban areas which were not represented in Parliament. In 1731 several Lancashire MPs were pressurised into supporting a petition from Manchester, which was not a parliamentary constituency, requesting a popularly elected Board of Guardians for the town's workhouse.[14] It was always open to extra-parliamentary groups to approach individual MPs to present petitions on their behalf or to sponsor private bills. Parliament spent a considerable portion of its time passing private and local bills which sprang from the desire of particular economic interests to enclose land, build turnpike roads, dig canals, improve harbours, clear rivers, or pave streets. Private and local bills were printed at the expense of their instigators. This requirement was deliberately designed to invite a measure of public participation in the debate on the proposed legislation. The printed bills were intended to serve the same purpose as modern 'green papers'; to act as a draft proposal for discussion by interested parties 'out-of-doors'.[15]

Remarkably well-organised extra-parliamentary interests, both economic and religious, were able to exert considerable pressure upon the policy of Walpole's government and the decisions of Parliament. Not surprisingly, some of the most effective interest groups were those closely linked to and clearly favoured by the ruling oligarchy. On several occasions Walpole's administration responded to the political demands of the

Bank of England and the great chartered trading companies.[16]
The directors of these great trading companies were close allies
of Walpole and hence part of the ruling oligarchy, but many of
the shareholders in these companies, who also helped to bring
pressure to bear upon the government, came from outside the
ranks of the privileged elite. Moreover, there is a great deal of
evidence to suggest that other interests without such close links
to the ruling oligarchy were able to exert pressure upon court
and Parliament. The West India interest did not have the same
close links with the government as the great chartered trading
companies. None the less, this combination of absentee West
Indian proprietors and London merchants trading with these
colonies made up for these deficiencies with the sophistication
of their pressure-group tactics. A carefully orchestrated petitioning and propaganda campaign was mounted to convince
MPs of the need to protect the trade with these colonies from
competition from the French West Indies. The planters,
merchants and their agents cultivated influential MPs, sol-
icited the government, secured favourable press comments and
submitted evidence to parliamentary committees and government officials. The result was a series of measures in their
favour including the Molasses Act of 1733 and the Sugar Act of
1739, both of which promoted the commercial interests of
planters and merchants.[17]

The dissenting churches could not apply the economic
leverage of the West India interest and could never claim the
popular support of the established Church, but their pressure-
group tactics were more sophisticated than that of any other
interest in the nation.[18] With very few friends in high places and
faced by considerable popular hostility the Quakers succeeded
on several occasions in securing amendments to legislation
allowing them to affirm rather than to swear oaths. They even
came close in 1736 to obtaining a Tithe Act which would have
relieved them from persecution for the non-payment of tithes.
The regular, constant and peaceful agitation of the Quakers
was concerted by a permanent central executive committee.
This committee kept a watchful eye on parliamentary legislation and co-ordinated the pressure from the local, county and
national meetings of the Quaker societies. The effective
lobbying of the Quakers encouraged the major dissenting sects

to imitate their organisation and their political tactics. In 1727 the three Boards of London Dissenting Ministers set up a joint committee which co-ordinated pressure in favour of Indemnity Acts to allow Dissenters to hold office without taking the sacrament in the Church of England. Acts to this effect were passed in 1727, 1728, 1729, 1731 and each year from 1733 to 1743. Such successes persuaded the committee to establish a lay organisation – the Dissenting Deputies – which aimed to secure the repeal of the Test and Corporation Acts. In 1736, and again in 1739, the Dissenting Deputies mounted major lobbying campaigns among MPs and peers. They gave an excellent demonstration of the techniques of peaceful political agitation, though they failed to achieve the desired repeal. While not without sympathy for the Dissenters' cause, Walpole bowed before the more powerful pressure exerted by the Anglican clergy. He warned the Commons that it must 'consider what was the opinion of people without doors, especially the Church'.[19]

During periods of national political crisis extra-parliamentary opinion went beyond the humble petition and the sophisticated lobbying campaign. Nationwide campaigns were mounted in an effort to dictate the conduct of MPs. In these co-ordinated and concerted movements petitions for the redress of grievances were combined with 'instructions' from constituents to their MPs, requesting them to vote in a particular way and to bring forward certain resolutions in Parliament. In 1733 there was a vigorous national protest against Walpole's Excise Bill, while between 1739 and 1742 there was concerted extra-parliamentary pressure of this kind against Walpole's political conduct in general and his handling of the crisis with Spain in particular. Walpole himself claimed that these campaigns were instigated and orchestrated by the disaffected leaders of the parliamentary opposition.[20] Some historians have endorsed this claim, but this view ignores the substantial evidence which suggests that these campaigns were generated by genuine popular hostility to Walpole's policies.[21] The parliamentary opposition undoubtedly used the press to alert public opinion of the dangerous implications and alarming consequences of the government's conduct, but both the press war and the instruction campaigns had a natural appeal at constituency level.

In 1733 some petitions were formulated by opposition MPs and by meetings of the county gentry, but even these had an impact beyond their particular constituencies. Many of the 54 petitions (and this is a conservative estimate) had instigators who did not belong to the landed elite.[22] The lead in this almost unparalleled display of public anger was given in fact by London where the campaign was not organised by the city's parliamentary representatives. In the Common Council it was the Lord Mayor, John Barber, who promoted the resolution which instructed the city's MPs to vote against the Excise Bill. This initiative was taken up by the Court of Aldermen and supported by a broad coalition of tobacco and wine importers, Dutch and Hamburg merchants, linen drapers and brewers, and a substantial section of the middling liverymen. The general populace also rallied against the Excise Bill, parading wooden shoes through the streets, manhandling Walpole himself at the door of the House of Commons and burning him in effigy. London's lead was soon followed in Westminster, Southwark, Bristol, Liverpool, Nottingham, Newcastle and Exeter.[23] Instructions even came from constituencies such as Wigan, Bath, Carlisle, Coventry, Harwich and York that were represented by supporters of the government not by opposition MPs. Eight towns, including Daventry and Towcester, also petitioned against the Excise Bill even though they were not parliamentary constituencies. There can be no doubt that much of this opposition came from the urban commercial classes; a sectional interest certainly, but a substantial one and one which appears on this occasion to have represented a very considerable body of extra-parliamentary opinion. The financial exactions of the Excise Bill and the army of investigative excise officers needed to enforce it aroused real hostility among the British people as a whole. Walpole's retreat on the issue did not immediately defuse the climate of excitement and bitterness. In the general election of 1734, when the Excise was the only significant issue, the government suffered over 20 defeats in the more open constituencies and in several counties the highest polls of the whole eighteenth century were recorded.

Although Walpole was saved by the results in the rotten boroughs, the general election certainly registered a popular defeat for his administration.[24]

Between 1738 and 1742 Walpole was faced by an even more popular and broad-based anti-ministerial coalition. This extra-parliamentary opposition originated in hostility to the government's conduct of commercial negotiations with Spain, but it was soon extended into a general and sustained attack on the policies and the methods of Walpole's administration. Once again the lead was taken by London merchants, this time those who traded in Spanish American waters. On 3 March 1738 Micajah Perry, a London alderman and tobacco merchant, seconded by Sir John Barnard, presented a petition to the Commons from the London American and West India merchants condemning the Spanish attacks on British commerce and demanding a tougher response from Walpole's administration. Within weeks there were similar petitions from Bristol, Liverpool and Glasgow and a well-orchestrated press campaign which drove the government onto the defensive. The convention which Walpole negotiated with Spain in 1739 confirmed the worst fears about his conciliatory policy and inaugurated a new wave of protests. Over the next few months the court Whigs lost control of the City of London, even of the Court of Aldermen. The independent opposition in London seized control of the city's political institutions, promoted a petition against the Spanish convention and delivered 'instructions' to the city's MPs on no fewer than five occasions by 1742. These instructions condemned Walpole's whole political system and adopted a programme of constitutional reform that included attacks on placemen in Parliament, on a large standing army in peace time, on septennial Parliaments and on the veto possessed by the Court of Aldermen. There were demands for a vigorous inquiry into Walpole's mismanagement of public affairs and for the implementation of reforms which would eliminate political corruption.[25]

In this campaign London gave a lead to popular opinion throughout the country. The livery's instructions of October 1739, which called for the introduction of a Place Bill, were copied by 12 other boroughs and 5 counties. The resolutions of Common Council in June 1740 rallied at least 36 other constituencies, while the City's instructions of 1741–2 encouraged even more constituencies to follow this lead.[26] In Bristol the petty merchants, drapers and tobacconists of the Steadfast Society asked Edward Southwell, a candidate in the election of 1741, to pledge himself in support of a Place Bill, a reduction in the size of the army and the repeal of the Septennial Act.[27] In November 1742 the merchants and tradesmen of Exeter dispatched instructions to their two MPs requesting them to support constitutional reform and to refuse to grant supplies until concessions were forthcoming.[28] In Scotland, where the tiny electorate was dominated by aristocratic influence, instructions were sent from Edinburgh, Aberdeen, Stirling, Kincardine, Dumfriesshire, Ayrshire, Aberdeenshire, Lanarkshire and Ross.[29] In Edinburgh the instructions were drawn up by the merchant companies and such tradesmen's corporations as the surgeons, goldsmiths, skinners and weavers.[30] This wave of protests undoubtedly represented genuine popular hostility to Walpole's administration and it certainly had a significant impact on government and Parliament. A contributor to *Common Sense* claimed that the electorate was the sovereign authority in the kingdom: 'If the electors of England should declare to you (the Parliament), you shall not make laws for us, we will do it ourselves: will any man say they may not do it?'[31] While rejecting such radical conclusions even the ministers themselves recognised the need to bow before this storm of popular resentment. The Duke of Newcastle acknowledged: 'If we go on despising what people think and say, we shall not have it long in our power to direct what measures shall be taken.'[32] Walpole himself confessed: 'If the City of London showed their inclinations against him in this public manner there was no standing against it, and he should think himself bound to yield.'[33] He did yield to the clamour for war in 1739, but his inability to prosecute this conflict successfully only incited the public to greater fury. In the general election of 1741 most of the open constituencies and a majority of the electorate voted against Walpole's candidates even though his majority in seats was not totally eroded. Walpole was eventually hounded from office early in 1742, as much because of public hostility out-of-doors as because of the greater effectiveness of the opposition within Parliament.

The extra-parliamentary pressure groups and these nation-wide instruction campaigns clearly show that an independent political culture was taking root among the urban bourgeoisie in particular and, to a lesser extent, among the lower orders. The urban bourgeoisie had their own social and economic reasons for resisting the authority and criticising the policies of the ruling oligarchy. Becoming politically conscious and politically active within their own communities they often resented the political and economic systems which threatened to reduce them to the position of clients dependent upon and submissive to their superiors. The intense struggle for local power and patronage, which fused at times with vigorous contests for parliamentary representation, provided the urban bourgeoisie with a focus for their political ambitions. The more open politics of the urban areas sometimes brought in the lower orders, usually when an economic crisis stimulated mass participation in popular direct action. Ordinary subjects caught up in crowd demonstrations or violent riots could exert at least a temporary influence on the ruling oligarchy. These bourgeois and plebeian political cultures could hardly have existed, still less have flourished, but for the activities of the press and a deep-rooted libertarian tradition which was nurtured by such publications. It was the free press which informed the public of the conduct of the ruling oligarchy and which acted as the main political medium for co-ordinating and expressing popular opinion.

In the large boroughs political power was dominated by local oligarchies and political disputes revolved much more around local than national issues, but the middling orders were not totally excluded from political influence and local disputes did occasionally become caught up in national affairs. This was most certainly the case in the metropolitan area. By virtue of its capital status, its commercial supremacy, its sheer size, its comparatively democratic system of government and its special privileges of petition and address, the City of London was virtually an independent political community. It certainly dominated the arena of popular politics. The city corporation, divided into a Court of Aldermen and a Common Council, had complete jurisdiction over its own territories and had considerable economic power and patronage at its disposal. Walpole could usually count upon the support of the rich financiers and merchants who dominated the Court of Aldermen, but he increasingly alienated the independent merchants and the middling sort who dominated the election of the Common Council and of the city's four MPs.[34] In the early 1720s most of the independent merchants and liverymen of London were critical of Walpole's close links with the monied interest and of his support for the Quarantine Act and the Westminster Bridge Bill, but it was the City Elections Act of 1725 that turned them strongly against the court. This measure sought to remodel the constitution of the city and to circumscribe its more democratic tendencies. The freeman franchise was defined more narrowly (disqualifying nearly 3500 voters), the control of elections was tightened up, the growth of the lesser livery companies was restricted, and the Court of Aldermen was given a veto over all legislative acts and resolutions of the Common Council. The act can be regarded as a sensible attempt to deal with long-standing abuses,[35] but its critics interpreted it as an assault on London's political independence and as a means of strengthening oligarchy. Walpole certainly hoped to inhibit the Common Council from adopting an independent role as a critic of the government and he aimed at increasing aldermanic control over local ward politics. The measure fired partisan disputes in which popular opinion cast Walpole as the villain. It was opposition to the City Elections Act that first encouraged the emergence of a broadly based anti-ministerial coalition in London. This opposition fought Walpole on two fronts. It endeavoured to oust the court interest in the city corporation, especially in the Court of Aldermen and, as we have seen, it gave a lead to the nationwide petitioning campaigns of 1733 and 1738 to 1742. By 1741 Walpole's opponents in London had severely reduced the court interest on the Common Council, had gained a clear majority on the Court of Aldermen, and had secured a complete victory in the election of the city's four MPs. For the first time since 1688 the court had lost political control over the nation's capital city. The popular champions of independent opinion in London had vindicated a more open concept of politics and had made a seed-bed for the radical libertarianism of the later eighteenth century.

The example of London spread to the other large boroughs. Westminster was more under the influence of the ruling oligarchy than London because of the presence of the court, Parliament, Whitehall and the houses of fashionable society within its boundaries; but it also had the largest urban electorate in the country. While the wealthy western parishes were generally pro-court in their political sympathies, the poorer eastern parishes were more resistant to aristocratic influence and more hostile to Walpole's administration. By the later 1730s the lesser tradesmen of these areas were becoming politically active and were beginning to wrest control from their social superiors. In 1741 this opposition formed a Society of Independent Electors and swept the polls against the court in a violent election.[36] Popular resistance to oligarchy was not confined to the metropolitan area. In many of the larger boroughs there were conflicts between the corporation party which represented the interests of the richer inhabitants and an independent opposition hostile to the political dominance of this local oligarchy. This was the case in Coventry, Exeter, Bristol, Colchester, Tiverton, Leicester, Liverpool, Norwich, Nottingham and Worcester. These local contests often involved a religious division, with the Anglicans usually forming the corporation party and the Dissenters active among the opposition. In Coventry and Nottingham, however, the Dissenters were the entrenched interest. In many of these towns local issues overlapped with national politics. In both Liverpool and Tiverton the town corporations tried to restrict the number of electors who could vote in parliamentary elections, while the opposition campaigned for wider franchises.[37] In Norwich in 1722 and in Chester in 1732 local and national political tensions fused and provoked considerable bitterness. The election of a sheriff in Norwich was the occasion for a demonstration of several hundred citizens shouting their opposition to the court and their support for the Jacobite Bishop of Rochester. This riot encouraged the local Whigs to suggest remodelling the city's charter in order to increase the power of the local oligarchy on the Court of Aldermen.[38] In

Chester there were a number of violent riots during the election of the town's mayor, though the real issue in dispute was whether the town should support a bill in Parliament seeking approval to deepen the River Dee.[39]

Direct involvement in elections, pressure groups, petitioning campaigns and borough politics was largely confined to the middling orders. Only occasionally did political activity of this kind involve the poorer sections of society. Nevertheless, as many historians have recently demonstrated, the lower orders did engage in direct action which could influence the political decisions of the ruling oligarchy.[40] In crowd demonstrations the poor revealed a strong sense of corporate identity and a capacity for effective collective action, though in the age of Walpole the populace failed to develop a coherent critique of society and never adopted a programme for the restructuring of the whole political system. Crowds did wear Jacobite colours at the Coventry election of 1722 and during the Cheshire contest in 1734,[41] while rioters celebrated the Pretender's birthday at Bridgewater in 1721[42] and protested on the anniversary of George I's accession at Harwich in 1724;[43] but these isolated and unconnected incidents were neither proof of serious disaffection among the masses nor the prelude to armed insurrection. Positive support for Jacobitism at grass-roots level collapsed after the widespread rioting of 1715–16,[44] though there is considerable evidence of plebeian hostility to the ruling Whig oligarchy continuing throughout the years of Walpole's ascendancy. Popular antipathy to the Whigs did not lead to violent measures to overthrow the Hanoverian regime, but it did express resentment against Walpole's intimate association with dissenters and monied men and against the corrupt tactics and anti-libertarian tendencies of his administration. Jacobite symbolism was little more than a gesture of popular defiance to the ruling oligarchy. The lower orders preferred to appeal to the English libertarian tradition and to adapt the ideology of the country opposition to their own conditions, but the limited nature of their political consciousness and the superior power of their social superiors prevented them from developing a radical programme aimed at transforming their own position in society.[45] Although the common people believed that they were free men, not slaves, they were usually on the defensive. They engaged in direct collective action in order to protect their traditional rights and to preserve their established customs. The poor did not expect to decide who should rule them, but they did seek to circumscribe how the ruling oligarchy should exercise its authority. Far from rising in armed resistance to overthrow established authority, most rioters were concerned to enlist the support of that authority in defence of their customary rights.

In some areas popular direct action was almost endemic, whereas the ability of the authorities to preserve law and order was severely circumscribed. In the East End of London, in forest and fenland areas, and in the manufacturing towns and villages, official authority was often weak and plebeian independence was strong. There was no long-established social hierarchy and no effective, professional police force to act as a substitute. Firm social discipline was lacking in such areas and, not surprisingly, the poor showed little respect for established authority. Indeed, in any area where the poor could gather together in significant numbers they could threaten the local authorities who had no effective civilian police and who could not always depend upon the intervention of the army. In such circumstances both central government and local magistrates had to tread a careful path between enforcing the law and restoring social harmony. Popular violence forced the authorites to choose between repression and concession.

Faced with the problem of considerable popular unrest Walpole's administration frequently resorted to a policy of coercion and ignored the genuine economic grievances which had often sparked off these violent protests. The government feared that riots might be the prelude to revolution or the first step to anarchy. Walpole's own correspondence shows that he was always predisposed to see the hand of Jacobite conspirators behind any manifestation of public disorder.[46] After a riot against turnpikes in 1735 Lord Chancellor Hardwicke argued that it was essential for the government 'to inculcate into men's minds the dangerous consequences, that must follow from suffering the people to get the better of the laws, &, as it were, to override the acts of the legislature'.[47] Ministers frequently encouraged JPs to make use of the unpopular Riot Act, which had been passed in 1715 following widespread rioting, and sent troops to their assistance. In response to a virtual epidemic of poaching across several counties Walpole's government passed the notorious Black Act of 1723 which created no fewer than fifty capital offences connected with poaching.[48] In similar fashion the administration responded in 1735 to a rash of riots against the new turnpike roads by making it a capital offence to destroy the toll gates.[49] The Porteous riot in Edinburgh in 1736 provoked Walpole into an attempt (largely unsuccessful) to punish the city and its magistrates,[50] while the appearance of effective workers' combinations among London tailors in 1720 and among Wiltshire weavers in 1726 propelled the government into passing legislation to ban both of these nascent trade unions.[51]

There were times, however, when Walpole's government clearly recognised the limits of its authority and endeavoured to placate those it could not subdue. In these instances the government's natural response was to retreat from a dangerous confrontation and to make the minimum concessions needed to restore law and order. In 1720, for example, when the popularity of foreign calicoes was creating unemployment among English weavers in London and elsewhere, an act was passed to forbid the wearing of printed, stained and dyed calicoes imported from abroad. Serious and persistent rioting and the presentation of over 90 petitions to Parliament persuaded the government to offer concessions on this occasion.[52] Serious rioting among the weavers of the south western counties in 1726 stirred Walpole's ministry into an even more impressive display of conciliatory tactics. Two commissioners were sent down by Townshend to investigate the causes of the riots. When they reported that the weavers had genuine grievances and that their employers were largely responsible for the crisis the government summoned representatives of both sides to London. There the Privy Council urged them to draw up articles of agreement about wages and the measures of cloth to be regarded as the unit of payment. This agreement was then embodied in an act of Parliament in 1727.[53] While insufficient efforts were subsequently made to render this measure effective, its enactment did indicate that the government would occasionally protect the interests of the poor in order to avoid serious disturbances. The dropping of the Excise Bill in 1733 and the embargo on grain exports following widespread food riots in 1740 were further demonstrations that the lower orders were not without influence on government policy.

The growth of an independent political culture among the urban bourgeoisie and even among the labouring poor in the towns was greatly aided by the expansion of the press and the constant public debate on the liberty of the subject. Although the political elite sponsored publishers, printers and journalists for their own ends in the struggle for power, they also helped the press to play an important role in encouraging popular involvement in national affairs. A substantial proportion of the public prints was devoted to political issues and this intense debate helped to bring politics out of the restricted arena of court and Parliament. The press brought political news and political opinions to that significant and growing sector of the middling and literate classes who lived in or near the larger towns. Nearly all the political literature of the age was produced in London and the large towns and it was in these urban areas that literacy rates among all classes were at their highest and the dissemination of the public prints was most efficient. Pamphlets, periodicals and newspapers flourished in London and were widely circulated in the coffee houses and taverns in the capital and in towns throughout the whole country. The choicest political items from the capital's press were often reprinted in the provincial press which grew in numbers and increased its interest in politics during Walpole's ascendancy.[54] Despite efforts by the government to control the press by the Stamp Act of 1725 and the persecution of hostile printers and journalists, and despite Walpole's attempts to subsidise the pro-ministerial press, the government frequently lost the propaganda battle.[55] No ministerial periodical could rival the influence of *The Craftsman*. No newspaper subsidised by the government was as popular as the *London Evening Post* which, from its inception in late 1727, was usually critical of the ministry. This influential newspaper played a major role in rallying public opinion against Walpole in 1733 and again from 1739 to 1742. During both crises it gave its readers the clear impression that the country was totally united against Walpole.[56]

In the provinces, where the number of newspapers grew from

24 in 1723 to 42 by the early 1740s, most of the press were critical of Walpole's administration.[57] The *York Courant* was perhaps the most outspoken provincial critic of Walpole. From 1729 onwards it reprinted each week the leading political essay from *The Craftsman* and from 1739 it bitterly attacked Walpole's policies, rejoiced at his fall and then campaigned for his prosecution. Similar views were expressed in many provincial newspapers, including the *Chester Courant*, the *Newcastle Courant*, the *Norwich Gazette*, the *Lancashire Journal* and the *Worcester Journal*. In 1740, when a virulent press campaign against Walpole was in full swing, the Bishop of Chester complained to the Duke of Newcastle of

> the unwearied industry of some to poison the common people with ill thoughts of the Administration, with fair pretences of great respect to the King. This poison is, by my observation, chiefly conveyed by a course of newspapers dispers'd all over these and neighbouring parts. We have a Printing Press here at Chester, another at Manchester, another at Leeds, and other places, all under the direction of seditious and disloyal men, scattering their papers all over the countys at low prices. . . . The authors pick their news out of the London Prints, and take care to publish everything that is against the Government, but give by half, or with some sneer, whatever is favourable towards it.[58]

The overwhelmingly anti-ministerial emphasis of the influential *London Evening Post* and of most of the provincial newspapers was due in part to the greater political excitement provided by opposition criticisms of the government. It owed much more, however, to the preponderance and popularity of 'Country' or 'Tory' attitudes throughout the nation. It seems clear that the vast majority of readers were generally hostile to the policies and the methods of Walpole's ministry. Even pro-government printers believed that their political views were not shared by a majority of their readers. Certainly in any local press war the opposition newspaper more often triumphed. This was the case at York, Bristol, Chester, Nottingham, Newcastle and other towns. Only at Exeter, Northampton and Norwich did the pro-government newspaper prevail. While such Whiggish newspapers rarely dared to launch into open praise of Walpole, the anti-ministerial newspapers in the provinces played a major role in promoting and concerting the nationwide and extra-parliamentary opposition campaigns of 1733 and 1739–42.

The opposition press did not just criticise some of the specific policies of Walpole's government. It increasingly upheld the liberties of the subject and condemned the executive's corruption and abuse of power. The demands for Place Bills and for more frequent elections and the attacks on the size of the national debt and the standing army were all propagated by the Opposition and the independent press. So were more radical political notions. In the early 1720s John Trenchard and Thomas Gordon, in their influential *Cato's Letters* published in the *London Journal*, defended government by consent, the liberty of the press, the freedom of the individual and equality before the law.[59] Many critics of Walpole demanded a return to triennial parliaments, while some even attacked the injustice of the existing distribution of seats. The rotten boroughs which returned so many MPs were condemned and proposals were made for increasing the representation of such rich and populous constituencies as Yorkshire, Middlesex, London and Westminster. It was even suggested that such growing towns as Birmingham and Leeds deserved direct representation in Parliament.[60] These proposals were made by critics of Walpole who believed that Parliament needed to be more representative of property and, at least to a greater extent than at present, more representative of the people as a whole.

While these demands for the redistribution of seats were not matched by a sustained campaign for the extension of the franchise, some of Walpole's critics were already suggesting in the early 1730s that every man had 'an equal right to nominate the makers and the executors of the laws'.[61] Less than a decade later the political rights of all men were being put forward in a more explicit manner. In 1740 an opposition propagandist defended the instructions sent to MPs even when they came from 'the meaner sort' rather than the propertied elite because all those who paid taxes on their beer, their shoes and their tobacco contributed to the support of the government. They therefore had a legitimate interest in public affairs.[62] Two years later, in 1742, another opponent of Walpole made the same connection between taxation and representation: 'as the lowest fellow in the kingdom contributes out of what he gets to the public service, so it seems but just that he should, if he has a mind, know what he pays for, and see if he can see, whether the public is well served or not'.[63] He concluded that since the British called themselves a free people then any creature in the country should have the right to question and judge the government. While such arguments did not carry the day they are a clear indication that the trend to oligarchy during Walpole's ascendancy did not go by default. Indeed, there were already the signs of those political tactics, methods and ideas that were soon to create a radical opposition to the aristocratic dominance of British politics.

IV

This essay has endeavoured to show that political life in the age of Walpole was not the preserve of a patrician oligarchy, but involved, in different ways and to varying degrees, the electorate at large, the middling orders in London and the larger towns, and even the labouring poor when they felt driven to combine in defence of their interests. While there was a trend towards oligarchy in these years there were other developments which were paving the way for the growth of urban radicalism. During Walpole's ascendancy it is impossible to understand fully the decision-making process in national politics without any reference to the needs, expectations and demands of the people 'out-of-doors'. The political crises of 1733–4 and 1739–42, in particular, can only be satisfactorily explained if extra-parliamentary opinion is examined and weighed in the balance. Concessions by the patrician elite to their supposedly submissive dependents are quite inexplicable unless we recognise that the people were rarely servile even when they were dependent, and on occasions they demonstrated their political independence in the clearest terms. Furthermore, too great an emphasis on the trend towards oligarchy and the exploitation of patronage shows only how stability was achieved but offers no explanation for the survival of political strife. Popular resistance to the Whig oligarchy took a whole variety of forms; from the willingness of voters to alienate their landlords, through the creation of pressure groups and the organisation of instruction campaigns, to violent street demonstrations and unrestricted press warfare. These actions all demonstrated that the people were conscious of their rights as free subjects in a free state and that they were determined to protect, even to extend, their liberties. Political stability did not rest simply on the absence of strife, tension and disputes. It was also the product of a political system that was flexible enough to contain the competing demands of different interests and rival pressure groups. Even then, the political system constrained, but did not completely eliminate, competition and dissension. Stability and strife were both characteristic features of politics in the age of Walpole and it is important to appreciate not only the existence of the two but their symbiotic relationship.

3. A Client Society: Scotland between the '15 and the '45*

BRUCE P. LENMAN

WALPOLE's Scotland was poised between the 1715 rising, a massive affair with active English support which might have succeeded but for the ineptitude of its leadership, and the '45, which came as a bolt from the blue and had only limited active support in Scotland. Even so, the Jacobite army reached Derby. It gave the Westminster establishment such a fright that they had by 1748 passed a package of measures designed to smash for ever the peculiar social and cultural patterns of the Highland clans, which were seen as the seed-beds of rebellion. General Wade's Highland military roads of the 1720s and 1730s had proved a convenience mainly to Prince Charles on his march to Edinburgh, but the post-Culloden measures hit home.

Walpole's working life as premier was free of active Jacobite rebellion (despite his carefully cultivated paranoia on the topic), and it was the Act of Union which governed his relations with North Britain. As a young politician Walpole had been a member of a government whose two main successes in the couple of years after he joined it in 1705 were the Battle of Ramillies and the Union.[1] The Articles of Union form the best introduction to the ground rules of the political game as it affected what had been before 1707 the ancient, independent kingdom of Scotland. The first three articles united England and Scotland into one new kingdom of Great Britain which was

* The author wishes to acknowledge generous help from the Carnegie Trust and from the University of St Andrews to help cover the expenses of research for this chapter.

to have a single parliament, and the succession to whose throne was to be a Protestant one vested in the Illustrious House of Hanover. The Scots were granted full rights within the English commercial system, a system which not only encompassed the British Isles, but which also spanned the North Atlantic. English coinage, weights and measures were adopted by the new United Kingdom of Great Britain. The reality was that England absorbed Scotland. Though Article 3 referred to the Parliament of Great Britain, ostensibly a new body, the English Parliament simply added a few Scottish members and carried on as before. To be precise, it added 45 Scottish MPs, and 16 peers, the latter laughably known as the 'Representative Peers'. To place the scale of the Scottish contingent in perspective it must be said that before the Union the House of Commons at Westminster had 513 members, and the 45 Scottish MPs just exceeded the 44 returned by the county of Cornwall.[2]

The Scottish Commissioners for negotiating the terms of the Union had been nominated by Queen Anne's English ministers. They therefore showed no serious interest in trying to protect Scotland's identity or its political tradition. Both were snuffed out by the Act of Union. What they were interested in, both personally and because they had to push the Union package through the Scots parliament, was the class interests of the Scottish landed aristocracy which dominated that legislature. At one level, the Scots aristocracy was moving towards the view that their interests might best be served by total absorption in the English political system. Hopefully this would help to solve the grave economic problems which had dogged Scotland since the terrible dearths of the period 1695–9,[3] and they expected it to offer to their own leading families a chance of assimilation to the envied life-style of the Westminster political elite. At a different level, the tough and avaricious men who made the Union settlement acceptable to the Edinburgh Parliament were well aware that total integration was not necessarily to their own advantage. Provided the Protestant Succession went through, and Scottish political life was abolished at a national level, Westminster was not fanatical about details. The upshot was that the Union was almost as interesting for what it kept apart as for what it joined together.

The established Churches were kept firmly apart. Since the

Commissioners nominated to discuss the Articles of Union had been forbidden to discuss matters ecclesiastical, that side of the Union settlement was embedded in two parallel measures; the 'Act for Securing the Protestant Religion and Presbyterian Church Government' in Scotland, and the 'Act for Securing the Church of England as by Law Established'. Had the Church of Scotland thrown its weight against the Union it might have provided precisely the organisation and mobilisation which was lacking in the great body of opinion hostile to the surrender of national identity. The greatest champion of the Presbyterian settlement of 1690, the Very Reverend Principal William Carstares, Principal of Edinburgh University from 1703 to his death in 1715, was by no means a rabid advocate of Union. He was much more anxious to secure the Protestant Succession, and could see dangers in a Union, but when it became clear that English politicians were determined to push an incorporating Union through and were willing to buy Presbyterian acquiescence with formal guarantees for the 1690 settlement, he wrote to Queen Anne's first minister, Harley, late in 1706 saying that 'the desire I have to see our Church secured makes me in love with the Union as the most probable means to preserve it'.[4] What Carstares was frightened of was the internal menace to the Kirk by Law Established in the shape of that large proportion of the Scottish landed classes who had retained strong Episcopal sentiments after 1690, and who usually combined them with equally strong Jacobite sympathies.

Law was another area where a strategically placed vested interest had to be conciliated by a guarantee of continuing separateness. The Scottish legal profession was closely linked to the landed classes because a very high proportion of the members of the profession were members of landed families. This fact has been demonstrated in rather general terms by an analysis of the membership of the Faculty of Advocates – a corporation of Edinburgh lawyers with a virtual monopoly of places as judges in the central courts of Session, Justiciary, and Exchequer, and in minor courts with national jurisdiction. After the abolition of heritable jurisdictions in 1748 they extended their empire to the county sheriffdoms. Sons of lairds, from all over Scotland were the hard core of the entrants. Along with members of higher echelons of landed society they composed roughly three quarters of all entrants in the eighteenth century. A significant increase in non-landed members came only after 1800.[5] Even when the calculations are repeated on a tighter basis, it appears that the titled classes made up a little under a third of all entrants to the Faculty in the period 1707–60, and that third included a small but significant number of members of the high nobility. A higher proportion of the titled classes – roughly half – can be found among Scots MPs, which reminds us where the priorities of the ruling class lay. If the 335 entrants to the Faculty of Advocates between 1707 and 1760 were not preponderantly members of titled houses, they all came from reasonably well-off backgrounds simply because of the cost of training. Until the 1740s this more or less had to include a spell at a Continental university, preferably a Dutch one, studying the Civil or Roman Law which was the usual topic for the entrance 'trial' to the Faculty.[6]

It is therefore hardly surprising that the Act of Union in its nineteenth article specifically guaranteed the survival of the Courts of Session, Justiciary and Admiralty in Scotland in their existing form and with their existing relationships to inferior courts. The central English courts in Westminster Hall (Chancery, Queen's Bench and Common Pleas were named) were banned from consideration of Scottish cases. The question of appeals from Scotland to the House of Lords was deliberately passed over in silence and later that procedure was established by assertion of right. The Crown's patronage of gowns on the bench of the Court of Session was specifically confined to members of the Faculty of Advocates, Principal Clerks of Session, and the group of senior Edinburgh lawyers known as Writers to the Signet (though the latter, if preferred, had to pass an examination in Civil Law before the Advocates). The arrangements were almost a paradigm of the Union settlement for they secured, within the British state, a private reserve of power and patronage for well-connected North Britons.

The Edinburgh lawyers, if important, were by no means the only important legal vested interest appeased by the Treaty of Union. Article 21 guaranteed the existing rights and privileges of the royal burghs of Scotland, and thereby appeased urban patriciates which were in practice dependents of the landed interest. Article 20, without which it is doubtful whether the Treaty would have been accepted, stated: 'That all heritable Offices, Superiorities, heritable Jurisdictions, Offices for life, and Jurisdictions for life, be reserved to the Owners thereof, as Rights of Property, in the same manner as they are now enjoyed by the Laws of Scotland, notwithstanding of this Treaty.' That swingeing provision guaranteed the continuation of perhaps the most radical single difference between the Scottish and English polities. England was an abnormally unified and centralised jurisdiction, with one taught Common Law for the whole realm (though other legal traditions also survived in specific courts). Central courts at Westminster exercised oversight everywhere except for one or two palatinates like Lancaster or Durham, which in any case either fell to the Crown or were held by Crown nominees, like the Prince–Bishop of Durham. Scotland was quite different.

Heritable jurisdictions were widespread in Scotland. At local level the baron court was basic. Though Justices of the Peace were introduced into Scotland by legislation of 1587 and 1609, they never assumed the importance they had in England by the Tudor period. Furthermore regalian jurisdiction, which literally implied royal powers, was very common in Scotland, where regalities ranged in size from the 500 square miles of Argyll held by the chief of Clan Campbell, the Duke of Argyll, to numerous small regalities in the Lowlands. The origins of the latter can often be traced to secularised ecclesiastical foundations which had been granted regalian rights when established. In Fife the town of Dunfermline was a regality. A more important town in the west, Glasgow, also had that status. Great Highland magnates like the Duke of Atholl were essentially regality holders rather than clan chiefs. The big regalities had Justice Courts at their *caputs* (Inverary for Argyll and Logierait for Atholl) and were self-contained little kingdoms where the King's Writ ran only for high treason. Smaller regalities did not have a Justice Court and functioned more-orless as private sheriffdoms. Regalities of some size went on being created quite late. Grant of Grant was given an extensive one in his main clan territory on Speyside as a reward for his firm support for the Glorious Revolution of 1688. However, it must be emphasised that the strength of heritable jurisdictions in Scotland is underemphasised by a survey confined to baronial or regalian jurisdictions. Many offices within the royal system of jurisdiction, and notably the sheriffs who were the king's principal officers in the localities, had become hereditary in noble houses. All the Border sheriffdoms, for example, were hereditary. When the heritable jurisdictions were abolished in 1748 4 of the 16 proven hereditary sheriffs, the Earls of Argyll, the Earls of Rothes, the Murrays of Philliphaugh, and the Agnews of Lochnaw, had been continuous since 1567. The oldest, the Agnews, originally a Norman family, held by a charter of 1451. Argyll's shrieval rights went back only to 1473.[7] This extraordinary system had begun to decay after 1688–90, when splits in the ruling classes over politics and religion deprived it of the homogeneous, interlocking leadership it needed to function well. The Edinburgh lawyers disliked its autonomy which they assaulted vigorously after the Union of 1707. Forfeiture of many Jacobite-held jurisdictions after the '15 further undermined the system, but it survived until Lady Day 1748, when for good or ill it was suppressed.[8]

Finally, it is clear that though the Scottish aristocracy wanted free access to English markets for the goods and products which helped pay their rents, they by no means accepted the idea that they must resign themselves to potentially destructive English competition in their own domestic markets, especially in activities into which they had sunk a lot of irrecoverable capital. Coal mines and salt works were the prime, and normally linked examples, for Scottish salt pans were coal-fired. The Treaty of Union contained extremely complex provisions, notably the lengthy eighth article, which had the effect of giving Scottish coal a temporary, and Scottish salt a long-term fiscal advantage in the Scottish domestic market. The Scottish upper classes were in fact very commercially orientated. The biggest single bribe used in the whole Union settlement was the repayment to them, plus five per cent p.a. interest, of the huge amounts of capital they had lost by speculating in the stock of the ill-fated Darien Company, the Company of Scotland for Trading to Africa and the Indies. A good deal of rent was still paid in grain, which the landlord collected in girnels or granaries and then marketed in bulk.

Many landlords were deep into coal and salt. Above all, they had since at least 1660 been increasingly affected by a consuming desire to become richer quicker. The Scottish economy had so far disappointed them. What was its nature?

We are fortunate in possessing an 'Account of the Number of People in Scotland, 1755' compiled by the Reverend Doctor Alexander Webster, an Edinburgh minister who combined evangelical, actuarial, demographic and bibulous interests with impressive catholicity. On the whole, 'Dr. Magnum Bonum's' estimate of 1,265,000 people holds up not badly to modern scrutiny. The first official census came in 1801 and showed that the Scottish population had grown to 1,608,000, but the exercise of working back from Webster to 1700 is infinitely more obscure than that of moving forward from him. Recent work using mortality indices has concluded cautiously that 'It is not impossible then, that Lowland Scotland in 1691 had much the same population as it had in 1755'.[9] Natural growth, on this interpretation, would have received a severe setback from the mortality crisis of the period 1695–9, and recovery would have been so slow as to take over fifty years. Whether this view will survive detailed current work on regional baptismal and poll tax records may be doubted, for it seems that a tentative picture is emerging which is far more in accord with the latest work on English demography i.e. a pattern of limited but real and significant population growth in the first half of the eighteenth century.[10] In demographic terms Scotland between 1710 and 1750 may have been a gently buoyant society.

It was also overwhelmingly an agrarian one. For geological reasons Scotland fell, then as now, into three main farming regions, with many smaller sub-regions further complicating the picture. Good, often sandstone-based soils were largely concentrated in the Central Lowlands, or Midland Valley, a quite narrow corridor between the two great geological fault lines; the Highland Boundary Fault and the Southern Uplands Fault. Both in the Southern Uplands and in the Highlands and Islands very ancient rocks gave rise to poor, thin soils which ensured that these regions, both endowed with heavy rainfall, were better suited for pastoral than for arable farming. One natural consequence was a brisk interregional trade which along the Highland Line helped to sustain a whole series of 'frontier' towns such as Dingwall, Inverness, Kirriemuir, Dunkeld, Crieff, Dunblane and Dumbarton. In these towns grain surpluses from the Lowlands moved north in exchange for a southward-moving surplus of pastoral products ranging from cattle on the hoof to goat and deer skins. In the far north another regional complex reproduced the same basic interchange. Caithness, the extreme north-eastern tip of the mainland, formed part of a single cultural and economic province with the Orkney Isles, sharing a Norse heritage and underlying sedimentary rocks, mainly sandstones and flagstones of the Old Red Sandstone series. Despite its climate, Orkney produced grain surpluses in the shape of oatmeal and bere (a hardy form of barley), which it exported to the west Highlands, Norway, and to the Shetland Islands. In the latter archipelago a harsh geological framework dictated a pastoral agriculture and a heavy emphasis on fishing in the teeming waters around the islands which ranked with the Faeroes as one of the great natural fisheries of the North Atlantic. Orkney's ruling class of lairds was an extreme example of the commercialisation of the Scots landed classes, for Orkney families such as the Baikies, Traills, Craigies, Richans, Youngs and others can only be described as 'merchant-lairds', starting out very often as businessmen in the small town of Kirkwall and moving into land on the back of profits from the export trade. Similar groups can be found elsewhere in Scotland. In Montrose, a coastal burgh south of Aberdeen, for example, the burghal oligarchy was heavily committed to the bulk export of salmon, and it had gradually bought up estates all around Montrose, primarily with an eye to their fishing rights. In a regional capital like Aberdeen centre of the North East, a mini-Lowlands behind the Highland Line, the apex of the burghal oligarchy consisted of landed families who found in the governance of a major royal burgh a source of both profit and power.[11]

The practice of agriculture in the first half of the eighteenth century in Scotland was less backward than the authors of the *Old Statistical Account of Scotland* written in the early 1790s were usually prepared to admit. In particular areas, of which the well-favoured Lothians around Edinburgh are a good example, systematic enclosure and consolidation of holdings into complexes of 250–350 acres was well advanced by 1710, being pushed forward from the late seventeenth century by landowners such as Lord Belhaven. In Galloway in the south-west the rise of large-scale cattle production for the English market produced quite large enclosed cattle parks of 1000–2000 acres. The formation of parks on this scale also produced a spectacular but unsuccessful popular protest against the displacement of tenants involved, in the shape of the Levellers who rioted extensively and cast down enclosures in the period 1723–5. Elsewhere communal farming on a 'run-rig' basis with common grazing and an infield and outfield system around the settlement was still standard. The settlement was a cluster of houses known as a 'ferm toun' in the Lowlands, or a 'clachan' in the Highlands, and the arable was divided into strips, with individuals normally holding a scatter of strips which were periodically redistributed.

The Highland Line was a cultural divide between a Gaelic-speaking world and the Scots speech of the Anglo-Saxon Lowlanders. It was also a division between differently structured rural societies. Whereas the rural society of the Lowlands was often rather complex, with considerable 'middling groups' in many areas holding direct of the Crown or by the virtual ownership known in Scotland as feuing, and with quite elaborate social layering both above and below them, that of the Highlands tended to stark simplicity. The magnates in the Highlands, who were usually clan chiefs, leased extensive areas to a gentry class known as 'tacksmen' (often related to the chief). A tack was the Scots term for a lease. Below the tacksmen came a mass of peasants holding their land by annual agreement of a verbal kind. In the Lowlands such evidence as we have suggests that by the early eighteenth century most tenant farmers had written leases and that leases of 10–19 years' duration were far from uncommon. It is clear that, perhaps for reasons of capital shortage, there was no very drastic and widespread reorganisation of even Lowland farming until well into the second half of the eighteenth century, but a 'pioneer' phase of tentative experiment has been identified between 1730 and 1750, and it is quite clear that within the old framework significant changes in outputs were possible.[12]

The most dramatic example of this was the rise of long-range cattle-droving. At the time of the Union perhaps 30,000 cattle were being driven south to England every year. Apart from a period of depression in the 1730s, their prices drifted gently upwards, though big increases came only after 1740. By 1750 the number of cattle moving south to England was up to 80,000 beasts a year, while the Scottish Borders were sending as many as 150,000 sheep south each year.[13]

Stock walked to England along rights of way rather than roads. Drovers were so important that they were exempted from the disarming acts of 1716 and 1748. Reduction of arable and the commutation of mill-dues or multures into grain rents increased the supply of grain needed to sustain the specialist stock-raising areas. Interregional trade, relying heavily on coastal shipping, produced something like a unified Scottish grain market by about 1730 when the standard deviation between counties in the annually calculated 'fiars prices' dropped below 10 per cent.[14] From all these developments landlords derived more buoyant rent rolls without the need to make heavy investments. Black cattle from the Outer Hebrides could be shipped and walked to London.

Another expanding trade in which the landed interest had a big stake was linen. When Daniel Defoe described Perth in the *Tour Through the Whole Island of Great Britain* which he published in 1724–6, he was emphatic that 'The chief business of this town is the linnen manufacture; and it is so considerable here, all the neighbouring country being employ'd in it.'[15] Both the coarse and the fine woollen manufactures seem to have been in decline, partly due to English competition, but linen soared from an average of 3.5 million yards stamped by the officials of the Board of Trustees for Fisheries and Manufactures in 1728–32 to an annual average of 7.8 million yards in 1748–52. The trade leaned heavily on the labour of entire rural families in periods when farm work was slack. Even the finishing end of the business, where alone in the early period of the industry heavy investment was necessary, tended to be sited in the countryside in order to have easy access to water power. Especially in the counties of Angus, Fife, Perth, Lanark and Renfrew, linen massively underpinned rent rolls.[16]

Towns or burghs were essential to rural society as markets or market-places, and outside the Highlands they were numerous, but they were completely dominated by the landed interest. Though towns were important as centres of specialist services, craft activity and mercantile capital, they were outclassed industrially by the sheer scale of such aristocratically controlled enterprises as the coal, salt and lime works, with their increasingly elaborate waggonway systems designed to transport the product to navigable water.[17] Nor were most burghs physically large. Glasgow had a population of 12,766 in 1708, increasing to 23,546 for a slightly larger area in 1755. Edinburgh grew from about 40,000 in 1722 to 57,000 in 1755, on a very cramped site. Dundee had 12,477 inhabitants in 1755, and Aberdeen 22,000. All others were much smaller, some indeed were urban units only by the grace of their charters.[18] Town councils were self-elected and susceptible to influence. From 1721 the Earl of Ilay and his aristocratic allies dominated Edinburgh town council, using it as part of their mechanism for controlling the Convention of Royal Burghs where Edinburgh's lion's share of burghal taxation gave it an exceptionally powerful voice.[19]

Education did not seriously undermine the fundamentally unequal structure of Scottish society. In the Lowlands parochial schools were relatively well developed but the Highlands were poorly provided for and the towns had much the same mixture of municipal and private-venture schooling as characterised many English towns. Literacy levels may not have been very different in the Lowlands from those prevailing in the nearby north of England. New industrial jobs by no means always required literacy. Five universities did constitute an exceptional endowment, but the percentage of the eligible population at those five universities did not differ much from the same statistic for England or Germany. Presbyterian clergymen dominated the teaching faculty and both they and their students were necessarily totally deferential to aristocratic social leadership, because they all wanted the preferment of which the aristocracy were the fount.

The Scottish aristocracy were therefore paradoxically placed. They totally dominated social and political life in Scotland, but as a class they showed unmistakable signs of discontent with their lot. By English standards they were poor. Since they were sitting in a country with about a quarter of

England's population and a taxable capacity more inferior still by several degrees of magnitude, this was hardly surprising, especially when it is borne in mind that the Scottish peerage in 1707 was roughly as numerous as the English. At the very top of the social scale a great magnate like the Duke of Argyll might have by 1770 an income of £9000 net from his Scottish estates, but his estates were uniquely vast, and even so he was not in the same league as the top echelon of the English Whig oligarchy. Many Scottish peers were quite poor by any standard. The Earl of Kilmarnock joined the '45 because he was starving. He later said that he would have rallied to Muhammad for bread. After 1707 it was notorious that almost none of the Representative Peers could afford to cover all their expenses for a parliamentary session in London. Nor were Scots MPs, most of whom sat as clients of a magnate or group of magnates, richer men. On the contrary, they were nearly all drawn from the social layer immediately below the peerage. A minority were younger sons of noble houses. The great majority were lairds, as the territorial form of their names showed. Names like Forbes of Culloden (an Argyll client), Oswald of Dunnikier, or Dalrymple of Hailes completely dominate the record. The odd rich merchant returned for a burgh can usually be shown to have been either a man of business to a powerful peer or a candidate sponsored by an irate government anxious to chastise a sitting MP. On top of the problem of low income levels, the Scottish political class also suffered from debt. This affliction could affect great magnates like the Dukes of Hamilton, whose infamous venality at the time of the Union was largely due to debt. It could also cripple the career of a man like Ludovick Grant of Grant, who retired from the Scottish bar in 1737 after failing to secure judicial preferment, to live cheaply at home in order to pay off family debt.

Desperately anxious as these men mostly were to match the life-style of the English upper classes, it is hardly surprising that they were disproportionately prominent in all the worst financial scandals and 'bubbles' of the era. The Darien Scheme of the 1690s, which started as part of the vicious duel between rival English East India Companies, ended up as a crazy speculation led by the Scottish nobility. They had to use the Union negotiation to recoup their losses. Undeterred, they were so heavily into the South Sea Bubble that the Secretary of State, the Duke of Montrose, himself a big plunger in the game, was convinced that the price of landed property in Scotland would be permanently raised by the enhanced prosperity of the North British political elite. As it was the Whig politicians ended up deeply grateful to Sir Robert Walpole for the shameless stonewalling with which he opened his premiership and which saved all but a few sacrificial lambs from the wrath of the public. Latterly the South Sea affair was little better than barefaced robbery of the nation by the political class including the royal family. John Law, the Edinburgh man who became Controller-General of Finance for France in 1720, was almost certainly sincere in his advocacy of the various credit-creating schemes which eventually culminated in the spectacular and disastrous Mississippi Bubble which was the French equivalent of the South Sea crisis. Nevertheless, it is significant that when he visited England in 1721 after resigning his offices in France he was received as an intimate by the Duke of Argyll. Outright theft as a means of making a fast buck had a recurring fascination for the smaller fry in the Whig ranks. In 1732 outraged Tory backbenchers blew the whistle on a ring of Whigs who were busy plundering the Charitable Corporation 'for the relief of the industrious poor' and Archibald Grant of Monymusk, a ringleader in this unsavoury business, was expelled from the House.

He had been MP for Aberdeenshire. After his expulsion he retired to his estates and became an agricultural improver, for which he has been embalmed in an odour of sanctity by modern economic historians. Contemporaries knew him to the end of his days as the notably unpleasant and greedy trickster he was. It was perhaps no accident that the knavery in the great East India Stock Crash of 1769, which people rightly compared with the South Sea Bubble, was led by Lauchlin Macleane, a member of the Maclean of Coll family. However, fully to grasp the implications of such a contingent of poor, unprincipled and greedy men in British politics, it is essential to examine the activities of one marginal member of the North British nobility in some detail.[20]

Fully to participate in politics naturally involved a public acknowledgement of the Hanoverian succession, so convinced

Jacobites were by definition non-players in this game. All other participants from North Britain were Whig. They tended to polarise around two party structures. One was the so-called Squadrone, originally christened the Squadrone Volante at the time of the Union, but keeping its identity thereafter mainly as the haven of all those who could not or would not find a place within the ranks of the other significant group, the Argathelians or followers of the Duke of Argyll. In practice, the Argathelians were normally managed by the duke's brother, who succeeded him in 1743, but who is known to history as the Earl of Ilay. The two machines were essentially geared to the pursuit of office for their leaders. Not every member of the Scottish political class was firmly committed to either party, but all had to live with them.

James Primrose, 2nd Earl of Rosebery (d. 1755), may serve as an example. His inheritance was such that his tutors absolutely refused to shoulder any further responsibility for him as soon as they could, despite his father's declared wish that they serve as curators as well.[21] Thereafter his lordship was continually tormented by his desire to be in fashionable London, Bath or Paris (anywhere but Edinburgh!) and a lack of the means to sustain such a style of life.[22] The obsession with the life of a man of fashion in London which was so strong in the young James Boswell, the future biographer of Dr Johnson, and which Boswell enshrined in his posthumously published diary, was equally strong in the mind of the 2nd Earl of Rosebery. The first earl had clamoured for some salaried sinecure such as the Chamberlainry of Fife. He felt he had shown total political subservience to Queen Anne's ministers in a way which more than merited reward.[23] His son sank to dunning political friends for cash needed to fend off creditors too powerful to ignore, like the President of the Court of Session.[24] By the late 1730s he had a state pension which Sir Robert Walpole once suggested might be paid on time, as an exceptional gesture, but even this did not spare him the necessity of touching Lord Loudon for £4. 10s. to stop the sale of his horse for debt.[25]

Rosebery whined and wheedled on the margin of Westminster politics. Walpole once personally gave him £25 to fund a trip from London to Scotland, whence Rosebery predictably petitioned for payment of a pension instalment. Rosebery hawked his vote at 'Representative' Peer elections with all the grace of a low-grade tart. At the end of a traditional British grovel to Walpole in February 1739 he swore that Sir Robert's humble memorialist would 'always vote for the court list'.[26] Awarding a pension but failing to pay it regularly was a wonderful way of reinforcing deference. Soon Rosebery was swearing to my Lord Ilay that he would always vote as Ilay instructed. He also enquired of Ilay about his pension arrears.[27]

There were by-elections for Scottish peers to replace those who died between the general elections which the government disliked so much that it spaced them at seven-year intervals. May 1739 saw Rosebery toe the government line and vote for Lord Morton to replace Lord Selkirk.[28] Despite such good behaviour Rosebery had to pawn most of his clothes in 1740 partly because he was an inadequate nincompoop incapable of ordering his affairs, but also partly because there was no shortage of instant servility to Walpole among British Whigs from the North. A devalued Rosebery begged Loudon to 'att least speak to Sir Robert Walpole' and tell him that if pension payments were not a little more regular 'I shall want bread'.[29] Always amusing, never edifying, Rosebery later lost a horse at a Grantham inn for want of £1. 5s. 0d. to pay his bill. His philosophy of politics was summed in a letter from Edinburgh of March 1741 saying: 'On Satterday I write Sir Robert and Lord Ilay, and if they don't pay me £150 instead of £100 this Lady Day I shall vote as my Interest directs me, and my Relations would have me.'[30]

The degradation of the so-called Representative Peers was universally acknowledged throughout Scotland. The Duke of Montrose wrote in 1719 to his friend Mungo Graham of Gorthie saying that only a downright time-server could be a Representative Peer. They were mostly tools of government. Repeated challenges to the Government List which made a mockery of the forms of election were all unsuccessful. Montrose was particularly bitter because in 1707 nobody had expected that most Scots nobles at Westminster would sit as ministerial nominees. Used to a much more personal kind of monarchy than the English, the Scots magnates had taken it for granted that the sovereign would be able to give them independent access to the House of Lords by granting them

British titles. The 16 elected peer seats were expected to be consolation prizes grubbed for by the second-raters and has-beens of the noble political class.[31] The decision of the House of Lords in the celebrated Brandon case of 1711, when that House refused to admit the Duke of Hamilton on the strength of his rank as Duke of Brandon in the British peerage therefore slammed a vitally important door in the face of the higher Scottish aristocracy. Motivated by a real fear of the venality of the Scots and their subservience to court influence, the legally indefensible decision of the House of Lords went far to reinforce that subservience. Court support, in the broad sense of government backing, was now the only means of access to the legislature for nearly all Scots peers.

The down-at-heel Earl of Rosebery was not atypical of his class. He was a gambler always searching for wealth in the shuffle of cards or the roll of dice. He expected to be staked out for life by the dominant political machine of the day. He was also a strong Angliciser who tried to scrounge a commission for 'Neil Primrose my second son' (aged 12), not in order to send him off to foreign wars, but because 'tho it were but a pair of Colours in any marching Regement it would enable me to goe forward with his Education at Aitoun School'.[32] Eton was not the only great school busy turning the sons of Scots peers into British gentlemen fully acceptable to the English Establishment. William Murray (1705–1793), later 1st Earl of Mansfield, the fourth son of David, 5th Viscount Stormont, was processed in turn by Westminster School and Christ Church, Oxford, then assisted by a schoolmate at Westminster, Thomas Foley, to turn to law rather than the Church (which had seemed the inevitable fate for the younger son of an impoverished Scottish peer). He rose rapidly, partly due to his Scottish connections, arguing before the Lords in the case of Paterson v. Graham in 1732–3. He addressed the Commons on behalf of the London merchants who were harrying Walpole into war with Spain in 1738, and after Walpole's fall entered Parliament as MP for Boroughbridge in Yorkshire, and office as Solicitor General. It was a truly remarkable career for a man from an actively Jacobite family, and his greatest days as an immensely important Lord Chief Justice of England lay well ahead. The use of educational structures with a view to anglicising the Scottish elites was in fact well established by 1707. A good example was the Snell Exhibition at Balliol College, Oxford, which brought a succession of able Glasgow University graduates to England. Its founder was John Snell (1629–79), a Scottish royalist refugee from the civil wars of his century. The provision that holders should return to take orders as Episcopalian priests in Scotland was not enforced after the Union of 1707 which was just as well for the young Adam Smith, who held a Snell Exhibition of £40 p. a. between 1740 and 1746. The future father of economics was of a decidedly secular turn of mind.[33]

Personal advancement to more money and better jobs than the Scottish economy could sustain was the normal goal of the Scottish Whig. By 1715 several of them had carved out careers which made their professional identity as British diplomats or soldiers far more important to them than their base as Scottish landowners. Charles (afterwards 8th Baron) Cathcart, who commanded the Hanoverian Cavalry with distinction at the battle of Sheriffmuir, that indecisive engagement which marked the end of any serious Jacobite hopes in the '15, is a case in point. A veteran of Marlborough's wars, he was a member of the Prince of Wales' Household in 1716–18, and after a spell of rustication returned to the court at the accession of his old patron as George II in 1727. Even more striking was the career of General Sir James Campbell of Lawers (d. 1745), a Campbell laird from the northern shores of Loch Tay who was a younger brother of the 3rd Earl of Loudon. He fought in nearly all Marlborough's major battles, with particularly dramatic experiences at Blenheim, Ramillies and Malplaquet. A cavalry officer, he commanded the Scots Greys; was decorated for heroism at the battle of Dettingen; and died of wounds received whilst commanding the British cavalry in the bloody action of Fontenoy in 1744, when he was about 85 years of age.[34]

In other men physical courage was perfectly compatible with bloody-minded egotism and nowhere more so than in the person of John Campbell, 2nd Duke of Argyll and Greenwich (1678–1743). 'Red John of the Battles' was not only Marlborough's outstanding subordinate, but also insanely jealous of him. Capable of statesmanlike moderation, as after the '15, when he saved Scotland for the Hanoverian dynasty at

Sheriffmuir, he was normally egregiously arrogant, abrasive and greedy. No reward was ever commensurate with his merits, and politics to Argyll was the pursuit of personal advantage, regardless of nominal consistency. He moved the dissolution of the Union in the Lords as a protest against the attempt to impose a malt tax on Scotland. In 1725, as part of a deal ousting the only rural Scottish party, the Squadrone, Argyll's faction imposed that tax on Scotland. The most visible figure in the military repression of a brewer's strike and widespread rioting against the malt tax was the Irish Commander-in-Chief of Scotland, General Wade, but the political and part of the military muscle deployed against the resistance came from the Campbells. Argyll and his brother Ilay (later 3rd Duke of Argyll) controlled the situation, with Ilay posting north to cabal with the leading Scottish law officers, Lord Milton (Ilay's acknowledged right-hand man in Edinburgh) and Lord Advocate Duncan Forbes of Culloden (another Argyll client). Sir James Campbell of Lawers, who was in Edinburgh, was given a commission to command all available troops. The old soldier said he would rather have commanded in Flanders.[35]

The initial hope of the Argyll men was that the brewers' will would be broken by threats of imprisonment. The arrival of 'the Great Man' (i.e. Ilay) in Edinburgh was expected to mark a swift end to the crisis.[36] It is interesting to see Walpole's own nickname ('the Great Man') being transferred to Ilay, his satrap for North Britain. Even after some brewers had been arrested, however, it became clear that, in Sir James Campbell's words, 'the folks seem to be in a very mutinous way'. He added, 'I hope that they will be wise'. He feared physical violence.[37] It came in the shape of massive rioting in Glasgow which was crushed by an equally massive display of military force by Wade and Forbes of Culloden. Thereafter the Edinburgh brewers 'submitted themselves to the King and parliament'.[38]

To say that Scotland was meaningfully 'represented' in that legislature is wholly to misconstrue the role of her 16 peers and 45 MPs. There were only about 2600 voters in the 33 counties of Scotland and most of them were subject to control by a few hundred landowners. The venal cliques in the town councils alone voted in the burghs, and it required the effrontery of

Edmund Burke to invent much later the lunatic theory that the voteless were 'virtually represented'. Scottish MPs rarely wanted to offend by representing grievances. Like Wade, they served the government for profit. After teaching Glasgow subservience to sovereign power Wade secured a Highland triumph when the Mackenzies, the most powerful of the clans north of Inverness, surrendered their weapons on a far greater scale than anyone had expected. They had a history of Jacobitism but their chief had decided to come to terms with Westminster.[39] For Argyll supporters the malt tax episode was crowned by hearing, towards the end of the crisis, of the final ousting of the Squadrone's Duke of Roxburgh from his position as Secretary of State for Scotland.[40]

Argyll continued on his usual erratic personal path. Having, in debates on the Mutiny Bill of 1717–18, insisted on the reality of the threat to liberty represented by a standing army in peace-time, he opposed any reduction in the army in 1733, when he was on good terms with government, and insisted that it was no menace at all. As his relations with Walpole degenerated under the strain mainly of his own megalomania, he tended to adopt 'popular' attitudes. He was applauded for defending the city of Edinburgh in 1737 against a bill of pains and penalties following on the Porteous Riots. Smuggling had become a national sport in Scotland after 1707, so when a popular smuggler was executed in Edinburgh it was hardly surprising that there was trouble, lethal trouble, between the town guard commanded by Captain Porteous and the town mob. Convicted of murder by a local court and understandably pardoned by the Crown, Porteous was lynched by a well-drilled crowd after being torn from custody. Judging by his track record on the malt tax, Argyll under different circumstances might have managed the daunting of Edinburgh. As it was, he went on to join the critics of Walpole who were baying for war with Spain in 1738, and after the bad harvest of 1740 went around blaming Walpole for the hard times. After the Great Man's fall in 1742 he was rewarded with office but shortly resigned in high dudgeon for his usual reason – a collection of offices and honours starting with being Master General of the Ordnance seemed to him grossly inadequate for his transcendant merits. He died, deranged, in 1743.[41]

Argyll, like his Squadrone rivals in the regional aristocratic ascendancy was a firm Whig, in the sense that he was committed to the Protestant Succession embodied in the House of Hanover. The most drastic alternative to the existing political system was Jacobitism, support for the exiled line of the Stuarts represented by the melancholic figure of James Francis Edward Stuart, the Old Pretender. As a cause, it seemed to be dying after 1715, shaken to its roots by the Earl of Mar's gross mismanagement of the initially promising rising of that year. Jacobitism was essentially a conservative backlash led by disgruntled lairds and nobles, and it did seem that the Scottish nobility as a whole were convinced that it had no future. The absurd episode of the 1719 rising in the north-western Highlands seemed to confirm this view. It was crushed almost as soon as it had started by government troops, and apart from some significant Mackenzie support it was the work of a small group of Scottish Jacobite exiles who were very obviously being used by the Italian first minister of Spain, Cardinal Alberoni, as pawns to mount a diversionary attack in the course of a quarrel with Britain which had no bearing on Scottish affairs whatsoever.[42] The real problem is to explain why Jacobitism survived at all as a potential force. For this there are several explanations, one of which must be the way in which Jacobite and Whig were inextricably interwoven in the close family networks of the Scottish aristocracy. A sinister example of this is James, Lord Grange (1679–1754), who while professing strict Presbyterian and Hanoverian principles and holding the post of Lord Justice Clerk in the Edinburgh judiciary nevertheless kept up a close and obscure connection with the Jacobite party, of which his brother the Earl of Mar was a leader. Grange manipulated his Whig acquaintances in an artful way which repeatedly corresponded exactly with the needs of the Jacobites. For example, he deprecated early news of the 1715 rising, suggesting there was no cause for alarm, and astonishment when it became clear that there was plenty of cause for acute concern.[43] Nobody was more assiduous in making touching appeals for clemency for rebels and their families in influential Whig circles.[44] He was active in the tacit conspiracy by the Scottish judges to make the forfeiture of Jacobite estates ineffective, or very difficult.

One of Grange's most interesting arguments in the course of the latter episode was that if the collection of forfeited rents were to be made ultimately to the Westminster exchequer there was real danger that English law would be used to decide disputes. From there, he argued, it was but a step to a general penetration by the English Common Law and the destruction of the Scots legal tradition.[45] Nothing of the sort occurred, of course, but Grange knew that his correspondent knew that the defence of the Scots legal tradition was essential if the Scots courts were to be kept clear of Englishmen (Scots like Mansfield were meantime making tracks towards English courts).

The Scots legal tradition as Grange understood it was, in fact, quite a recent formation, drawn into its Romano-Dutch framework in the *Institutions* (1681) of a great jurist, Sir James Dalrymple, 1st Viscount Stair (1619–95), and rendered accessible to hard-riding lawyers in the slim text book, Sir George Mackenzie's *Institutions* (1684). Both Stair and Mackenzie changed the traditional legal usages of Scotland considerably to suit their own prejudices and professional interests, thereby obscuring to future generations the nature of the very mixed system of law traditionally practised in Scotland. Mackenzie's slim volume was edited in its seventh edition by an academic lawyer in Edinburgh University, Alexander Bain, who also produced supplements to Mackenzie in 1731 and 1749. The next major institutionalist, Andrew McDouall, Lord Bankton (1685–1760), produced his *Institute* in the early 1750s, which may help explain why the 8th edition of Mackenzie in 1758 was the last. Mackenzie was a Jacobite, Stair a Whig, but their mutual enthusiasm for a distinct Scottish legal tradition, defined so as to suit Edinburgh advocates, underpinned a vested interest transcending party.[46] Grange's own underlying respect for any meaningful concept of Justice was clearly nil. Any man who could, with the co-operation of a clique of rascally Highland chiefs like Lord Lovat, Sir Alexander MacDonald and MacLeod of Muiravondale, kidnap his own wife in 1732, publicly celebrate her funeral rites, and keep her an isolated prisoner in St Kilda, Sutherlandshire, and Skye until she died mad in 1745, was primarily interested in ends, not means.

It would nevertheless be wrong to imagine that the Jacobite cause did not include men of honour, integrity and patriotism. It was one of the enduring strengths of Jacobitism that it appealed to just such men, especially when they were outraged by the venality and the lack of principles, scruples and identity which tended to characterise the higher Whig leadership. Both Ilay and Walpole were an affront to any informed person who accepted the traditional Christian view that government was and ought to be a moral process. With the establishment in 1690 of a purely Presbyterian form of governance in the Kirk, nearly half the ministers in the country were left disgruntled, attached to episcopal governance, and north of the Forth often still in control of their pulpits due to staunch support from the nobility and gentry. After a test case in 1712, the power of the Presbyterians to prosecute episcopalian clergy simply for liturgical deviation was curbed. Episcopalian ministers could be squeezed out of their pulpits, slowly over time, for failure to pray for King George, but often this simply drove them into the households of the nobles and lairds whose children they taught and to whom they preached a passionate compound of Jacobitism and religious fervour.[47] The 1690 religious settlement was doomed if the Jacobites were to seize power, as was the Union, of which they were the leading opponents. One result of this situation was that committed Presbyterians were 'the King's (i.e. King George's) hearty Friends'. Intellectual Presbyterian trouble-makers like John Simson, a mildly progressive but apparently orthodox professor of divinity at Glasgow, were regarded by some as more of a menace to political solidarity than to Gospel Truth.[48] After 1729 he was placed in the ideal academic position of retaining his salary, but being forbidden to teach.

In one sense, the political management of Scotland in the early eighteenth century was not difficult. Jacobite members of the ruling class were excluded from politics except in rebellions, while both the other significant groups, the Argyll men and the Squadrone were universally recognised as Whigs.[49] Neither the Argathelians nor the Squadrone were over-burdened with political principles. The main problems were their deadly rivalry with one another, and the extremely brash and unpleasant style which these nobles employed when demanding jobs and money. English ministers like Godolphin and his successor Harley do seem to have found these ghastly North Britons difficult to stomach, but their own response, which involved balancing Squadrone Secretaries of State such as Montrose or Roxburgh against the much stronger Argathelian block, whilst trying to concentrate patronage decisions in the Westminster Treasury (which lacked the local knowledge to take them), simply led to confusion and paralysis. Once in power, Walpole broadly accepted the facts of Scottish life, while making sure Ilay never developed into an autonomous political boss.

The Campbells, led by the Argyll interest, simply had to be allowed to be top dogs, because as long as the Argyll leadership was intelligent, nobody else could match them, and they could make life miserable for any ministry at a general election where the outcome was finely balanced. The various branches of the Campbells showed remarkable coherence, which was a major source of strength. Apart from Argyll and his principal rival for the Campbell leadership, Breadalbane, there was Campbell of Cawdor, whose estates lay in the Laigh of Murray, far from the main bastions of Campbell power, but very much with them in spirit. Finally, there were the Ayrshire Campbells represented by the Earls of Loudon, magnates closely related to the Montgomeries (Earls of Eglinton) and the Dalrymples (Earls of Stair), and therefore able to lead a massive western block into the Argathelian camp. Argyll was personally impossible, but even here the Campbells had Ilay, who never broke with Walpole and who with his brother maintained an effective 'hard-man, soft-man' act guaranteed to squeeze all allowable concessions out of Walpole.

Ilay, an Englishman by education, residence and preference, knew full well that Walpole's own Scottish expert, John Scrope, Secretary to the Treasury, had to be allowed a key role in patronage decisions, and that the whole system was about power and patronage, not representation. The last thing Walpole wanted to hear was a voice articulating the needs and grievances of Scotland.[50] Intelligent contemporaries knew full well that the role Ilay played so successfully in politics was limited and highly personal. The ultimate source of authority on North British patronage still lay with Walpole and Scrope, though in practice they delegated much of their power in these matters to Ilay.[51] The placing of the Secretaryship of State for Scotland (technically simply a third Secretaryship) in abeyance was perhaps a symbolic way of underlining the limits on the status of Walpole's Scottish satrap. The post was revived for the Squadrone's Marquess of Tweeddale in 1742, only to be suppressed indefinitely after his monstrously inept handling of the '45.

It was a standard Jacobite gripe that the Whig regime was excessively influenced by the 'democratical tendencies' of Presbyterian rabble-rousers. The reverse appears to have been the case. With the restoration of lay patronage in 1712 Presbyterian clergymen needed nomination from nobles and lairds for advancement, and they knew that the extensive patronage of the Crown was in practice at the disposal of Whig politicians. Ilay deliberately adopted a tougher line on Crown nominations, which before his ascendancy had been handled with some respect for parishioners' views. He concentrated exclusively on the political usefulness of ecclesiastical patronage, narrowly construed, and manipulated the General Assembly of the Kirk (still theoretically opposed to lay patronage) through his clerical manager, the very erastian Patrick Cumming, who dominated the Assembly in 1737–42 and 1746–51.[52] Lairds and lawyers were in any case massively present in the General Assembly, thinly disguised as Ruling Elders.

The Solicitor General, Sir James Steuart of Goodtrees, assured the Duke of Montrose early in 1715 that he had not directly opposed strong expressions of grievance in the Assembly because they were irresistible, but he hoped subtly to divert and confuse the issues, the better to serve the government.[53] Goodtrees is often described as a hard-line Presbyterian. He was more of a hard-line Whig who deemed all episcopalians Jacobites. In this world, secession by Presbyterians passionately opposed to lay patronage merely strengthened the vice-like grip of the politicians on the remaining Church of Scotland. This was certainly true of the Original Secession by four ministers led by Ebeneezer Erskine in December 1733. A 'Moderate' party determined to come to terms with lay patronage did not exist until the early 1750s, but a divided and weakened Kirk had been in no position to offer serious resistance to domination by lay politicians for decades by then.[54]

So powerful had the Campbell political machine become within a North Britain made safe for Whigs that by the late 1730s it was able to indulge in the luxury of internal division without actually committing suicide. The stages by which the 2nd Duke of Argyll drifted into formed opposition to Walpole until he was deprived of all his offices in 1740 remain disappointingly obscure. Walpole seems to have regarded Ilay as his loyal ally to the end, and he was in a position to know, but Argyll himself, in unprecedented co-operation with the Squadrone, helped to ensure that crucial swing against Walpole in the Scottish constituencies which, along with a similar swing in Cornwall, placed the premier in an untenable position. Walpole's fall in 1742 made very little difference to the political system and certainly did Argyll no great good, but Ilay, who succeeded as 3rd Duke of Argyll in 1743, was able in the long run to reassemble his political troops and to exploit the errors of the Squadrone leadership to recapture most of the political clout he had enjoyed in the 1730s.[55] For those who had hoped for a new moral order in politics after the fall of the 'sole minister' it was all very depressing. Cynical power-brokers like Ilay and Walpole made official rhetoric about a 'Protestant Constitution' and 'Revolution Principles' sound hollow. Both men had a sense of the limits to what they could get away with, but this was realism, not the 'Civic Virtue' peddled by university orators.

Andrew Fletcher, Lord Milton, Ilay's principal Edinburgh man of business, seems to have been the exception which proves the rule, for he really tried to practise the Public Virtue and Improvement which he preached. Most North British Whig politicians were egotists happy to make representation a joke, and to leave patriotism to Jacobites. From the disgruntled Whig Grant of Grant to the crypto-Jacobite Lord Lovat, there was a consensus by 1745 that the regime lacked moral justification, Henry Pelham, himself a future premier, said at the start of the '45 that the real threat to the regime was the lack of will to defend it.[56] Not much wonder that Prince Charles was able to walk from Glenfinnan to Edinburgh in 1745 without the additional burden of having to ask his tiny army to fight.

4. Walpole and Ireland

DAVID HAYTON

I

WALPOLE, in common with every other English politician in the first half of the eighteenth century, usually accorded Irish business a low priority. Even at the height of the gravest crisis in Anglo-Irish relations in this period, the affair of 'Wood's Halfpence', he displayed the superciliousness that characterised the fashionable Englishman's attitude to all things Hibernian. 'I have weathered great storms before now and I hope I shall not be lost at last in an Irish hurricane.'[1] Nevertheless, the way he and his colleagues tackled the Irish questions they were posed can tell us a good deal about the man and his administration, as well as about the nature of the Anglo-Irish political connection.

Walpole's Irish policy has been viewed differently on either side of the Irish Sea. English historians have claimed that after defusing the furore in Ireland against Wood's Halfpence, Walpole reacted by seeking to exclude Irishmen from the government of their country, peopling Dublin Castle instead with party hacks from England, and that he thereby alienated the 'natural rulers' of Ireland, the Protestant squirearchy, and unwittingly paved the way for the 'nationalism' of Flood and Grattan.[2] Irish historians, by contrast, have viewed Walpole's premiership as the beginning of the age of the 'undertakers', when the government, anxious for a quiet life, contracted out Irish parliamentary management to Irish politicians, who 'undertook' to carry through the king's business in return for a say in policy and a sizeable piece of the patronage pie.[3] Each of these conflicting interpretations contains part of the truth.

II

The wars, confiscations and migrations of sixteenth- and seventeenth-century Ireland had left the 'Anglo-Irish' land-owning and governing class in a dominant but exposed position. The English settlement of Ireland had been largely a plantation of gentry, lacking the necessary substructure of yeomanry and freeholders, so that although by 1700 Protestants controlled over 80 per cent of Irish land, they formed no more than a quarter of the population. The Anglo-Irish saw themselves as a beleaguered minority, vastly outnumbered by the Catholics, whose inveterate hostility, on national and religious grounds, reinforced by the bitter grievance of dispossession, was taken for granted. Furthermore, the only province in which Protestants had arrived in substantial numbers, Ulster, was dominated not by English settlers but by Presbyterian Scots, many of them recent immigrants, who were viewed by the Anglican establishment with almost as much enmity and suspicion as were the Catholics. Threatened from two sides, the Anglo-Irish were aware that their security depended on English military aid. It was an army from England that had sent King James packing in 1690, and English governments had maintained large standing forces in Ireland ever since (albeit for strategic, financial and political reasons of their own). Mobilisation of troopers to deal with outbreaks of banditry or agrarian disturbances acted as a regular reminder to Irish Protestants of their ultimate reliance on England.

On the other hand, there were limits to this feeling of dependence. While the Anglo-Irish accepted the insuperable hostility of their Catholic fellow countrymen, they were equally conscious of the improbability of any Catholic uprising. The Jacobite war and its aftermath, the exile of the so-called 'wild geese', had resulted in the 'destruction' of the Catholic 'gentry', and without their 'natural leaders' it was unthinkable that the common people could rebel. The only real chance lay in the importation of leadership from France and the Jacobites. Reports that the Pretender was on the sea let loose panic among the Anglo-Irish. In normal circumstances, however, even the fear of the Pretender was slowly coming to be discountenanced. When the young William Fownes proposed in 1730 to invest all his capital in Irish land, and was advised by his grandfather that "tis good to have an estate in England for fear of another Irish revolution', a friend commented drily, 'he may as well frighten you with the Day of Judgment, and 'twould do you more good'.[4] The Anglo-Irish also realised that in their relationship with England the dependence was not all on one side. They were, after all, the only allies the English possessed in Ireland, and were not going to be thrown over. An Irish politician, observing in 1724 that only by force would Ireland be made to accept Wood's Halfpence, could state categorically, 'that is what will never be used'.[5]

The niceties of this complex interrelationship, with the ultimate dependence of the Anglo-Irish masked by a degree of give and take in practice, was well expressed in the constitutional machinery through which Ireland was governed. Theoretically English control was strict. The executive in Dublin Castle (the Lord Lieutenant, and in his absence a commission of Lords Justices) was appointed from England and responsible to English officers of state. The Crown enjoyed a large 'hereditary revenue' in Ireland, and the Irish Parliament was only called to vote 'additional duties' to make up the shortfall. When it did meet it had no right to prepare legislation, that being the task of the Irish Privy Council, whose bills had to be approved by the Privy Council in England, and were then presented for acceptance or rejection by the Irish Parliament, with no possibility of amendment. The Westminster Parliament also possessed the power to legislate itself for Ireland if need be. That was the letter of the law; the practice was somewhat different. By the reign of George I Irish Parliaments had come to develop a power of the purse. The military budget required regular injections of 'additional duties', and Irish MPs were careful never to vote these for periods of longer than two years. When the Tory ministry failed to secure a supply in 1713 the arrears that quickly accumulated resulted in the establishment of a permanent Irish 'national debt'. Nor, apart from a moment of desperation on the part of Bolingbroke in 1714, was the taxation of Ireland by the British Parliament ever envisaged. Secondly, there had been an important development in the process of legislation. Aside from the measures needed to start off a session, bills actually began their lives not in the Irish Privy Council but in the Irish Parliament, as 'heads' of bills. Tampering with 'heads' by either Privy Council, though not infrequent, did lead to difficulties and sometimes to the rejection of a returned bill, especially in the case of money bills, over the drafting of which the Irish Commons claimed a monopoly: these were seldom altered. The crucial debates of any session came when the money bill 'heads' were considered. Here, and indeed generally in the Commons, the viceroy was obliged to employ Irish political managers, 'undertakers' of one sort or another. As yet no standing court interest, no body of 'King's friends', had emerged to take responsibility for government business. Certainly the Lord Lieutenant and his Chief Secretary, nearly always Englishmen, would lack sufficient local knowledge to cope on their own, nor would they be at their posts long enough to acquire it.

These kind of constitutional arrangements were well suited to the peculiar fledgling 'patriotism' of the Anglo-Irish. Still conscious that they represented the 'English interest' in Ireland, and capable of thinking of themselves both as 'English' and 'Irish' in different contexts, they were fond of exuberant statements of Irish patriotism, and denounced what they saw as English economic exploitation while realising that the possibilities of action and remedy were restricted. William Molyneux's *Case of Ireland Stated* (1698) which denied the right of the English Parliament to legislate for Ireland, and was to be so influential on the 'patriots' of the later eighteenth century, received little public support from Irishmen when it first appeared. Naturally enough, the subtleties of the Anglo-Irish position were lost on English ministers, who gave little thought to Ireland until they had to, and tended to accept effusions of patriotism at face value. Like Queen Anne, they believed that the Anglo-Irish had 'a mind to be independent, if they could; but they should not'.[6]

The requirements of a ministry from its Irish policy were simple: 'additional duties' to pay for the army; and peace and quiet in the Irish Parliament and in the kingdom at large. Attacks on the British government or Parliament, which could lead in turn to difficulties at home, were especially to be

avoided. Otherwise Irish issues made little impact at Westminster. There were relatively few Irishmen in either House,
and, unlike the Scots, their collective opposition could not
hazard the court's majority. An Irish lobby organised itself, as
in 1731 under Lord Perceval, to promote measures in the
British Parliament that would benefit Ireland, mostly in the
realm of trade and industry, but was active only on these
specific issues. It was often joined and sometimes led by the
Chief Secretary himself or other officials of the Irish administration, showing that the real political dividend to be gained
was the satisfaction not of the 'Irish lobby' itself but of
Parliament back in Dublin.[7]

Changes in the pattern of Irish politics following the
accession of George I made it easier in some respects for
English ministers to get what they wanted.[8] In Anne's reign the
Dublin Parliament had been infected by English-style 'party'
politics, as Irishmen fought the battles of Whig and Tory as
lustily as their English counterparts. The existence of such
hard-and-fast divisions had tended to cramp the viceroy's
freedom of manoeuvre. Each party provided a ready-made set of
'undertakers', with prejudices and commitments that were not
easy to override. After 1714, however, the two-party structure
broke up quickly in Ireland. The frightening implications of the
succession issue for the Anglo-Irish tended to shift the centre of
gravity in Irish politics decisively over on to the Whig side. So
comfortable was the Whig majority returned at the 1715
general election (and without an Irish Triennial or Septennial
Act this Parliament lasted the whole reign) that the party could
enjoy the luxury of a schism in the very first session, with
discontented Whigs joining Tories in Opposition. The Tories,
for their part, also split. Toryism had struck shallower roots in
Ireland, and without the prospect of a return to power by their
allies in England the more moderate, more ambitious and
needier Tories came over to the court. The bulk of Tories
probably remained in Opposition throughout the 1720s, and
although party distinctions were not entirely lost sight of even
later, in terms of management the family- or territorial-based
'connection' soon came to be the significant unit of parliamentary organisation – the 'clans' of the court party in 1729, for
example, the 'Boyleites', 'Wynneites' and other 'tribes' of the

later 1730s, the 'Cork squadron', the 'north-countrymen', and even at one point the 'toopees', set apart by the cut of their hairpieces. Having individual magnates and heads of families to bargain with rather than party caucuses gave the viceroy a more positive role in the political game. There were, however, unpleasant side-effects. The party conflict of Anne's reign had temporarily deflected Irish emotions from national questions, which now reared up again. The hybrid Opposition naturally looked for 'popular' but non-party grievances, and the most obvious were matters of 'patriotic' concern. As the Englishman Bishop Godwin observed in 1717, 'now the Tories are brought low I find the distinction between English and Irish grows more wide'.[9]

This refocusing of Irish political concern was not the only invidious result of the breakdown of the two-party system. Another chronic problem arose from the rivalry of the two most prominent Irish Whig politicians, Alan Brodrick and William Conolly. This was still unresolved when Walpole and Townshend took over the ministry in 1722. The quarrel had originated in the division of spoils in 1714. Brodrick became Lord Chancellor while his former colleague succeeded him in the Chair of the Commons. In Ireland the Speakership was an overtly political office and Conolly therefore assumed the role of 'undertaker'. Brodrick, a passionate egoist, would brook no rival, and his antagonism was sharpened by the fact that Conolly, in his secondary capacity as chief revenue commissioner, controlled more valuable patronage than he himself did. Conflict between the two began in 1715 and continued unabated. Conolly's strategy was to make himself useful at all times; Brodrick's to behave himself but to foment trouble in the Commons through his son, St John. Not surprisingly, Conolly proved consistently the more attractive to the court. Even the Duke of Bolton, viceroy in 1717, who came to Dublin as a close friend of the Chancellor and began by favouring him, had by 1719, in Brodrick's words, 'taken other people entirely into his bosom'.[10] Bolton's replacement the following year by the Duke of Grafton made matters even worse for Brodrick (now Lord Midleton). While Conolly was in high favour, one of the 'secret council', the viceroy held the Brodricks at a distance, blamed them for his troubles, and pressed for them to be disciplined.

However, the extent of their support in the Irish Parliament, and the complications of English politics, kept Midleton in office. For he and his son, and brother, were Members of the British Parliament as well. In the Whig Schism they had sided with Sunderland and Stanhope, but by 1719 Midleton had broken with Sunderland, and expected dismissal.[11] Uncertainty as to how much damage this might cause in Ireland postponed the decision, and then the balance of English politics shifted again with Walpole's return to office. Regarding the Brodricks as potential allies at Westminster, he was willing to protect them from Sunderland.

Although with hindsight the central problem of Irish policy in the period 1715–22 appears to have been the management of the Commons and the resolution of the struggle between Conolly and the Brodricks, for the ministers all else was overshadowed by the goings-on in the Irish House of Lords. It was unusual for the Lords to claim such attention. Attendances were small, including always a high proportion of bishops, and little important business was transacted. In normal circumstances there would be sufficient poverty among the lay lords, sufficient cupidity on the episcopal bench to form an automatic government majority. But the early years of George I's reign were exceptional. The Whigs had inherited in 1714 an upper House so dominated by Tories that a batch of new Whig bishops was not enough to turn the scale and there had also to be a creation of peers. The trouble was that these were mostly Irishmen, and first-rank politicians at that, rather than mere lobby fodder. And although many of the new bishops were Englishmen, one or two able Irish clerics were promoted, including friends of the forceful Archbishop King of Dublin, himself an arch-patriot. For a time Irishmen outnumbered Englishmen in the House, and when any 'national' issue arose the patriot coalition headed by King and the Tory primate Lindsay would stand a fair chance of defeating the court. It was thus doubly unfortunate that the Lords should become embroiled in a constitutional conflict over the cause of their appellate jurisdiction, brought into question by an appeal from Ireland to the British House of Lords. The case culminated in the passage in 1720 by the Westminster Parliament of a Declaratory Act reaffirming its rights both to hear Irish appeals and to make laws for Ireland. Reactions among the Anglo-Irish were bitter. Lord Abercorn called this 'an amazing bill': 'I venture to say that Ireland never yet received so stunning, or rather fatal, a blow.'[12]

By the summer of 1720 passions were running so high in Ireland that few Irishmen believed their Parliament would ever sit again.[13] Sunderland responded with a characteristically bold initiative, tackling the two chronic problems together. Midleton was to be dismissed in a round of legal promotions. More radically, Irish government finances were to be reorganised so that 'additional duties' would no longer be required, and thus, as Dublin opinion had divined, 'His Majesty [may] not be under the necessity of calling a Parliament every two years'. Some bizarre expedients surfaced in ministerial discussions, including a transfer of army officers to the West Indies, and most extraordinary of all for a Whig government to suggest, a farm of the hereditary revenue. Sunderland did, however, secure the prior consent of the king to whatever was proposed.[14] At this point Walpole stepped in. Using his friendship with Grafton to secure the Lord Lieutenant's backing, he argued that it was now too late to avoid calling a Parliament in 1721, and therefore that it would be too risky to remove Midleton or tamper with the Irish establishment.[15] Both schemes were dropped. Walpole's alternative policy soon became clear. He assisted St John Brodrick's return to the British Parliament, and persuaded Grafton to bury his ill-feeling far enough to seek Midleton's co-operation for the next Irish parliamentary session, and to show him 'visible favour and credit'.[16]

The 1721–2 session in fact proved comparatively quiet. Both Houses were distracted by a controversial project for setting up a national bank, and the Declaratory Act, surprisingly, was not disputed. But this did not mean that the underlying difficulties had been resolved. Conolly and the Brodricks were still at daggers drawn, and the *entente* Grafton had established with the Chancellor proved too fragile to last the session. Before long Midleton was looking around for support against Grafton and Walpole, and after Sunderland's death in 1722 found it in one of the leading lights of the Sunderland faction, Lord Carteret. Nor had the patriotism of the Anglo-Irish suddenly shrivelled.

The rapturous reception given to the playwright William
Philips's allegorical representation of his country's woes,
Hibernia Freed, when performed on the London stage in
February 1722 to an audience composed of 'the wild Irish',
testifies to the continuing vigour of national sentiment.[17]
Should sufficient provocation be given it was ready to burst
forth again; and that the ministers themselves promptly
supplied.

III

To the English there seemed nothing particularly controversial
in the patent obtained in July 1722 by the Wolverhampton
ironmaster, William Wood, to mint copper coins for Ireland.
But this 'obscure, inconsiderable, insignificant, ill-designing
mechanic' and his 'wicked project', came to be viewed in
Ireland both as a symbol of English oppression and as a real
threat to the Irish economy. Much of the violence of this
reaction can be explained by circumstances. Not only was Irish
patriotism rampant, and any English interference likely to be
interpreted in a sinister light, Ireland was also gripped by an
acute financial crisis, which made interference with the coinage
of all things the most alarming. In 1720 it was reported that 'the
extreme scarcity of money . . . is so great that it has put a
general stop to trade and must in a short time to the payment of
our rents'; a year later, that 'above 6,000 . . . weavers and other
manufacturers of the wool' were 'actually starving'.[18] The
bursting of the South Sea Bubble had poisoned the public mind
in Ireland, as well as in England, against government-inspired
financial schemes of any kind, and even the most level-headed
Anglo-Irishman could see in the new 'brass money' a trick to
'ruin' his country and 'every private man's estate'.[19] Furthermore the way in which Wood had acquired the patent, buying
it for £10,000 from the original grantee, the Duchess of Kendal,
reeked of jobbery. Following the gift of Irish titles to Kendal
and to George I's half-sister Kielmansegg, and of Irish
pensions to Hanoverians at a cost of some £11,500 p.a., here
was the crowning evidence that the new dynasty was selfishly
plundering Ireland's resources.[20]

The campaign against the Halfpence in 1722–5 can be compared to that in England against the Excise, in its scope and eventual success. Already by the time the Irish Parliament met in September 1723 unrest was mounting, fuelled by a pamphlet, *Ireland's Consternation*, which depicted the draining away of the bullion of the kingdom in return for the worthless Halfpence: the recurring nightmare of opposition writers. But it was in Parliament that the explosion occurred. Both Houses addressed the king against the Halfpence; and even when the royal reply promised inquiries, the Commons reiterated a demand for directions to Irish revenue officers 'that they do not, on any pretence whatsoever, receive or utter any of the said halfpence'. The parliamentary fission set off a chain reaction. Swift added his satirical talent to the 'clamour' with the so-called 'Drapier's Letters', in which, during the following year, he excoriated Wood, attacked Walpole, and explored the wider theme of Ireland's constitutional status and the rights of the Anglo-Irish as 'a free people'. Lesser writers followed suit, and the stream of tracts, squibs and ballads became a cascade. Molyneux's *Case of Ireland* was reprinted, in an attempt to catch the patriotic mood. Even more worrying for the ministry than this bombardment from the press was the response of public opinion, expressed by the propertied classes in addresses from grand juries and corporations, and by the populace in demonstrations and rioting. The current of addresses had been set in motion by the Irish Privy Council itself, prompted by patriot leaders there, and by Dublin; by the autumn of 1724 towns as far apart as Londonderry in the north-west and Wexford in the south-east had joined in. Wood had also been hung in effigy by the Dublin '*mobile*', and a consignment of his coinage had been turned back from Cork after threats to the ship carrying it. The Englishman Judge Hale described how 'the people' had vented their emotions in 'a furious and extravagant manner ... nothing but burning of shops, pulling down houses, and tearing in pieces the persons of such as should import, receive or conceal any of this coin'.[21]

Walpole's reaction was compounded of surprise, outrage and alarm. Although the patent had not been of his devising, he was determined at this stage to support it, in the words of one historian, partly from 'his concern for the royal prerogative' and partly from 'his conviction that a sound economic proposal was being wrecked by interested politicians and fanatical demagogues'.[22] He believed in the merits of the coinage and the honesty of Wood, especially after Sir Isaac Newton, no less, had assayed samples. The first printed attack on the Halfpence, *Ireland's Consternation*, Walpole dismissed as 'the most arrant Grub Street paper I ever read in my life'; the 'chief objections', transmitted by the Irish government, were in his opinion 'frivolous', the outcry in the country manufactured rather than spontaneous.[23] At the same time, he took the affair very seriously, stung by criticism of himself and by hints of impeachment in the Irish Parliament, embarrassed by the involvement of the Duchess of Kendal, and anxious at the opportunity Carteret had grasped to 'fling dirt'.[24] In the context of Anglo-Irish relations, there was also the underlying fear that the Irish, 'both friends and foes', wished to 'shake off' their 'dependency' on England.[25]

According to Walpole's interpretation, which Townshend and Newcastle shared, the situation demanded a reappraisal of policy, though as yet no repudiation of Wood. The ministry's difficulties were seen as stemming from Grafton's incompetence, the continuing intrigue of Carteret with Midleton, and the Anglo-Irish desire for 'independency'. Walpole's impatience with the viceroy boiled over early in the Irish parliamentary session of 1723–4, when he fired off two letters sharply reminding Grafton of his responsibility: 'upon whom the consequences of this Irish storm will fall most heavily I will not say; I shall have my share, but if I am not mistaken there are others that will not escape. I hope your grace is not mistaken, when you are persuaded to be thus indifferent.'[26] Townshend was even more angry, rebuking the viceroy so roughly that Walpole felt obliged to intercept and suppress his letter.[27] Only Newcastle treated Grafton sympathetically, not because of any higher opinion of his abilities but out of concern for 'the child's good heart'. It was through Newcastle's mediation that Grafton's ruffled pride was smoothed down in order to maintain ministerial unity while the Irish Parliament was sitting.[28] But when the session was over he was dismissed.

Getting rid of Grafton improved matters only in one limited respect. To do more required coming to terms with the chronic

problems which had beset ministers and viceroys since 1715,
the rivalry between Midleton and Conolly, and the apparent
strength of the 'patriotic' element in Irish politics. Attention
focused first on Midleton, because of the Chancellor's dealings
with Carteret, of which Walpole was very well informed. Their
correspondence was opened by his agents, copied and then
resealed.[29] The effects of the intrigue on proceedings in the Irish
Parliament were graphically described in Grafton's
despatches, in which St John Brodrick figured as 'the most
open manager against the court', and the Chancellor himself,
despite professions of loyalty and claims that St John was 'not
under my control or correction', was said to have been much
less discreet than usual in his own opposition.[30] The viceroy
repeated his emphasis on the utter necessity of replacing
Midleton. He obtained Newcastle's backing, and Townshend's, and finally, in January 1724, a promise from the
king.[31]

Yet Walpole hesitated. He did not accept Grafton's assurances of the weakness of Midleton's following and the corre-
sponding strength of Conolly's. To most Irish observers, the
1723–4 session was not primarily a struggle between court and
Opposition, or even for and against the Halfpence, but between
Conolly and Midleton to see who should 'govern'. And the
Brodricks had scored considerable successes. The supply was
contested 'inch by inch'; there were embarrassing inquiries into
pensions; a move to censure Midleton for neglect of his judicial
duties elicited a vote of confidence from the Commons.
Conolly's worst moment came in a division he actually won, on
the County Westmeath by-election, in which he and the
Brodricks had backed opposing candidates. After making this a
public test of his position the Speaker scraped home by the
narrowest of margins, an outcome the 'Midletonians', and
Dublin society in general, regarded as a humiliation.[32]
Walpole had thus good reason to doubt Grafton's sanguine
hopes. Moreover, he entertained suspicions of his own about
Conolly. Walpole viewed the rivalry of Conolly and Midleton
with detachment. After all, Conolly was as much an Irishman
as Midleton (more so, since he was of Gaelic stock and
Midleton the son of a Cromwellian planter), and therefore just
as unreliable. He had failed to press the arguments for the

Halfpence in the Parliament and the Privy Council, and in his capacity as a revenue commissioner had been actively obstructive. So instead of removing Midleton, Walpole permitted the Chancellor to be reappointed a Lord Justice in 1724, and tried to convince the other Brodricks of his goodwill towards them.[33]

Walpole's final solution to this perennial question was to hand over the decision to the new viceroy; a neat touch, since Grafton's successor was none other than Carteret. His appointment was a stone that massacred a multiplicity of birds, and the Irish fatalities were a by-product of the main purpose, the defeat of Carteret's challenge for control of the English ministry. One minor consequence, as Walpole pointed out, was that in Ireland Carteret would 'be forced to . . . take his party, betwixt the two great men there'.[34] When the lord lieutenant arrived in Dublin in 1724, far in advance of the next parliamentary session, all eyes were on him. What they saw was the careful steering of a middle course. No one was taken into his 'entire confidence': 'it's observed that Lord Carteret is not particularly great with any, very few or none are admitted to his closet . . . but wait till he comes to them in the drawing room'.[35] The decision was eventually taken for him, as a result of Midleton's inflexibility over the issue of Wood's Halfpence. Having refused to support the viceroy in insisting on the patent, and under pressure from England, the Chancellor resigned in April 1725. Even then Carteret did not throw himself into Conolly's arms. As late as the meeting of Parliament in September he was still acting as his own 'chief minister'. A second *faux pas* on the part of the Brodricks pushed the two men together. St John's ham-handed efforts to repair the damage done by his father's resignation, in offering to undertake for the court but only if Carteret 'trusted all to their conduct and management', misfired badly. Conolly had made no such demands, and the leadership of the court party fell into his hands.[36]

As far as Walpole was concerned, Carteret's most important duty was not to decide between Midleton and Conolly, but to clear up the imbroglio over Wood's Halfpence. Walpole was sure the viceroy would fail, and destroy himself in the process: 'he will be under a necessity of either helping us through in this affair, which I think it will be impossible for him to think of, after the part he has already acted, or of losing himself with the King, when he shall see that he falls in entirely with the Irish politics, and the independency that is so much aimed at.'[37] In this he misjudged Carteret, and underestimated him. True, the viceroy's first reaction to expressions of Irish hostility to the Halfpence – opposition in the Privy Council and the refusal of the Dublin grand jury to make a presentation against Swift's *Seasonable Advice* – was to recommend the withdrawal of the patent, but after being slapped down by the English ministers he faithfully carried out their wishes. He was willing to lose himself with Midleton but not the king. So he threw the ball back into Walpole's court, doing his best but advising ministers that antagonism towards the Halfpence was such as to imperil the granting of taxes when the Irish Parliament reassembled. Whatever went wrong would not be his fault. When colleagues at the Castle, defenders of the 'English interest' and men that Walpole trusted, gave the same advice, the ministers were forced into a corner and recalled the patent.[38] This concession, followed by rumours of war in January 1726, inspiring a surge of loyalty, enabled Carteret and Conolly to overcome the endeavours of the Midletonian–Tory patriot coalition. Parliament was dissuaded from crowing over the abandonment of Wood, and an ample supply was voted. Contrary to Walpole's expectation, even intention, Carteret was able to report in March 1726 that 'our affairs have taken a happy turn again'.[39]

The appointment of Carteret had resulted in the resolution of a long-standing dilemma, whether Midleton or Conolly was to be the chief 'undertaker', and the extraction of a painful thorn from the government's side in the shape of Wood's Halfpence, but it had not been calculated with these ends in view: its mainspring had been the high political manoeuvres at Westminster. Furthermore it did nothing to counter what minister's understood to be a spreading of the notion of 'independency' in Ireland. There was, however, a positive element in ministerial thinking in 1724–5, and one in which considerations of Irish policy rather than English politics were paramount. This was centred on two key appointments, both of Englishmen, Hugh Boulter to the Primacy in place of the Tory Thomas Lindsay in 1724, and Richard West to be Lord Chancellor in place of Midleton the following year. West died after only 18 months

but was succeeded by another Englishman, Thomas Wyndham. The Primacy and Lord Chancellorship were posts of
vital importance in three areas: parliamentary management,
patronage and government. In the Lords the Chancellor was
Speaker, and the Primate could act as unofficial 'whip' for the
episcopal contingent; in patronage matters the advice of the
two men would carry great weight in recommendations in the
law and Church respectively; and there was a tradition that
both were included, *ex officio*, as Lords Justices, a tradition only
broken since 1714 because Lindsay had been such a vehement
Tory, and to which ministers reverted at the first opportunity
after Boulter's appointment. In each of these areas the new
Primate and Chancellor were expected to support the 'English
interest'; in opposing the 'patriots' in the Lords; in finding
English candidates for important vacancies; and in carrying
out policy. The advantages of appointing Englishmen had been
urged for some years by the English-born bishops and judges
already resident. Even Grafton, in his anxiety to be rid of
Midleton, had on occasion adopted this line.[40] To men like
Walpole and Newcastle, convinced of the Irish determination
to seek 'independency', these promptings scarcely needed
reinforcement, but the antics of the Brodricks and the refusal of
the Irish Privy Council to uphold Wood's patent certainly
provided it. The responsibility for initiating the redirection of
policy cannot be attributed solely to Walpole. The choice of
Boulter, for example, was originally Bishop Gibson's, backed
by Newcastle. But the Prime Minister's personal commitment
to the policy of building up the 'English interest' cannot be
doubted.

It is ironic that while the appointment of Carteret, conceived
in English terms and actually made in the hope of a messy
failure, was to prove a success, the appointments of Boulter and
Wyndham, especially Boulter, who was much the more forceful
personality, and the policy associated with them, brought as
many difficulties as advantages. There was really no need to go
to these lengths to cope with manifestations of Anglo-Irish
patriotism. Ample resources were at the disposal of the Dublin
administration to manage both Houses of the Irish Parliament,
provided that the one basic rule was obeyed: that the chosen
undertaker or undertakers be afforded clear and unequivocal

support. This ought to have been the lesson of the Wood's Halfpence fiasco, but for various reasons – the background of the jurisdictional dispute, the stridency of opposition to the Halfpence, the obsession of ministers and their Irish correspondents with the theme of 'independency' – Walpole and his colleagues concentrated their attention elsewhere. They persuaded themselves that, first, the management of the Lords required a particular effort, whereas in normal circumstances – now that death and episcopal appointments had eroded the Tory and 'patriot' cohort – it did not; and, secondly, that no Irish politician could be trusted. While it was sensible to name an Englishman to the Primacy in 1724, all the suitable Irish candidates, from Archbishop King downwards, having identified themselves as too 'national' over the Halfpence, there were a number of Irish lawyers who could have been placed on the woolsack without endangering the maintenance of English government in Ireland. Discrimination ran the risk of alienating valuable support. Worse still, the establishment in Dublin of an alternative channel of communication and patronage threatened to undermine the positions of viceroy and 'undertaker'.

Although there is no direct evidence, it is reasonable to infer that the ministry *intended* Boulter and Wyndham to act as a check on both Carteret and Conolly. Walpole's suspicion of Carteret had not diminished; and Grafton's earlier reliance on the Speaker was thought to have been a serious handicap on his endeavours to ride out the storm over the Halfpence. There was a desire to prevent the same thing from happening again. The most effective way in which Boulter carried out his commission was in transmitting his own recommendations to vacant offices, which were accepted in preference to others. At first this ploy seemed to be aimed at mortifying Carteret, as when Wyndham was named to succeed West as Lord Chancellor at Boulter's suggestion without the Lord Lieutenant being consulted, but since many of Carteret's nominations originated with Conolly, the struggle took on a wider significance: Primate and Chancellor ranged against viceroy and 'undertaker'. And apart from the isolated victory, Carteret and Conolly suffered a sorry time of it. Had it not been for Conolly's influence over the extensive patronage of the revenue commission, he would have been unable to reward his supporters, and would have suffered in the Commons in consequence.[41] Fortunately for Carteret, the determination of Walpole, Newcastle and Boulter always to pursue the 'English interest' seems to have faltered in 1727. The ministers may have come belatedly to appreciate Conolly's worth. Boulter's inability to make much impression on the Commons, where management by 'undertaker' was as vital as ever, and Conolly's success there in the 1725–6 session, seem to have influenced the Primate himself, who was relieved to see Conolly re-elected as Speaker in the new Parliament in 1727.[42] Boulter continued to recommend Englishmen to office, but now took into consideration the repercussions on Commons management. And in the following year Conolly's position improved further as both Midleton and St John Brodrick died, and Thomas Carter, another prominent 'patriot', defected to the court.

The importance of having a capable Commons 'undertaker' was amply demonstrated after Conolly's death in 1729. A man of his 'long experienced services, great fortune and numerous dependants' was hard to replace, and there was no obvious heir among his cronies in the court party. Instead two of them, Sir Ralph Gore and Marmaduke Coghill, 'the next persons to Mr Conolly', agreed on a joint 'undertaking'. Gore became Speaker, while Coghill took over Conolly's leadership of the revenue commission. The partnership was promising, but needed time.[43] Instead of helping, the English ministry offered a gratuitous provocation to the Irish Commons by altering the heads of a money bill. The timing was extraordinary, and the episode reveals once more Walpole's ineptitude at handling Irish public opinion. In dealing with Wood's Halfpence he had underestimated the depth of Irish feeling, aggravated it by his obstinacy, and, when obliged to back down, had over-reacted and seen more in the patriotism of the Anglo-Irish than actually existed. This time he showed the same high-handedness but the skill and exertion of the viceroy prevented a climbdown. 'I never took more pains in my life', wrote Carteret, and it was only his endeavours in closeting so many MPs that secured the supply.[44] Carteret had made a great success of his lord lieutenancy, for all the mines Walpole had laid in his path, and even those who disagreed with his objectives paid tribute to his performance as a wire-puller. This was not of course what had been envisaged on his appointment.

IV

It was typical of Walpole's approach to Irish affairs that Carteret should have been dismissed on his return to England in 1730, to be replaced by an inferior politician with no experience of Ireland. Nothing could better illustrate the use of the viceroyalty as a pawn in the power-game at Westminster, with no heed for the consequences in Dublin. Dorset, Carteret's successor, was a man of 'mediocre abilities'. His nomination as viceroy, an aspect of the ministerial reshuffle of 1730, may in part have been intended, as was Carteret's before him, as a means of putting him out of the way.[45] In Irish terms it was a risky manoeuvre, given the recent upheavals in the court party which had necessitated Carteret's intensive personal involvement in management in his last session. And this kind of politicking was not in Dorset's character. 'He appears very steady', was the view in Dublin, 'and not so loquacious as Lord Carteret, nor so intriguing.'[46]

The effects of Dorset's unfamiliarity with the landscape of Irish politics were soon observed. Departing from the practice of engaging an 'undertaker' in the Commons, he hoped instead for the general support of all men of goodwill, an approach based on archaic assumptions about political conduct. 'He hath a civil, genteel way of looking, but speaks very little to anybody, so that he doth not give offence by distinguishing persons.'[47] This ostentatious impartiality was supplemented by a conscious effort to play up the prestige of the viceroyalty. Dorset's equipage was extravagant; his social calendar a whirlwind of banquets, balls and entertainments; and there were forays into the provinces, to Kilkenny, for example, with a 'great retinue', and to Drogheda, to receive the freedom of the city in a gold box.[48] Pomp was not enough, however, and many of Dorset's parsnips were destined to remain unbuttered. By failing to channel his favour in one direction, and to signal that direction clearly enough, he had broken the cardinal rule of management, and in consequence his first parliamentary

session, in 1731–2, was an unhappy one. True, the supply and
accounts were passed 'with great unanimity', but a request for
a long-term grant of duties to pay the interest on the national
debt was refused without a division. By the end of the session
even Dorset's friends were speculating on a new chief gover-
nor.[49]

For Walpole it was not the general unsoundness of Dorset's
management that mattered, so much as his particular failure to
carry a repeal of the Irish Test, a proposal to which the Prime
Minister had given his personal backing, no doubt as a stage in
his wooing of the English Dissenters, to whom this would be a
token of good faith. It had ever been so with English Whig
ministers since the imposition of the Irish Test in 1704, and
previous attempts at repeal had been launched in 1707, 1709
and 1719. All had foundered on the staunch opposition of the
Anglican majority in both Houses of the Irish Parliament. In
1731 Walpole and Newcastle swallowed what Presbyterian
lobbyists told them, against all informed advice to the contrary.
The method they chose was based on the project of 1709, to
repeal the Test in the way it had been imposed, by a clause
tacked by the English Privy Council to a popery bill sent from
Ireland.[50] The flaw in this tactic was that for all their virulent
anti-Catholicism most Irish MPs seem to have realised that
there were now few loopholes in the penal code that were worth
closing, while at the same time they were as hostile as ever to
the Ulster Presbyterians. When the idea of repeal was mooted
members of the Irish administration protested, and there was a
rush of MPs back to Dublin in case a snap vote was called.[51]
Walpole, who had remarked airily to Dorset that 'I do not see
how a clause of this kind added by the council here can
embarrass your affairs', gave way, and no insertion was
made.[52] The scare weakened the viceroy's position still further,
and even the unamended popery bill was thrown out by the
Irish Parliament. Walpole did not, however, drop repeal, since
he had not been shown starkly enough that the assurances he
had accepted were illusory. He prepared to return to it when
the Irish Parliament met again.

Meanwhile life had been made even more difficult for Dorset
by the death of Sir Ralph Gore, though ultimately the election
of a new Speaker in the next session, in 1733, was to pave the

way for the restoration of stability to Irish parliamentary management. There were only two candidates. Coghill had decided against standing, as had Thomas Carter, who as a relatively recent convert to the court still enjoyed support on both sides, but whose hauteur and vanity made him insufferable. That left a straight fight between Henry Singleton, the ablest of the surviving Conolly clique, and Henry Boyle, leader of the 'patriots'. Boyle had the more powerful following, but in Coghill's opinion Singleton might still have been elected had it not been for the intervention of Carter. Unable to obtain the Chair himself, he assumed the role of king-maker. He had kept up his friendship with Boyle, and almost certainly, though incorrectly, saw the other man as the junior partner in any collaboration. It did not take long to draw Chief Secretary Carey and Primate Boulter into a 'cabal' for Boyle. Singleton's Tory past could profitably be contrasted with Boyle's record of resolute Whiggery in the dark days of Queen Anne's reign; and Singleton also represented the old gang at the Castle, of which Boulter was wary. Even before Dorset arrived back in Ireland the Lord Lieutenant, and the ministry in England, had been convinced that Boyle's interest was unassailable. Dorset declared for Boyle as Speaker, offered him Gore's old office as Chancellor of the Exchequer or a revenue commissionership, and promised to use 'all his influence' to have Boyle appointed a Lord Justice subsequently. Boyle opted for the Exchequer, as the less onerous and more remunerative office, though he was later to change his mind. A bargain had been struck.[53]

Unfortunately, viceroy and Speaker did not understand their agreement in quite the same way. While Boyle saw himself as the new 'undertaker', the heir to Conolly, Dorset had no intention of giving up his previous strategy. Boyle complained bitterly of 'my Lord Lieutenant's private and reserved behaviour, his not communicating his pleasure to any, and keeping those who are most ready to serve him at a distance from his councils'.[54] As the session wore on the ranks of the 'patriot' Opposition were refilling. Whether this was a cause or the effect of Boyle's resentment cannot be determined. There were those, diehard Tories and younger pretenders to Boyle's 'patriotic' mantle, who regarded him as an apostate. But the Clonmel election in December 1733, in which he had allowed his reputation to become involved, showed that his personal 'interest' was still strong, and the fact that his supporters seem to have delayed coming over the court in large numbers only until he had reached a better understanding with Dorset in 1734 is highly suggestive.[55]

The showdown that preceded this *rapprochement* came with a renewed attempt on the Test, again at the insistence of the English ministry. Repeal was something that Boyle could not easily have supported even if he had wanted to. There is every indication that, as well as his discontent with the Lord Lieutenant, which made him generally less amenable, he was personally averse to it, and beyond his own inclinations lay the certain opposition of many of his followers. The Tory element among his 'patriots' would be galvanised by this issue, and it was a step that the Brodricks, whose party Boyle had inherited, had themselves opposed in 1719. The tension in Dublin, where 'every tongue is employed about taking off the Test, either pro or con', acted as a catalyst on the Speaker's smouldering *amour propre*, so that when the Chief Secretary reproved him for not keeping his parliamentary forces in better order, he responded with indignation. He was no court tool, he declared, having stood as Speaker 'on the foot of the Country Party' and having only been adopted by the court when they found they could not stop him. 'Whatever the court suffered was by their own mismanagement, having no confidence or intimacy with anybody, and by throwing among us a bone of contention about the Test.'[56] This outburst, followed by the decisive rejection of repeal in the Commons, appears to have settled Dorset's mind. Early in 1734 he adopted a new attitude towards the Speaker. We may possibly see the effects of this in the court's massive victory (by 102 to 27) in January over a 'patriot' plan to alter the system of drafting 'heads of bills', and in February Dorset redeemed his pledge to recommend Boyle as a Lord Justice. The repeal episode had drawn to a head Boyle's seething resentment, and made Dorset face up to the implications of their concordat over the Speakership. For the remainder of his lord lieutenancy, until 1737, his partnership with Boyle was harmonious and successful, reminiscent of Carteret's with Conolly.

This did not put an end to all Boyle's problems, however, for he still had Walpole to reckon with. Just as the Prime Minister had frustrated Conolly's exploitation of patronage, so he began to do the same to Boyle. The case concerned a valuable revenue collectorship, that of Cork, which Boyle wanted for an associate. This was in the spring of 1734, while Boyle was still Chancellor of the Exchequer, with no say himself in the appointment. He obtained Dorset's recommendation, but the revenue board was responsible to the English Treasury and Walpole was able to put in his own nominee, leaving Boyle once again 'full of resentments'. In a memorable letter to an English correspondent, the Speaker made these plain:

> Where's my credit, where's my influence, or what business have I here, when I can no longer be of use or service to His Majesty's affairs. . . . You, Sir, very well know the difficulties I laboured under at my first setting out . . . to persuade my troops to fight in a cause foreign to their own principles or natural inclinations; and now, just as they are brought into good discipline, I can expect no less than a revolt, if they find their endeavours to support me have proved altogether ineffectual.[57]

The story has a familiar ring, even to the extent of the Primate and Chancellor siding with Walpole against the viceroy, and it is tempting to suppose that, as with Conolly, this snub to Boyle was part of a campaign to inhibit the independent strength of the undertaker. Dorset had discovered that the ministers were cautious of including Boyle in the commission of Lords Justices, lest the practice of naming the Speaker harden into a convention.[58] But if it was really intended to try to prevent Boyle becoming an 'over-mighty subject', the effort was quickly abandoned. The affair of the Cork collectorship seems to have been an isolated incident. A year later the atmosphere was different, Primate, Chancellor and Speaker joining to make their recommendations.[59]

Dorset and Walpole had been fortunate, through no efforts of their own, to find a worthy successor to Conolly. Boyle himself has remained a somewhat enigmatic character despite the length of his political career (he was to have 23 years as Speaker and an active parliamentary after-life in the Upper House).

Many had discounted him as a fit candidate for the Chair 'by reason of his natural modesty, and his little application to the knowledge of parliamentary proceedings'.[60] But the latter deficiency could soon be overcome, and Boyle's low-key performance in debate could be an asset in an undertaker. His disabling speech in 1733, delivered 'with as much indifference and as little concern as if it had been at a tavern amongst a few of his friends', was typical. It was not the passionate orator but the man able to talk to MPs on their own terms that was likely to carry the sense of the House. Boyle was essentially 'a country gentleman of great good nature and probity, well beloved but not of extraordinary abilities'.[61] He did not dazzle the Commons, or bully them as Carter did. He was also an easy man to underestimate, which may have helped him harness stronger personalities under his leadership. Whatever the reason for his success, the 1735–6 session, with ministry, viceroy and Speaker pulling together, proved the calmest for years: 'no faction stirred'.[62]

And yet Walpole could not let this particular sleeping dog lie. The replacement of Dorset by Devonshire in 1737 repeated the mistake of 1730 in removing for reasons of English politics a viceroy who had learned how the Irish political system worked, in favour of someone who was no more talented as a politician and who as yet knew little of Ireland. Walpole was not insensitive to Irish concerns. He was willing to support measures to assist the Irish economy: in 1739 the British Parliament legislated to open up new markets for Irish woollen yarn.[63] But he was always likely to subordinate the needs of Irish parliamentary management to the exigencies of domestic politics, or even to the advantage of family and friends. Devonshire's first three chief secretaries were successively Edward Walpole, the Prime Minister's son, Thomas Townshend, a favourite nephew of the Pelhams, and Henry Legge, Walpole's personal secretary, who was actually given the job on the understanding that he would never have to go to Ireland.[64] Devonshire himself was not especially unprepossessing, but his lord lieutenancy did result in a recrudescence of factionalism within the Irish administration. The trouble came from his close friendship with Brabazon Ponsonby, one of Conolly's former lieutenants. Under Devonshire, Ponsonby was brought into government, and like a cuckoo in Boyle's nest began to take over: he was given the Speaker's place on the revenue commission; the vacant Lord Chancellorship was filled according to his recommendation. He cemented his position in 1739 by marrying off two of his sons, William and John, to the viceroy's daughters. William later became Chief Secretary and John succeeded his father in the revenue. Although Devonshire went out of his way to conciliate Boyle and to 'show proper regard . . . to all that do service to the government', the rapid rise of the Ponsonbys and their allies could not fail to disrupt the smooth working of the 'undertaker system'. As Devonshire admitted, there were 'great animosities amongst those who compose the government interest'.[65] In this respect, the situation in Ireland at the end of Walpole's premiership was substantially the same as it had been when he had come to power.

V

Neither of the traditional interpretations of Walpole's Irish policy, what we might call the 'English' and 'Irish' versions – one suggesting a ruthless imperialism and the other a resignation of responsibility to local agents – presents the whole truth. It is probably true that Walpole came to distrust Irish political managers almost as a matter of course, largely on account of their failures in 1723–4 over Wood's Halfpence. Despite his sang-froid, the affair did embarrass him and shake him into a rethinking of his Irish policy. His determination that the patronage plums should thenceforth be given to Englishmen reflects this hardening attitude. It served several purposes, underlining Ireland's dependence, reinforcing the 'English interest', particularly in the Lords, and creating a political counterpoise to the influence of the Commons 'undertaker': hence the part played by Boulter as an alternative medium of patronage. This line was not, however, followed consistently or rigorously: some Irishmen were still preferred for top jobs, and the experiment of deliberately slighting Conolly, and later Boyle, as a means of stunting their authority, was in each case short-lived. It had to be. The results of the ministry's failure to come down decisively in favour of either Conolly or Brodrick before 1725; of Dorset's refusal to 'distinguish persons' in 1731–2 and of his merely half-hearted backing of Boyle in 1733; all demonstrated the *sine qua non* of keeping the court united and the chosen undertaker strongly supported. As long as the Irish Parliament met regularly it would need irrigation by the waters of patronage, and conditions dictated the use of some kind of 'undertaker system'. On the other hand, far from instituting this 'system', Walpole accepted it only reluctantly and on occasion actively worked against its operation. 'Undertakers' had existed in the Irish Parliament before 1720. If anything, Grafton's troubles convinced Walpole of the undesirability of a viceroy relying on local managers. His contribution to the history of the 'undertaker system' was an unavailing effort to stifle its development.

Walpole's political management of Ireland cannot really be termed a success. His interventions, guided nearly always by English considerations, were rarely helpful and often damaging. Even the choice of Carteret as viceroy in 1724, the ablest occupant of the post since Wharton in 1708–10 and arguably also the most effective, was primarily related to domestic politics. And doing well in the office did not prevent Carteret's dismissal. The use of Boulter and an accompanying English Lord Chancellor as a resident English political agency in Dublin was one instance of a more considered approach, but its effects on management were mixed, and in the long run probably unnecessary. In this period any English Whig ministry could manage the Irish Parliament, Commons and Lords, easily enough, simply by allowing the machinery to tick over. Until the demise of Jacobitism and the development of a more powerful sense of national identity gave the Ascendancy the confidence seriously to challenge English constitutional and economic paternalism, Anglo-Irish relations would remain fundamentally stable. Such troubles as Walpole endured were for the most part of his and his colleagues' own making.

5. Economic Policy and Economic Development

MICHAEL JUBB

I

IN recent years there has been a resurgence of interest in the economic history of the early eighteenth century, as historians have sought to understand the nature and determinants of economic growth in the years preceding industrialisation. The pace of growth in the third and fourth decades of the century has become a matter of some controversy. Deane and Cole in their pioneering work of quantification saw the period as one of relatively slow growth, with total real output rising by only 6.5 per cent between 1720 and 1740.[1] Other economic historians, including J. D. Chambers and C. H. Wilson, have developed this theme, which achieved its fullest statement in Anthony J. Little's *Deceleration in the Eighteenth-Century British Economy*. Little characterises the second quarter of the eighteenth century as a period when economic growth slackened as a result of the checks imposed by low agricultural prices and demographic reverses.[2]

New economic historians, however, have not found this picture convincing. They have substantially revised Deane and Cole's figures to show the national product rising from £57.5 million in 1720 to £64.1 million in 1740, a rise of 11.5 per cent. This revision stems partly from new estimates of the population growth rate in this period. The Cambridge Group for the History of Population and Social Structure now estimates average annual population growth rates for the years 1700 to 1740 at 0.30 per cent, compared with an earlier widely accepted estimate of 0.05 per cent.[3] This has obvious implications for analyses of the growth of demand, a subject in which historians have shown increasing interest. The other major factor behind the revision of growth rates has been a reassessment of the influence of rising agricultural productivity. Agricultural prices fell in the early eighteenth century and the 1730s and 1740s especially have been seen as decades when long runs of good harvests reduced agricultural incomes, and brought a widespread agricultural depression. Agriculture accounted for about 40 per cent of national income, and associated with this depression there was, it is argued, a stagnation or even a contraction in the home market for manufactured goods.[4] This view has not been universally accepted, however, and a much more optimistic picture presented by A. H. John and E. L. Jones has received some confirmation from new economic historians. They suggest that relatively rapid population growth and the rising real incomes resulting from falling agricultural prices brought in their train a rapid increase in the demand for food. This was met by an even more rapid increase in agricultural output, helped by unusually favourable weather conditions and by cost-reducing innovations like the introduction of fodder crops into rotations. These innovations enabled farmers, at least in the light-soil areas of eastern England, to maintain or increase their incomes by producing more livestock and grain at lower unit costs. Agricultural output was thus probably rising in the first half of the eighteenth century much faster than previously thought, and the consumption of food probably rose slightly faster than the domestic consumption of manufactured goods.[5]

Concentration on overseas trade as an engine of economic growth in the early eighteenth century has, as a result of these revisions in estimates of national output, been replaced by an increasing emphasis on the interdependence of the home and overseas markets: the expansion of foreign and colonial trade was related to increasing domestic demand for imports.[6] Measurement and the construction of models of the early eighteenth-century economy are hampered, however, by the lack of adequate quantitative data; the earlier emphasis on overseas trade was much influenced by the availability of statistics collected by customs officials, although their interpretation presents problems which have not been adequately resolved. Domestic consumption presents almost intractable problems, and the models are particularly inadequate for dealing with the short-term developments which most interested contemporaries. In concentrating on long-term trends the models often lack temporal specificity. For population, the Cambridge Group has provided annual estimates and identified two demographic crises in the Walpole period: one from 1727 to 1730 with deaths peaking at 80 per cent above normal in 1729; the second from 1740 to 1742.[7] For other factors in the economy we are much less well equipped with time-specific information.

II

The promotion of economic growth, although not, of course, stated in those terms, was a major preoccupation during Walpole's period. Much attention, then as later, focused on overseas trade, which many believed was stagnating. Walpole clearly shared the belief that it was the government's duty to promote overseas trade, although in the 1730s he was increasingly attacked by merchants and others for not doing more. He gave overseas trade an important place in his first and in many subsequent King's Speeches, and one of his first measures was to remove remaining export duties on manufactures and import duties on raw materials.[8] Apart from such general measures, however, the ministry was not an initiator in trading and industrial policy. It lacked the necessary information to form a legislative programme. But it did regard itself as having an important role, along with Parliament, in regulating trade and industry in the best interest of the nation as a whole – a matter on which there was considerable debate: 'some branches of trade, though beneficial to individual merchants may be prejudical to the publick'.[9]

In regulating such trades Walpole had potent new instruments to hand: the greatly increased levels of taxation imposed during the wars of the 1690s and 1700s. Under Walpole increasing efforts were made by various economic interest groups to modify a taxation system constructed under the severe financial strain of wartime so that it fitted better with peacetime economic objectives. Parliament and the ministry became accustomed to hearing and adjudicating between the arguments of various interest groups and increasingly aware that taxation involved more than the simple collection of revenue. In dealing with such problems, they referred to the national interest, the conception of which revolved around doctrines generally termed 'mercantilist'. But mercantilism did not involve a fixed body of doctrine: there was always room for disagreement about the relative importance of different concepts and prescriptions. The pursuit of wealth and the demands of national security, to take an obvious example, often conflicted, and there were differing views on wages and on the importance of domestic consumption. There was also a constant process of adjustment between general concepts and individual cases.

The key to economic growth and national prosperity was generally seen as the creation and preservation of employment, to be achieved primarily by promoting the export of manufactured goods. And since trade was still generally conceived of as bilateral, there was particular emphasis on those trades which exported British manufactures and imported in return raw materials which could themselves be manufactured. Contrariwise, British raw materials and skilled labour were to be exploited to the full and their export to other countries prevented. Finally, British manufacturers were to enjoy protective tariff barriers around their domestic market.

Woollen manufacturers were the most successful in persuading Parliament and the ministry that their industry fitted into this scheme for economic advance. This is not surprising, since in both output and employment woollen manufacture was still by far the largest industry in England.[10] Output was probably fairly static in the 1720s and 1730s, and the industry was already losing its earlier overwhelming predominance, as others expanded more rapidly. But woollen manufacturers' 'political' dominance continued, and their difficulties served to strengthen their voice. A link was often made between declining woollen manufactures and rising poor rates. Simon Smith claimed in 1735 that in several clothing areas the poor rate had risen to between six and ten shillings in the pound.[11] But it was difficult to secure agreement, especially between wool growers and clothiers, on what would revive the industry and the employment it brought.

Clothiers generally took it for granted that the industry's health depended on its exports. There was even a tendency to judge the health of foreign trade as a whole by the volume of woollen exports. Merchants often argued that their particular trades benefited the country by providing markets for woollens. In 1738, for example, during a dispute over the differential tariffs on imported Valencia and Smyrna raisins, both the Levant Company and Spanish merchants argued that their raisins were returns for woollen exports.[12] The scope for such special pleading was extended by the woollen industry's difficulties. Exports of woollens stagnated in this period, as new woollen industries were established in countries such as Germany and Italy and the French increased their penetration of important markets such as the Levant: by the late 1730s the Levant Company feared the loss of its trade in English cloth. French success was the more galling since it was widely believed that they depended on an admixture of English or Irish wool in order to make marketable cloth at all. Clothiers thus argued that French competition could be disarmed by an effective embargo on the export of English and Irish wool; they even argued that since such an embargo would increase the demand for English cloth, it would bring higher prices for English wool growers.[13]

There were intense lobbying campaigns in 1720, 1731 and 1739 for the introduction of a 'universal registry' to record all movements of wool from shearing to cloth manufacture in order to prevent illegal exports. Some projectors even urged a government monopoly of wool purchasing. The 1720 campaign was overtaken by the South Sea Bubble. In 1731 it became entangled with proposals to remove the duty on Irish yarn imports, which had fallen drastically in the late 1720s. English clothiers persuaded Horatio Walpole and other members of the ministry that the yarn duty should be removed, in order to discourage Irish wool-running, to check the growth of the Irish cloth industry (about whose competition English clothiers were increasingly complaining), and to induce the Irish Parliament to introduce a registry in Ireland. But English sheep-farmers feared that increased yarn imports would lower the price of English wool. The ministry itself was divided, although Walpole himself was in favour of removal.[14] But when the Bill was dropped in the Lords, there ended any hope of an Irish, and thus an English, wool registry: clothiers had to be content with an increased customs guard on the Irish coast.

There was some attempt to make the failure to help the woollen industry an issue in the 1734 election, but further campaigning was desultory until 1739, when the yarn duties were actually removed. In the late 1730s west country clothiers had begun to import Irish yarn in significant quantities. Its low cost made it attractive in a relatively high wage area: removing the duty could make it more so and help relieve their labour problems. But there was still opposition to Irish wool or yarn imports from sheep farmers who argued that they had lowered wool prices and ruined them and brought great distress to English woolcombers and spinners.[15] The strong west country representation in the Commons, however, won for the clothiers the abolition of the duty, and in 1741 pressure mounted once more for the introduction of a wool registry. Graziers in Romney Marsh, who were themselves subject to a registry covering their particular area, joined in the pressure, arguing that a country-wide registry was the only remedy for the continuing fall in wool prices.

That schemes of elaborate controls upon the movement of wool were so widely canvassed and seriously considered (Walpole himself chaired a committee which resolved in 1741 that a registry should be introduced) shows the strength of the clothiers' lobby. English and Irish wool was undoubtedly sent to France in large quantities, and English cloth exports suffered badly from French competition. But even when exports had revived during the outbreak of plague in Marseilles in 1720–1 which halted French trade, English wool prices had stayed depressed. This cast doubt in many minds on the assumption that the health of the woollen industry as a whole depended on its exports. Further, there was little evidence behind the clothiers' insistent claims that French cloth depended on an admixture of English or Irish wool. The French produced fine wool themselves, and could secure additional supplies of the finest wool in Europe from Spain. The belief that French woollen exports could be checked merely by depriving them of English and Irish wool was wishful thinking, the product of sectional interest masquerading as patriotism. It was an extremely powerful belief, however, and assiduous pamphleteering and lobbying succeeded in persuading many politicians and even some graziers that it was true. The introduction of a wool registry was averted only by Walpole's downfall.

Other industries, including textile manufactures such as silk and linen, found it difficult to match the woollen industry's political weight. The silk industry grew prodigiously in the early eighteenth century, but was dependent upon imports of raw silk from the Levant and Piedmont. Both sources were unreliable and there were moves in the 1730s to stimulate imports of Chinese silk by reducing the prohibitively high import duty it bore.[16] The Board of Trade favoured the abolition of *all* import duties on silk, but the Levant and Italian merchants, whose raw silk imports were returns for woollen exports, defeated any such move. The interests of woollen exporters outweighed those of silk manufacturers. Similar worries about woollen exports prevented any moves to check the import of thrown (as against raw) silk, despite the distress caused by the rise in such imports to those formerly employed in silk throwing.[17]

Silk manufacturers were on much stronger ground in defending their home market. They campaigned in 1720–1 against the fashion for printed calicoes and linens, and successfully claimed that calico and linen printing, while itself employing only a few hundred people, prejudiced the employment of many thousands in both the silk and woollen industries. This worry about employment was strong enough to secure a ban on the wearing of printed calicoes, defeating even the East India Company, which imported the calicoes to be printed.[18] English and Scottish linen drapers, however, were able to persuade the Commons that any ban on printed linens would prejudice employment in the linen industry. The linen industry certainly benefited from the consequent increase in the demand for printed linens, but both English and Scottish linen drapers continually complained that they received insufficient encouragement. They suggested that linen manufacture should be encouraged in order to overcome Britain's over-reliance on the woollen industry. The Scottish industry did receive some support but in the late 1730s discontent focused upon British linens' lack of success in colonial markets. This was attributed to the drawback (repayment) of import duties on the re-export of foreign linens. Removing the drawback would reverse a six per cent price advantage which foreign linens enjoyed in the colonies. Merchants trading to Germany and Austria, whence most imported linen came, however, raised the spectre of reprisals against English woollens, and they and the powerful West India lobby prevented any move against foreign linens. Only in 1742, after commercial negotiations with Austria had been dragging on for five years and after the outbreak of the Austrian Succession War, was an ingenious scheme introduced to give a bounty on British linen exports, paid for by an additional duty on imported cambrics.[19] This helped the British industry while avoiding colonial protests and the appearance of discriminating against German and Austrian linens – cambrics were imported mainly from the Austrian Netherlands, about whose interests officials in Vienna were little concerned. Woollen exports, for which linens provided a return, were thus not threatened.

The colonies played an important part in the economic thinking of the period, being regarded essentially as providers of raw materials and as secure markets for British manufactures. The southern colonies and the West Indies fitted relatively well into this system; but the northern colonies did not. Colonial raw materials which could provide employment in manufacturing or processing were 'enumerated' and allowed to be exported from the colonies only to Britain. The growing colonial lobby in London made several attempts in this period to loosen these restrictions, trying to secure both a full 'drawback' of import duties when colonial goods were re-exported and the freedom to export directly to Europe. From a British point of view, however, such moves endangered not only the revenue and Britain's position as entrepôt, but the manufacturers, merchants and shippers who supplied the colonies.

The West Indian lobby was the most powerful and there were protracted lobbying campaigns to ease the restrictions on their trade as sugar re-exports declined dramatically in the

1730s. It is notable, however, that the initial campaign was directed not against the enumeration of sugar or the protection of British refiners but against the succour provided from North America and Ireland to the French sugar islands. The result of the campaign was the 1733 Molasses Act; but this failed either to stem the decline in sugar re-exports or to check the trade between the northern colonies and the French sugar islands.[20] The major benefit accrued to British sugar merchants and refiners: for a ban on the direct export of sugar to Ireland made it henceforth into an extension of the home market for them. Sugar planters had to wait until 1739, when there was fear of disaffection in the West Indies during the war against Spain, to prevail against the British refiners and secure an act allowing direct export to Europe.

The problem with the North American colonies, apart from those which produced tobacco, was that they produced raw materials very similar to those produced in Great Britain. The accepted remedy for this was that they should be encouraged instead to produce 'naval stores'. This would not only avoid competition with British products and manufactures, but reduce Britain's embarrassing dependence on the Baltic for supplies of timber, tar, hemp and iron. These strategic considerations made the government particularly anxious to encourage the production of naval stores in the colonies.[21] Bounties on the import of colonial tar tended, however, to produce tar of very poor quality, while the hemp bounty was unsuccessful in reducing dependence on Russian supplies. Measures to encourage the colonial timber industry were inhibited by the interests of British timber growers, and such as were implemented were notoriously unsuccessful.

Colonial iron raised particularly difficult issues. The British iron industry claimed to be second only to the woollen industry as an employer, maintaining at least 200,000 people. The cutlery, nail and other iron-working trades, however, depended on imports of pig and bar iron from Sweden and Russia. This had posed particular problems during the Great Northern War: measures to encourage colonial iron were included in Naval Stores Bills of 1719, 1720 and 1721 but defeated by forgemasters and others who feared colonial competition. The Board of Trade failed similarly in both 1729 and 1735, despite renewed worries about the state of Anglo-Swedish trade and complaints of shortages of pig iron. But by the 1730s there was heightened concern over the threat to employment in Britain.[22] The colonists were already producing bar iron, nails and other iron products, as well as pig iron. This brought a depression in the West Midlands iron trades, with the poor rate in Dudley at twelve shillings. John Bannister, the Crowleys' agent, argued that measures to encourage colonial imports would deflect the colonists from iron manufacture; but most forgemasters were unconvinced, fearing that such imports would supplant English rather than Swedish iron. The forgemasters presented instead a Bill to prevent the increase of bar iron and iron manufactures in the colonies. The Bill was defeated, but not until 1750 were the import duties on colonial iron removed.

The colonies were not only prevented from competing with British manufacturers; they provided a secure market for them. Even when colonists were allowed to export direct to Europe, their returns had to come from Britain and import duties on British goods were forbidden. And where, as with linen, re-exports from England to the colonies attracted drawbacks of import duties there was strong pressure for their removal. The general proposition that the colonists could import British goods only if Britain would accept their exports in return attracted little sympathy. The protection of British employment was paramount.

The 'export of labour' was widely regarded as the key to national prosperity. Trades like the East India Company's, which exported bullion more than manufactured goods, faced continuing hostility, with frequent attempts to compel the Company to export more manufactures. But the poor had not so much a right as a duty to labour in the cause of national prosperity.[23] They were prevented from taking their skills abroad, and the Workhouse Test Act of 1723 was but one of many measures designed to imbue the poor with correct habits of industry. There were also attempts at statutory control of the quality of goods produced by labourers, especially in areas where capitalist control was weak. Such regulation of the quality of cloth produced in Yorkshire seems to have had some success;[24] but in general it was difficult to establish effective regulatory machinery, and attempts to revive and enhance livery companies' powers were unsuccessful.

Attempts at statutory suppression of combinations, such as that of the London tailors were similarly fruitless. Labour disputes in the west country cloth industry were endemic but it is notable that at least in the 1720s the statutory intervention was more even-handed: weavers' combinations were banned but so was truck. This was largely successful in the Devon serge industry, but agitation continued in the more rural broadcloth areas of Wiltshire and Somerset, where troops were used to suppress weavers' riots.[25] Many landed gentlemen, however, clearly sympathised with the weavers' grievances, and the JPs brusquely rejected the clothiers' attempts to smear them as Jacobites. Privy Council mediation in 1727 was notably sympathetic to the weavers. But attitudes hardened in the 1730s when new riots were suppressed with little attempt to discover the weavers' grievances.

Views about wages hardened similarly in the 1730s. Writers such as Josiah Child and William Petty might propound high wage theories, but the general consensus was that, as Sir John Barnard put it, 'the prosperity of trade depends . . . upon the low rate of wages': high wages had undermined national prosperity.[26] It was further generally assumed that wage levels were determined by the cost of subsistence, measures that might increase which should thus be avoided. It was denied that this implied low food prices as well as low wages: for high wages induced a high leisure preference among labourers. Lower wages would simply compel the poor to work harder and thus to produce and to consume more. Food prices would be unaffected. Such arguments encountered remarkably little opposition from the landed classes, although Townshend and others complained of the subsidising of low wages, and thus foreign trade, from the poor rate. But attitudes to the poor rate hardened, too: writers such as Sir Matthew Decker argued that it should be abolished in order to discourage idleness.[27]

An increasingly assertive mercantile and manufacturing community persuaded a majority of the political nation that national prosperity depended on an expanding foreign trade. In 1739 they forced an unwilling Walpole into a war in defence of British trading rights and it is remarkable how little the landed gentry, who would pay for the war through the land tax, participated in the debate which preceded it. Resistance to those who, like Decker, argued that 'the gradations from the encouragement of trade to the benefit of lands are settled and certain' was, at least, muted. When John Smith argued in 1743 for a foreign trade regulated so that its benefits passed to labourers and landed gentlemen and not solely to merchants, he was clearly aware that merchants had had some success in achieving quite the reverse.[28]

III

In addition to the use of taxation for the regulation of industry and overseas trade there were structural difficulties relating to government finance as a whole. The huge cost (£130 million) of waging the wars of William's and Anne's reigns had necessitated the development of a system of taxation and public credit, the major features of which remained unchanged for the greater part of the eighteenth century. The new system of public credit required that long-term loans were secured on funds created by the imposition of specific taxes appropriated by Parliament for that purpose. This *funding* of the National Debt was crucial in securing the confidence of public creditors and thus in enabling the nation to pass on a substantial part of the cost of the wars to future generations. Between 1690 and 1714 new customs and excise duties were created at an unprecedented rate to create funds for new loans. By the end of Queen Anne's war nearly all customs and excise duties were appropriated in this way: they could not be abolished, reduced or used for other purposes without some compensating move to ensure the continued funding of the Debt.

The costs of civil government were met from the Civil List, a yearly fund created by the appropriation of certain customs duties and set at the beginning of George I's reign at £700,000. Military and other expenditure not to be met from the Civil List was decided upon each year in an annual act detailing 'current services' for the year – an annual scrutiny regarded as an important safeguard against the dangers presented by a standing army. Current services were funded from two sources: the malt duties, which raised £700,000–750,000 annually, and the land tax, whose rate was set each year. The land tax had been intended, when first imposed in 1693, as a proportionate levy upon personal and real income. It soon became, however, a levy almost wholly upon landed income, and the amount raised at any given rate – approximately £500,000 per shilling – remained fixed for a century from 1697. Four shillings in the pound was regarded as a maximum wartime rate, two shillings a normal peacetime rate. That did not, of course, mean that landowners paid a tenth or a fifth of their income; for they paid only a proportion of a fixed amount levied on their county. Moreover, local control of the assessment and collection of the tax was vested in commissioners annually appointed and drawn from the landed classes themselves. This was crucial in securing continued acceptance of the land tax.[29] Nevertheless, there was continued resentment of a tax levied directly on landowners, and one of Walpole's major aims was to reduce the unfair burden he felt it imposed on the landed classes.

The constraints imposed on fiscal policy by the appropriation of customs and excise duties and the direct link between the level of current expenditure and the rate of the land tax only added to resentment of the 'monied interest': public creditors regarded as profiteers from the war. The return to peace was accompanied by the twin but conflicting desires to reduce taxes and to reduce, if not to liquidate, the National Debt as soon as possible. Only gradually did the Debt come to be accepted as permanent. Besides understandable resentment at the payment of taxes to service the Debt – payments frequently characterised as transfers of wealth from the productive landed and merchant classes to the unproductive drones who made up the monied interest – there was a widespread fear that by 1714 the limits of borrowing had been reached and that the nation's power and influence in Europe had thus been dangerously reduced. Reductions in taxation and in the Debt and the burdens it imposed were thus of major political and economic importance.

Reducing the costs of servicing the Debt began relatively soon after George I's accession. The bulk of the Debt carried interest at over six per cent, though the legal maximum for private individuals had in 1714 been reduced to five per cent. In 1717 Walpole planned a scheme to reduce the interest on the Debt to five per cent. The savings thus achieved were to be used not to reduce or abolish taxes but to discharge the principal of the Debt *via* a newly created Sinking Fund.[30] Walpole's resignation in 1717 meant that only part of his scheme was actually introduced: the debt conversion dealt only with redeemable stock and not the irredeemable annuities which imposed the heaviest burdens. But the creation of the Sinking Fund at least brought the prospect of progressive annual reductions in the Debt.

The South Sea Company brought about an even more significant reduction in the costs of servicing the Debt while Walpole was out of office. The basic features of the Company's scheme to take over the National Debt were straightforward: public creditors were offered the opportunity to exchange their government stock for South Sea stock. For the government there was the prospect that this exchange would deal with the problem of the very costly irredeemable annuities since it would have to pay interest of, at most, five per cent (and, from 1727, four per cent) on the new South Sea stock; for the South Sea Company there was the prospect of a huge increase in its stock, great profit and prestige.

Unfortunately, the scheme as implemented contained two major flaws. First, instead of being restricted to the irredeemable annuities, it was extended to cover all government stock. Secondly, and more importantly, although the Company was allowed to increase its stock by fixed proportions for each unit of government stock exchanged, the ratio at which the exchange was to be made was not fixed. The Company was thus encouraged to inflate the price of its stock; for if public creditors could be persuaded to exchange their stock for South Sea stock at, say, three or four times its nominal level, the Company could then sell large amounts of stock on its own account. The directors were so confident of being able to do this that they made two issues of stock even before the first exchange. In the wild speculative boom which followed, exchanges were made on three separate dates, and on terms which were twice changed.[31] Stock was issued at such a high price that easy terms for payment were needed, and a huge number of exchange receipts circulated on the market. By 24 June 1720 South Sea Stock was at 1050 and it stayed at over 1000 until late in August. But by mid September it had fallen to 520 and by 1 October to 230.

The Bubble made many fortunes and ruined many more as the country was overcome by speculative fever. The bursting of the Bubble brought panic and anger, and those who had lost heavily clamoured for relief. Much of the anger was directed at the government. But from the government's standpoint the scheme was a success: 80 per cent of the irredeemable annuities were converted, as well as 85 per cent of the eligible redeemable stock (Bank of England and East India Company stock had been excluded). In the financial and political reconstruction which Walpole led after the Bubble, the subscribers were thus compelled to keep their bargains. They received some relief through a distribution of the remaining South Sea stock and of £2 million confiscated from Company directors; but they suffered losses of up to two-thirds in their income. The conversion of the National Debt brought some real hardship.

In the first five years after the Bubble Walpole was fairly conservative in dealing with both the Debt and the structure of taxation. The Sinking Fund (enlarged by the further reduction in interest payments) was used to repay Debt and current expenditure was low enough to be met by a two-shilling land tax. The rapid return of financial confidence was indicated by the government's ability to borrow increased amounts in anticipation of the land and malt taxes. From 1725, however, Townshend's diplomatic responses to the Treaty of Vienna brought increased expenditure. Walpole avoided an increase in the land tax in 1726 by borrowing £500,000 funded by a new duty on victuallers; but in 1727 he had to increase the land tax to its wartime level of four shillings – an increase which explains in large part Walpole's growing estrangement from Townshend.

By 1727, however, the interest payable on all South Sea stock had fallen to four per cent, and Walpole could begin to use for current services the resulting surpluses in funds appropriated to the Debt: he borrowed £370,000 for current expenditure, funded on surplus revenues from the coal duties. Many expressed doubts about this additional borrowing, arguing that the surplus ought to have been used for Debt repayment. But to Walpole the speedy liquidation of the Debt was no longer paramount. Rather, he wanted to use indirect tax surpluses to offset the hitherto direct relation between the level of current expenditure and the rate of the land tax. Walpole reduced the land tax to three shillings in 1728 and 1729, by again borrowing on revenue surpluses, exciting Opposition complaints that he was endangering public credit. A Committee of the Whole House, however, found public credit in a good state: government creditors did not wish to be repaid, since their investments were both secure and worthwhile. A further sign of the improved financial climate was the East India Company's acceptance in 1730 of a reduction in its annuity, which released further revenue surpluses. The remarkable recovery since the Bubble and falling military expenditure after the Treaty of Seville in November 1729 brought the possibility, for the first time in most men's memory, of significant reductions in taxation.

The falling cost of servicing the Debt had enlarged the Sinking Fund, and the King's Speech in 1730 asked MPs to judge if it might be reduced in order to give 'ease where the duties are most grevious'.[32] Walpole was ambivalent. His major aim was to reduce the burdens on land, rather than indirect taxes. But there arose widespread pressure to abolish the salt duties, which were characterised as especially burdensome to the poor. The proposal was undoubtedly popular, and Walpole acquiesced. But he noted with especial interest that those who had earlier argued that all revenue surpluses should be used to repay the Debt now urged that the Sinking Fund be reduced to 'relieve the people'. Walpole wanted to relieve the landed classes, by transferring some of the cost of current services from the land tax onto the newly available surplus revenues from indirect taxes, which he believed to be more equitable.

Ever since excises had been introduced in the 1640s, there had been disagreement about whether they should be confined to luxury goods or extended to articles of general consumption. The new scope for reductions in taxation added new stimulus to this debate. The idea that public expenditure should be met out of 'a tax upon luxury or superfluity' had obvious attractions.[33] Consumption of luxury goods was clear evidence of ability to pay; it also showed a dangerous spirit of luxury and debauchery which ought to be checked. Both these arguments were directed increasingly at the poor, although then as now there was little agreement about what were 'luxuries' and what 'necessaries'. But there was a growing feeling among both landed and merchant classes that labourers were living above their station, and that they should therefore be taxed. These notions were particularly evident in the campaigns to get an effective prohibitive duty imposed upon spirits, although a strong landed lobby fought against such duties because they feared the loss of an important market for their barley and malt.

Most excise duties, however, were levied on articles widely regarded as necessaries: there were heavy duties on beer, soap, candles, leather and salt. These were, of course, highly regressive, but theorists like William Petty had introduced the idea that duties should in equity be imposed on articles 'nearest the common standard of expense': the poor, after all, as well as the rich, benefited from the state's activities.[34] In fact, since most indirect taxes were appropriated to service the Debt, the taxes paid by the poor went mostly into fundholders' pockets. Walpole wished to use indirect taxes instead for current expenditure, so that he could reduce the land tax; and he quickly came to regard the abolition of the salt duties as a mistake. In 1732 he revived them for three years to raise a £500,000 loan. He was then able for the first time to meet the year's services with a land tax of only one shilling. His major themes in introducing this scheme were to stress the disproportionate burden of the land tax on landowners and to argue that 'that tax which is most equal and the most general, is the most just and the least burthensome'. Since the salt duties were paid by everyone, the amount levied on individuals was hardly noticeable: there was no evidence that they imposed an unacceptable burden on the poor. Pulteney, however, led the Opposition in arguing that it was wrong to tax those who received only subsistence wages: and any increase in their wages would worsen Britain's trading position and harm everyone, including the landed classes.

The land tax was not, of course, abolished altogether, although Walpole did consider its 'disuse' for a few years.[35] But the landed classes were reluctant to give up their control of its local administration and their participation in setting its rate each year: they were too apprehensive of what might replace it. A revised land tax with a more equitable distribution across the country would have been especially unwelcome to many. A reduction to the minimum practical rate of one shilling was thus more attractive than outright abolition. In reducing the land tax to one shilling, however, Walpole was planning a significant shift in fiscal policy. Since the Sinking Fund was no longer a reassurance to public creditors – rather, they feared repayment sooner than they wished – it might now be used for current services. Indeed, if, by collecting indirect taxes more efficiently, the Fund could be further enlarged, the land tax might thus be kept at one shilling indefinitely. The Sinking Fund could be used both to repay the Debt and as the means to transfer current expenditure costs onto indirect taxes. This was the thinking behind the excise scheme.

Walpole kept the land tax at one shilling in 1733 by, for the first time, taking £500,000 from the Sinking Fund for current services, to furious Opposition complaints that the Fund should never be used other than to repay the Debt or abolish taxes. Walpole simply replied that he *was* using the Fund to abolish taxes – one shilling on the land tax. Long-term use of the Fund in this way, however, required that there be further measures to enlarge it.

In essence there was little remarkable about the excise scheme. It simply changed the duties on wine and tobacco from customs duties payable at import into excise duties payable when goods were released from a warehouse for domestic consumption. Collection would thus be more efficient: the excise service was more efficient than the customs and (although the evidence is by its nature difficult to quantify) more effective in combating fraud and evasion. Many customs duties were high enough to present a substantial incentive to smugglers, and they were also very complicated to administer. There were regular administrative and legislative efforts to combat smuggling and fraud, and Walpole saw the excise scheme as another such attempt to deal with two of the most extensively smuggled commodities.

Wine duties were especially complicated, their level depending on the wine's origin and place of landing, and allowances for leakage, damage and wholesale traders all presenting opportunities for fraud. Discriminatory duties on French wine were an added incentive to smugglers, and in places like Romney Marsh there was a thriving trade in illicit wool exports and wine imports in return. Frauds in tobacco duties centred mainly on collusive underweighing at import by landwaiters who were given large bribes. Evidence of such frauds regularly came to light but they proved difficult to check: they probably accounted for 10 per cent of English tobacco imports, and much higher levels in north-western ports like Liverpool and Whitehaven. A second major source of fraud arose from the drawback of import duties on the two-thirds of imported tobacco which was re-exported: underweighing at import was matched by overweighing at re-export.[36] Such frauds were on an especially massive scale in Scotland. English tobacco merchants had complained since the early 1720s of Scottish frauds so extensive that prices had fallen to levels inconsistent with payment of the duties. Scottish tobacco merchants' success arose partly from their superior organisation, but fraud clearly played a part, too: Treasury investigations in 1722 and 1723 found some Scottish merchants re-exporting twice as much tobacco as they had entered at import. The Act of Union precluded discriminatory measures against the Scots, but the Scottish Customs Commission was amalgamated with the English in order to tighten up its administration. These measures did not succeed, however, in depriving Scottish merchants of their competitive advantage in fraud. The position was worsened by a stagnating domestic demand for tobacco: prices fell rapidly in the late 1720s, to below the break-even level for legal traders. This put great pressure on them to adopt illegal practices.[37]

Falling prices also brought complaints from American tobacco planters, who particularly resented having to pay commission to British merchants not just on the selling price of their tobacco, but on the customs duties as well. This raised the total commission nearly four-fold, which seemed particularly inequitable when customs duties were drawnback on re-export; and most merchants did not even pay the duties, but entered into bonds – discharged at re-export – for their future payment.

Planters' agents in London thus joined enthusiastically in the pressure to reform the tobacco duties.

The proposals in the excise scheme were not new. In 1724 Walpole had introduced an 'inland duty' to replace most of the existing customs duties on coffee, tea and chocolate. This change was combined with compulsory warehousing: after paying or securing the remaining customs duty, importers had to store their goods in secure warehouses until they either re-exported them or paid the new inland duties. Further, the movement of goods once removed from the warehouse was subject to detailed control, and retailers were licensed. The scheme aroused little comment, and brought some increase in revenue and an improvement in re-exports. Tea, however, remained one of the most heavily smuggled commodities. Shortly after the scheme's introduction, John Crookshanks, a former comptroller-general of customs in Scotland with first-hand knowledge of tobacco frauds, wrote to Walpole advocating a similar scheme for wine and tobacco.[38] Walpole took no action at the time, but the idea of using indirect tax revenue for current services, together with renewed merchant interest in warehousing schemes and some orchestrated pressure from American planters, brought the proposal to life once more in the early 1730s.

Walpole presented the excise scheme as a simple measure to increase the revenue from existing taxes by collecting them more efficiently. His major theme was that this would enable him to reduce the burden of the land tax. But the excise scheme and effective action against smugglers would bring benefits both to fair traders and to tobacco planters as well. Some ministerial writers went further, arguing that all customs duties discouraged trade and should be abolished: their replacement by inland duties structured to encourage the export of manufactures would make Britain a 'free port' and bring a great expansion in her trade and manufactures.[39]

The Opposition did not attack the plan to reduce the land tax by increasing the revenue from existing indirect taxes. They sought rather to show, first, that the plan would not work, since the total amount of fraud was only a tenth of the £300,000 Walpole hoped to raise through the excise scheme. They rejected Walpole's claim for the success of the inland duty on coffee, tea and chocolate, and contended that controls on the movement of goods once released from warehouses were unworkable. And they dismissed the supposed move towards making Britain a 'free port' as absurd: the scheme would instead bring merchants more trouble and expense and lead to a stagnation in trade.

The main emphasis in the campaign against the excise scheme, however, was on the threat to Englishmen's liberties. Excise officers had powers to enter houses and to inspect accounts which made them 'hateful . . . to the inferior people'.[40] Moreover, under excise laws there was no right to trial by jury. The Opposition cited numerous cases of excise officers' arbitrary actions, and arbitrary judgements by Excise Commissioners, to reinforce the fear that Englishmen's fundamental liberties were at stake. The danger was the greater, they claimed, since excises on wine and tobacco were merely the prelude to a 'general excise': duties soon to be introduced on 'food and raiment and all the necessaries of life'.

Walpole certainly did believe that 'equal' taxes would be both popular and equitable. The ministerial *London Journal* had in 1731 contended that 'most men of sense in the Kingdom are of opinion that a general excise would be the most equal way of taxing, for then every person would pay taxes in proportion to what he consumed'.[41] But the clamour against general excises brought a retreat. By 1733 the *London Journal* was claiming that it was a 'sacred maxim' never to tax necessaries, and Walpole renounced any intention to introduce a general excise: more 'equal' taxation meant more effective taxes on luxuries. The retreat came too late, however; Walpole could do little to counter the insistent claim that there was to be a general excise and armies of excise officers tyrannising the country. He had to withdraw the excise scheme altogether.

Walpole's major fiscal aim after withdrawing the excise scheme was to ensure that he could continue to use surpluses from existing taxes for current expenditure and thus to keep down the land tax. The precarious European situation brought rising military expenditure in the mid 1730s, and an increase in the land tax to two shillings. But Walpole avoided additional increases by twice extending the salt duties for further periods (borrowing in anticipation of their produce) and using the

Sinking Fund for current services. The Opposition deprecated the continued peacetime borrowing and the use of the Sinking Fund, but focused its attack more on the expenditure itself than on the means used to meet it. There was especial disquiet (shared in the ministry) about the need to repay large accumulated and unfunded navy debts: many argued forcefully that the naval forces' full cost should have been met each year.

By the late 1730s, however, when easing tension in Europe enabled Walpole to reduce military expenditure, the three main elements of government finance – the funding of annual military expenditure; the funding of civil government through the Civil List; and the servicing and repayment of the Debt – were all operating with notable efficiency. Current military expenditure was met with unprecedented ease and the land tax maintained at two shillings by using the Sinking Fund (or, in 1737, loans on remodelled duties on liquors). Only after the outbreak of war, in 1740, was Walpole compelled to increase the land tax to four shillings.

The Civil List was similarly healthy. George I's Civil List had caused continual problems, since he had consistently spent more than the £700,000 income it guaranteed him. But George II had been guaranteed at his accession an annual Civil List income of at least £800,000; while Parliament had to make good any deficiency, the king could keep any surplus. This settlement had inspired widespread unease at the time,[42] and later one of the Opposition complaints about the excise scheme was that it would enlarge the power of the Crown by increasing the Civil List. George II's Civil List revenues were consistently in surplus, which made the Opposition all the more angry when Walpole insisted – as, for example, with the introduction of the prohibitory duty on spirits in 1736 – that the king be compensated when there were fiscal changes which might reduce Civil List revenues. It looked as if Walpole counted pleasing the king more important than reducing taxes or repaying the Debt.

Walpole used the Sinking Fund for current expenditure every year after 1733, and even the Opposition ceased to argue that this endangered public credit. And if urged to use the Fund to reduce taxes, Walpole replied that he was using it to keep down the most burdensome tax of all – the land tax. In 1736 he went so far as to raise three per cent annuities funded on the Sinking Fund's produce. The final development in the use of the Sinking Fund for current expenditure came in the following year, when Walpole dismantled the barrier between Debt repayment and current services. Henceforth all appropriations of the Fund's produce were treated as supply. Debt repayment was merely a part of the year's current services; both were payable either from the Sinking Fund or from the annually voted taxes. The repayment of the National Debt through the Sinking Fund had lost its special importance.

The increasing acceptance of the National Debt can be seen in the debates in 1737 on Sir John Barnard's scheme to reduce the interest payable on it to three per cent. The interest rate on almost all the Debt had fallen from six per cent in 1717 to four per cent by 1730, and Walpole raised short-term loans at three per cent in 1732 and in 1736–8. Barnard argued that new three per cent loans should be raised in order to repay existing fundholders. This would both allow further reductions in indirect taxes and influence a general lowering of interest rates, benefiting both landowners and merchants. Barnard's opponents argued, with more ingenuity than logic, that lower interest rates would bring no such benefits; but more interestingly, fundholders now attracted more sympathy than before. Even the *Craftsman* joined in their defence. Particular attention focused on widows and orphans who depended on the funds for their income, and Barnard was forced to modify his scheme to accommodate them.[43]

Barnard's major difficulty, however, arose from his central aim, to reduce taxes: a reduction in interest payable on the Debt would mean, he argued, that duties on necessaries such as coal, candles, soap and leather could be abolished. He rightly argued that taxes on essentials were higher in Great Britain than in France or Holland where, as a result, goods were produced more cheaply.[44] But by 1737 taxes on necessaries had become much less contentious than even five years earlier. Both those who wanted the more speedy repayment of the Debt and those who welcomed the use of indirect taxes to offset the land tax warned of the dangers of too precipitate reductions in taxation. Despite Barnard's arguments about their baleful effects, many had come to accept that high taxes would remain until the Debt was repaid. Walpole engineered the defeat of the scheme, since it endangered his plans to use the Sinking Fund for current expenditure. It is notable that in so doing he excited popular demonstrations in his favour.

In his management of the national finances Walpole enjoyed, despite Opposition claims to the contrary, a fair degree of success. There was a net decrease of £6¼ million in the National Debt during his period of office and, more important, interest payments fell from £2.57 million to £1.89 million.[45] The Debt was not liquidated, but it was made much easier to live with. The reduction in interest payments was insufficient to allow wholesale reductions in the taxes imposed between 1690 and 1713, but it did provide scope for their modification. There were various and competing pressures for such modifications, and many lobbyists. But although the government lacked the information to formulate a detailed programme for economic growth, it did not meekly succumb to lobbyists' pressures. It judged their claims against a system of ideas which emphasised the productive employment of the poor and the export of the goods they produced (especially woollens) as the key to economic growth and national prosperity. But Walpole also had wider objectives: he wanted not just to modify the indirect taxes appropriated to service and repay the Debt, but above all to reduce the land tax which bore the major burden of current expenditure. He sought to shift that burden onto the existing indirect taxes, so that the landed classes, as well as traders and manufacturers, could benefit from the stable financial administration. The Revolution Settlement and the Hanoverian succession could then be more securely founded.

6.   Foreign Policy in the Age of Walpole*

JEREMY BLACK

THE dramatic changes in British foreign policy produced by the Glorious Revolution, and in particular the full-scale commitment of British resources to European conflicts, were further stressed by the accession of the Hanoverian dynasty. The Electorate of Hanover was not only one of the leading north German states; it was involved also in a series of legal and territorial disputes in northern Germany that engrossed the attention both of George I and of George II. Furthermore, both monarchs were well informed and concerned about European affairs. These royal interests provided a dynamic for British foreign policy that helped to ensure that during their reigns foreign policy was a leading issue of political debate and conflict in the court, the ministry, Parliament, the press and the political nation.[1] It is the object of this essay to explain and assess the significance of this situation, and to investigate the light that struggles over foreign policy throw upon the operations of the political system of this period.

I

Royal concern over foreign policy placed an enormous strain upon the political system, because the various policies advocated by the monarchs conflicted with both traditional British interests and the considered opinions of a large number of politicians and the vociferous view of much of that most

* I should like to thank Eveline Cruickshanks, Grayson Ditchfield, Harry Dickinson and Derek McKay for commentary on earlier drafts of this chapter.

ambiguous of eighteenth-century entities, public opinion. Britain and Hanover were but one example of the early eighteenth-century yoking, under a common monarch, of a German state with a non-German state possessing a representative system. Hesse–Cassel with Sweden, and Saxony with Poland were the other instances, and, in each case, the attempt ran into major difficulties partly stemming from the absence of shared interests.[2] Although Ragnhild Hatton, in her excellent studies of George I, has made a valiant attempt to defend the monarch from accusations of subordinating Britain to Hanover, and has made much of supposed common interests, it was no accident that most informed contemporaries believed the opposite.[3] Attempts to develop commercial links failed – possibly British manufacturers missed an opportunity to increase their penetration of the German market, though Hamburg was too attractive an entrepôt for the Hanoverian ports to offer much competition.[4]

Hanoverian territorial interests, in particular her struggle with Prussia for control in the neighbouring Duchy of Mecklenburg and for the succession to the Duchy of East Friesland, her attempt to gain recognition of her acquisitions of the former Swedish Duchies of Bremen and Verden, and her support for the Danes against the Russian-backed Duke of Holstein-Gottorp, led to Britain herself being opposed for much of the period to Prussia and Russia. This was unfortunate given that the most significant development on the European international scene in the first half of the century was the growing strength of these states, and that a struggle to gain their alliance occupied much of the attention of other European powers. Profoundly unhappy about the growth of Russian power, George I and his favoured Secretary of State, James Stanhope, tried to organise a coalition in 1720–1 aimed at forcing Russia to hand back some of the Swedish Baltic provinces that she had conquered. This has been described as 'a Peace Plan for the North', and defended on the grounds that the growth of Russian power threatened the Balance of Power and the supply to Baltic naval stores. It was a foolhardy scheme, and displayed the naïve optimism that characterised so much of George I and Stanhope's foreign policy. British naval power and British subsidies, supported by fine talk about the ever nebulous

Balance of Power, could not create a coalition strong enough to intimidate Russia. Peter the Great kept the Baltic provinces, and the legacy for Britain was a period of poor Anglo-Russian relations. This was only ended by the commercial treaty of 1734, and by British diplomatic support the following year for the movement of Russian troops to the Rhine in support of Austria against France.

Hostility to Prussia was another consequence of royal influence over foreign policy. Frederick William I of Prussia, George I's son-in-law, and Frederick II (the Great), George II's nephew, were not easy men to co-operate with, but efforts were made to link Prussian strength to British interests. Stanhope sought to use Prussia against Russia and at times against Austria, Townshend had similar interests in the mid 1720s and Walpole's brother Horace argued, in the second half of the 1730s, that it was in Britain's interest to develop Prussia as a continental counterweight to France.[5] Once his anti-Prussian Hanoverian minister Bernstorff had been disgraced in 1719, George I, at a time when he was allied to France, sought to improve relations in order to use Prussia to aid Hanoverian views against Austria and Russia. George II thwarted to a substantial extent a series of attempts to improve relations, such as Hotham's mission to Berlin in 1730. The attempt to develop a Protestant Alliance in 1735–6 was blocked largely by George II, and it could be argued that his personal stance goes far to explain why the Anglo-Prussian alliance that it had been hoped would be heralded by the accession of Frederick II was abortive.[6]

The views of George I also played a major role in the development of the Anglo-French alliance of 1716–30. George I wanted French support against Jacobite schemes, while the Regent of France, the Duke of Orleans, needed support against Philip V of Spain. Furthermore France was expected to support George I and his policies as Elector whether it be an anti-Swedish stance in 1716 or an anti-Russian one in 1716 and four years later. In addition, the French army became the ultimate deterrent to any attack on Hanover, a function that could not be fulfilled by the British navy. In 1727, 1729 and 1730 when Austrian and Prussian action against Hanover was feared, British diplomats persuaded the French to threaten military retaliation, and joined in detailed planning for a French invasion of the German Empire.

Thus, in two major respects the policies associated with George I and Hanover represented a major challenge to traditional assumptions about British foreign policy, first in the degree of commitment to European quarrels, and secondly in the Anglo-French alliance. These policies had consequences in southern as well as northern Europe. Concerned to preserve both the peace and the essentials of the Utrecht settlement, which as Whig politicians they had condemned but which they saw the necessity of supporting, the British, in league with the French, became involved in war with Spain in 1718. The origins of this war lay in Austro-Spanish territorial quarrels in Italy that meant nothing to British taxpayers, and that had detrimental consequences for British trade. Stanhope had thought that Spain would back down but his poor judgement was covered by Admiral Byng who sank most of the Spanish fleet off Sicily in 1718. This victory at Cape Passaro – a victory in no way inevitable – helped to increase British confidence in both their naval capabilities and their consequent diplomatic strength.

However, being the leading naval power in Europe did not give Britain the diplomatic weight that she expected. The navy could not drive the Spaniards from Sicily in 1718 nor the Russians from Livonia in 1720. In 1728 the Duke of Parma, then in dispute with Britain, pointed out that the British fleet could not reach him at Parma, whilst in the previous year the Austrian Chancellor mocked the ability of the British navy to intimidate Austria, declaring that a few burntdown houses in the Austrian possessions of Naples or Palermo would have little impact.[7]

The system devised by George I and Stanhope, in which Britain was to serve as the European policeman, orchestrating opposition to any attempts to disrupt the European system, was an unrealistic one. Britain could not afford to engage in protracted confrontation simultaneously with Russia and Spain. The complex system of mutual guarantees underlying international treaties was not proof against the dynastic luck of European politics and it remained difficult for any British ministry to win parliamentary support for the system when its consequences included a growth in the armed forces at a time of national phobia about standing armies, and a land tax of 4 shillings in the pound (equal to the wartime rates of the War of the Spanish Succession) at a time when the political nation clamoured for cheap government. Stanhope died in 1721 but his system – the Anglo-French alliance, and extensive commitments in European affairs – was continued by Secretaries of State such as Townshend (1721–30), and, although he was less keen on the French alliance, Carteret (1721–4). The Austro-Spanish alliance of 1725–9 led to reinforced emphasis on the French alliance and a high level of expensive armaments. Parliamentary and press criticism, strong in the late 1710s, created major problems for the ministry in the late 1720s as well, particularly in the session of 1729. Then the ministerial majority in the House of Commons fell to 35 during the debate over the government's failure to protect British trade from Spanish depredations. In that of 1730 there was a major political crisis when the Opposition claimed that the French were repairing the port of Dunkirk contrary to treaty.

One half of the Stanhope system – the Anglo-French alliance – was jettisoned in the summer of 1730 when, unbeknownst to the French, the British approached Austria for an alliance. This alliance, the Second Treaty of Vienna, signed in March 1731, was weak from the outset. Largely due to Hanoverian interests, Britain and Austria clashed in Germany,[8] whilst in 1732 the British refused to heed Austrian requests to send a squadron to the Mediterranean to protect Austrian Italy from a threatened Spanish invasion. The British repeated this refusal the following year when a contested royal election in Poland touched off the War of the Polish Succession (1735–5), pitting Austria, Saxony and Russia against France, Spain and Sardinia. Austria claimed British assistance under the terms of the Second Treaty of Vienna, and the British refusal to aid Austria marked the jettisoning of the second half of the Stanhopian system – the widespread involvement in European affairs. In January 1736 Walpole informed the French envoy in London, Chavigny, that he was at last free from the system that Stanhope had left him and that he had been obliged to follow hitherto.[9]

II

Walpole's position on foreign policy contrasted sharply with that of George I and Stanhope. In March 1718, attacking in the Commons the decision to grant funds that would permit an anti-Spanish naval commitment, he spoke of the need to attempt to avoid war, the dangerously high level of the National Debt and the political dangers presented by levels of wartime taxation.[10] Walpole's endorsement of Tory views on foreign policy was not restricted to periods, such as that of 1717–18, when he was seeking to win Tory support in Parliament against the ministry. In 1723 he acted, with great success, as Secretary of State in London, during the absence of the two secretaries in Hanover. He wrote then to the Duke of Newcastle of his opposition to 'very rash engagements' and, in the context of foreign policy, 'my politicks are in a narrow compasse . . . foreign disturbances . . . alone can confound us here'.[11] Walpole displayed an acute sensitivity, born of a long parliamentary experience, to the interrelationships of foreign and domestic politics. His awareness of the political and fiscal costs of interventionalist foreign policy schemes lay behind his attitudes, such as his opposition to intervention in the War of the Polish Succession. Though he disclaimed particular knowledge of foreign affairs and was described often as the 'tool' of his diplomat brother Horace,[12] his speeches, letters and conversations on foreign policy were both well informed and perceptive.[143] He was more sceptical about the French alliance than Horace, and in the summer of 1730 when he took an active role in the drafting of instructions to envoys,[14] he ignored Horace's advice to maintain the alliance. During the late 1730s Walpole conducted a confidential correspondence with the British envoy at Paris, Earl Waldegrave. In London he personally conducted many crucial interviews with foreign diplomats, such as that on 19 May 1729 when Count Kinsky, the Austrian envoy, argued in favour of a renewed Anglo-Austrian alliance.[15] He played a major role in the appointment of diplomats and in the discussions of foreign policy in Council and Parliament.

During the 1720s Walpole's views were subordinated largely to those of his brother-in-law Townshend, but the struggle between the two men in the winter of 1729–30, a struggle that centred on contrasting diplomatic strategies, and the subsequent resignation of Townshend in May 1730, was followed by a period when Walpole's influence was greater. Land tax, 4 shillings in the pound in 1727 and 3 in 1728, was cut to 2 in 1730 and 1 in 1732. To a substantial extent British policy after the resignation of Townshend was characterised by a reaction against the policy of the preceding years, a reaction expressed in terms of a wish to minimise entanglements and avoid expense. This was a foreign policy more in accordance with the views propounded by the Opposition in the late 1720s, and it would be attractive to suggest that in foreign policy, as in other spheres, Walpole had tempered Whig primacy to accommodate traditional Tory attitudes.

However, such an interpretation does justice neither to the role of George II, nor to the international situation. After the death of Peter the Great in 1725 Russia became less of a threat, and from 1733 relations improved appreciably. After 1731 Austria was less willing to challenge the position of powerful Protestant Princes of the Empire, such as the Elector of Hanover, and she abandoned her attempt to challenge the dominance of the East India trade by western European powers by establishing an oceanic trading company based at Ostend. The unwillingness to contest essential British interests, such as the *status quo* in the Austrian Netherlands (modern Belgium) and English control of the Celtic lands, that had characterised the administrations of the Dukes of Orleans and Bourbon in France, was maintained by the pacific Cardinal Fleury, premier minister in France from 1726 to 1743. The international situation permitted, therefore, a more relaxed British stance, and British neutrality in the War of the Polish Succession and the subsequent relatively low level of involvement in European affairs that characterised the second half of the 1730s stemmed in part from the absence of any clearly perceived threat to British interests. French success in the War of the Polish Succession and the subsequent French influence in European diplomacy was worrying,[16] but France was in no way the aggressive power that it had been under Louis XIV or was to become in 1741. It is significant that in the sessions of 1736–7 Parliament devoted less attention to Euro-

pean affairs than it had done over the previous decade,[17] whilst
in the following two sessions interest was restricted largely to
Spanish depredations on British Caribbean commerce. The
foreign policy of the late 1730s associated with Walpole both
reflected a less threatening international situation and received
less parliamentary criticism than that of the 1720s.

The relationship between George II and Walpole and the
influence of George II in general are difficult to evaluate. A
major problem is presented by gaps in the evidence. Little of
George II's correspondence survives, and it forms a woeful
contrast to the serried ranks of his grandson George III's
published correspondence. Extensive wartime damage to the
Hanoverian archives makes it difficult to estimate the influence
of Electoral interests. Walpole's papers are a very incomplete
series, and little remains for several important ministerial
figures, particularly Lord Harrington, Townshend's successor.
Divisions within the court or ministry, or between the king and
his ministers were not publicly debated. These disputes were
conducted within a small group who had many opportunities to
meet. Conversations took the place of memoranda. There was
no institution that recorded the audiences ministers had with
the king, and there is no equivalent for the British council of the
records of the Austrian Privy Conference which note separately
the views of the individual ministers. Isolating the views of
George II is not easy and in the instructions to British diplomats, George's own ideas are always intertwined with those of
his ministers.[18] It is no accident that historians have hitherto
neglected George as the subject of a scholarly biography.

These problems make it difficult to establish George II's
views during the War of the Polish Succession. The standard
view is clear – George II was keen to aid the Emperor but was
persuaded by the contrary views of Walpole. Unfortunately
this view rests on little more than the unreliable though
extraordinarily vivid *Memoirs* of Lord Hervey, a favoured
courtier of the queen, who occupied the far from politically
crucial post of Vice-Chamberlain. Hervey's account is substantiated by the despatches of the Austrian, Hessian and Saxon
envoys, and it is clear that George was concerned to demon-
strate publicly his loyalty to the Emperor, and ready to blame
Walpole for preventing assistance being given.

However, it is clear that there were other factors confusing the situation and omitted by Hervey, either through ignorance or because they qualified his dramatic account. As Elector, George II was free to assist the Emperor, but in 1732–3 relations between George, as Elector, and the Emperor were in a very poor state, and George was bitterly angry with what he saw as the Austrian thwarting of his scheme for royal marriages with Prussia. In 1734 George sent his Electoral contingent to the Rhine, but he delayed doing so for several months, despite massive Austrian pressure and a threatened French crossing of the river, because he was more concerned by Prussian troop movements in northern Germany and by the unstable situation in Mecklenburg. George II's concern about Prussian intentions rather than the French threat – the situation that was to so exasperate his ministers in 1744 during the War of the Austrian Succession – again played a large role in his attitude to 1735.

It is far from obvious that there was a clear-cut difference of opinion between George and Walpole during the Polish Succession War, and there is insufficient evidence to show that George was forced to adopt a policy of which he disapproved. The first few years of his reign had revealed that George was an independent and pugnacious figure capable of advancing his own views forcefully both to his own ministers and to foreign envoys.[19] There is no reason to believe that he lost this ability during the 1730s. In the late 1730s he drove Horace Walpole, who accompanied him as acting Secretary of State to Hanover in 1736, to despair by his firm stance on relations with Prussia and on Hanoverian territorial interests in East Friesland. Horace angered George and lost all his influence.[20]

It would therefore be mistaken to present British foreign policy in the 1730s as the policy of Walpole. Rather it could be suggested that in some spheres, particularly in the Baltic and in Germany, as in Britain with the army, George was of great influence,[21] but that in other spheres, particularly maritime disputes, he displayed less interest. Policy was not greatly influenced by British diplomats, apart from the ubiquitous Horace, but the Secretaries of State were of importance. Harrington had close links with Opposition figures, such as his relative the Earl of Chesterfield, and adopted an independent stance during the Excise Crisis. His replacement by Horace

Walpole was frequently rumoured, but never occurred, and he appears to have been protected by George II. Newcastle, Secretary of State from 1724 until 1754, displayed increasing independence in the 1730s.[22] In the late 1730s a major difference of opinion developed in the ministry over reaction to the sustained political agitation produced by exploitation of the continued problem of Spanish depredations.[23] This had been a major parliamentary issue in the late 1720s and its successful revival a decade later saw the same press agitation and identical arguments of the importance of British commerce and the ministerial failure to defend vital British interests. The ministry arranged a settlement with Spain – the Convention of the Prado – and defended it successfully against virulent Opposition attacks in the session of 1739, but difficulties over the diplomatic settlement arose and the ministry, its options limited by parliamentary considerations and its unity shattered by Newcastle's willingness to fight, drifted into war.[24]

This war, popularly known as the War of Jenkins' Ear after a Spanish atrocity allegedly inflicted on the captain of a British merchantman, placed Britain in a very difficult position. It was widely supposed that France would join Spain (although Fleury proved unwilling to take this step)[25] and, as a result, the British launched a search for allies. The traditional foreign allies of a Whig ministry were unavailable: the United Provinces was militarily weak and unwilling to anger either France or Spain with which they had close commercial links,[26] whilst Austria, an ally of France since 1735, had just been beaten by the Turks. As a result major efforts were made to win the alliance of Russia, and of Frederick the Great who succeeded in Prussia in 1740. Thus, the relative isolationism that had characterised British policy in the latter half of the 1730s,[27] was replaced, due to the need to offset probable French aid for Spain, by an active search for allies *before* the death of the Emperor Charles VI in October 1740, and the subsequent Prussian invasion of Silesia, posed fresh problems for Britain in the War of the Austrian Succession. Lord Hardwicke referred to the need to 'form such a confederacy upon the continent, as will make it dangerous for any power in Europe to disturb the tranquillity thereof'.[28]

The British response to Austrian demands for assistance –

George II had guaranteed the inheritance of the Austrian lands by Charles VI's elder daughter Maria Theresa – was an unsuccessful attempt to reconcile Prussia and Austria, and an attempt to create a grand coalition of powers that could put pressure on Prussia and France. Active attempts to win Russian assistance were continued, subsidy treaties were offered to states such as Sardinia and Hesse–Cassel. These diplomatic efforts were wrecked in the summer of 1741 by Hanoverian vulnerability. The military weakness of the electorate was well known – in 1738 the Prussian Grumbkow informed the British envoy in Berlin that an invasion would be easy, 'it would only be a breakfast', and in December 1740 Field Marshal Schwevin threatened an invasion if George II provoked Frederick the Great.[29] This weakness had for long affected British foreign policy but never more dramatically than in 1741. A French invasion of Westphalia and a Prussian military mobilisation led to the ignominious negotiation by George, as Elector, of a neutrality convention that bound him to vote for the French supported claimant to the Imperial succession, the Elector of Bavaria.

From the Hanoverian point of view this convention was essential, and in a persuasive defence of this viewpoint Uriel Dann has drawn attention to the perils posed for Hanover by her British connection, though possibly he makes too little of the contrast between the usually passive policies of the Hanoverian ministry and the schemes of territorial aggrandisement beloved by the Electoral masters.[30] For the British ministry the convention was disastrous in every aspect apart from the fact that it was negotiated during the parliamentary recess. It was concluded without consulting the ministers in London, undermined their attempts to create a pro-Austrian coalition and discredited British foreign policy in the eyes of domestic opinion. Opposition criticisms of policy, such as Bolingbroke's claim 'that the foreign interests of Britain' were being 'conducted in a certain subordination to those of Hanover', were matched by ministerial complaints. Every failing of foreign policy, such as the British navy's inability to prevent Spanish troops sailing to Italy in order to join the general attack upon the Austrian inheritance, was ascribed, unfairly, to Hanoverian interests, and the issue helped to poison the discussion of foreign policy in Walpole's last session as first minister.[31]

When Walpole fell in February 1742, British foreign policy was in difficulties. The widespread feeling that Spain could be easily defeated, a feeling fortified by Vernon's capture of Porto Bello in November 1739,[32] had proved mistaken. The resilience of the Spanish imperial system and Britain's need to maintain naval strength in European waters thwarted the bold schemes of extending British power in the new world. Austria had resisted with some success the 1741 attacks of France, Spain, Bavaria and Prussia, but it was a success to which British assistance, bar the ever important factor of finance, had proved of little value. As a war ministry the Walpole government was not a great success, although credit is due for the good state of the navy.[33] However, the war years, which lasted until the 1748 Peace of Aix-la-Chapelle, vindicated to a great extent the British foreign policy of the 1730s that had been subjected both at the time and subsequently to bitter criticism. France's total failure to overcome Austria is an important comment upon the claims that by remaining neutral in the War of the Polish Succession Britain had permitted a fundamental alteration in the balance of power in favour of France.[34] The difficulties encountered by the British in the War of the Austrian Succession in forming a coalition of allies that would do more than quarrel vindicated partially the traditional Tory distaste, also associated with Walpole, for alliance politics. It proved harder to control George II's Hanoverian predilections in wartime than in peacetime, as George sought to use the war to serve Hanoverian territorial objectives. French support for the Jacobite cause underlined the danger that the ministry of the 1730s had feared. Arguably the most successful feature of the war from the point of British diplomacy – the movement of British subsidised Russian troops to the Rhine in 1748, a move that, though tardy, helped to persuade the French to peace – originated in a policy devised during the Walpole years.[35] In short, the over-ambitious and unsuccessful record of British participation in the war of the Austrian Succession did much to justify the foreign policy of the 1730s from the criticisms it faced, just as the political history of the period 1742–8 – Jacobitism, ministerial instability, the 'ratting' of most of the

Patriots – did much to justify the Walpolean system from the assaults of its critics. War proved to be a major fiscal strain, a disrupter of commerce and a provoker of ministerial conflict, political strife and parliamentary difficulties.

III

Throughout the Walpole ministry significantly different options for the purpose and conduct of foreign policy existed. This was not, however, enough to ensure that quarrels over issues of foreign policy should be confined solely to the very small group whose task it was to formulate and conduct it. It is necessary to explain why these issues could provoke or serve as an occasion for major political debates. The political experience of George I and II and of most of their politicians was greatly influenced by their experience of nearly constant warfare, and of the attendant internal political struggles during the preceding two reigns. These wars, and in particular that of the Spanish Succession, provided a series of issues whose impact was still significant in the 1730s and which, because they had been linked, often fortuitously, to the party strife of the period continued to be of great importance in the definition of party views on foreign policy during the years of Walpole's influence. At times, the key Tory view on foreign policy appeared to be the defence of the Treaty of Utrecht, the peace treaty of 1713 negotiated by the Tory ministry and vilified by the Whigs both then and subsequently, although the Whig ministry was forced to use it as the basis for much of its own diplomacy. Defended by Tories, such as Stratford and Trevor in 1718 and Wyndham in 1739, and by Opposition Whigs wooing Tory support, such as Pulteney in 1739 and Argyll in 1740, and vilified by Whigs, such as Peterborough in 1730 and Walpole in 1739, who declared that it was 'a treaty that has been the source of all the divisions and distractions in Europe ever since', the treaty symbolised the manner in which different traditional stances on foreign policy, and contrasting positions in the past, help to define the political parties and to ensure that the need to justify their legacies was a major factor in political debate.[36]

The importance of foreign policy issues was clear. Britain was a major trading power whose fiscal strength and national credit system were closely linked to international commerce, whilst the location of the capital at London, the centre of trade, was of great importance. Various historians have argued that British foreign policy in the eighteenth century was dominated by commercial considerations, principally a search for markets, colonial and European, and a firm opposition to competitors.[37] An examination of parliamentary, pamphlet and press debate would appear to vindicate this claim. All politicians could agree in praising the virtues of trade, and all could see the advantage of expounding foreign policy in the light of commercial considerations. Thus, the Treaty of Hanover of 1725 was, according to the ministry, an attempt to thwart Austrian schemes for oceanic trade, whilst Opposition publicists could castigate British neutrality in the War of the Polish Succession on the grounds that Naples and Sicily in Spanish Bourbon hands posed a threat to Britain's Mediterranean trade.[38]

An examination, however, of diplomatic records reveals that the Walpole ministry's diplomatic commitment to the interests of British trade was patchy. Relations with minor states could be greatly influenced by the issue, whether it involved complaints against Venetian legislation threatening the interests of British sugar refiners, attempts to protect British trade with Hamburg from Danish attempts in 1734–5 to blockade the city, or moves in 1732–3 against Hamburg's efforts to benefit from the East India trade.[39] However, with larger states, from whom Britain sought political advantage, the picture was very different. The 1720s and 1730s saw most European states passing protectionist legislation that harmed British trade. British diplomats were instructed to complain, and threats of parliamentary retaliation were made, but these complaints were subordinated to the need for good relations. This was certainly the case with Sweden, Denmark and Sardinia.[40] Trade with Russia was sacrificed to political considerations in the 1710s and 1720s, and the important commercial treaty of 1734 negotiated only after political relations had improved markedly.[41] Moreover, the government failed to give much support to schemes for developing British trade with Austria.

Thus, the failure to protect Caribbean trade from Spanish depredations could be seen as but part of a more general disinclination to sacrifice political to commercial considerations. The ministry had close links not only with financial circles but also with some mercantile groups: the Russia Company played a major role in the negotiation of the commercial treaty with Russia, and links with the East India Company were close.[42] However, it was a mistake to claim that Britain was 'governed by a parcel of merchants', or, as in 1718, that the Spanish trade was so essential that the ministry would not risk war with Spain.[43] Mercantile lobbying was vociferous[44] and left much documentary evidence but this has led to an exaggeration of its importance. Much of the lobbying was at cross-purposes[45] and neither the diplomats nor the secretaries of state had much sympathy for merchants.[46] Possibly the failure to distinguish itself by a conspicuous support for trading interests was a political weakness of the Walpole ministry. It was certainly exploited to good effect by the Opposition, but it would have been unrealistic diplomatically to adopt commerce as a guiding principle. As Horace Walpole pointed out, 'if a merchant of London, and one of Amsterdam were to be the ministers of the political conduct to be observed between England, and Holland, instead of preserving a union between the maritime powers, the two nations would be constantly in a war with one another'.[47]

IV

Jacobitism helped to ensure that foreign policy was contentious. The Jacobite threat was a device that was used by several powers when their relations with Britain were bad. The failure of the 1715 Jacobite rising had owed much to the lack of significant support it received from foreign powers, particularly France, and the British ministry was well aware that foreign support was of great importance in assessing the Jacobite threat.[48] The issue was of particular importance in the decade 1715–25, when George I's Hanoverian-dominated policies led to the threat of Swedish and Russian support for the Jacobites, whilst Spain provided assistance in the late 1710s. The French alliance was clearly of great importance in minimising the Jacobite threat,[49] for although pro-Jacobite invasions could be threatened from other areas, such as Ostend and Corunna, it was France, with its nearby ports, large navy and army and traditional links and interest in Scotland and Ireland, that represented the greatest threat. The French played a major role in providing the Walpole ministry with information during the Atterbury plot, and moved their Irish troops away from the Channel coast, in response to British fears.[50] In 1731, in contrast, the effect of the end of the Anglo-French alliance was clear – French troop movements towards the Channel and reports of Jacobite activity led to a major British military mobilisation to prevent a feared invasion.[51]

The end of good Anglo-French relations and the major growth in the French navy in the 1730s made the Jacobite threat more serious in the 1730s though the French chose to ignore Jacobite pressure for assistance. In 1733 the Jacobites hoped to exploit the Excise crisis and French naval armaments by persuading the French to invade, but they were refused.[52] The British ministry did not doubt French hostility and were aware of the French notion, 'that we are to be frightened into any-thing by threatening to play the pretender upon us'.[53] It is unclear how far this influenced British neutrality during the War of the Polish Succession.[54] It was arguably easier and more effective for European states to threaten Hanover, as Austria did in 1726–7 and France in 1741, than to support the Jacobite cause. Despite Jacobite claims of massive support in Britain,[55] the Austrians and the French were aware that James III's Catholicism was a major negative factor.[56] Nevertheless, the Jacobite card was to be used with great effect by France in 1744–6, forcing a diversion of British strength, army and navy, to home defence. The 1745 rising vindicated Walpole's warnings of the potential dangers of Jacobitism.

v

The massive expansion of the national and provincial press during the early eighteenth century owed much to, and in turn helped to stimulate, public interest in foreign, principally

European, affairs and foreign policy. The quality of press reporting was high, critical evaluation of reports was stimulated by newspaper rivalry, and informed and perceptive comment was widely available. Xenophobic sentiment and anti-Catholicism were naturally common, but they did not vitiate the quality of the reporting. Indeed as Britain was commonly in alliance with at least one major Catholic power, anti-Catholicism, however much it might serve as a context within which to evaluate foreign countries (and it certainly did for most tourists),[57] could serve but rarely as a guide for discussing foreign policy.

The landowner, merchant or craftsman who busied himself reading and speculating about European affairs was a standard figure of fun.[58] It is difficult to assess how representative he was and how far or how readily concern about foreign policy could be translated into political pressure. There is little evidence of such issues being discussed in election campaigns, and though they are repeated often in Instructions or Addresses, such as those that greeted George II's accession, it is not clear how representative these were. 'My observation as to foreign affairs is, that the less one knows of them the better', wrote Henry Pelham in 1735,[59] and this view could certainly be substantiated by a detailed consideration of the general election campaign the previous year. Foreign policy related issues, such as the Folkestone fishermen who feared the press gang, were rare despite the fact that the election of 1734, like the following of 1741, was fought in the midst of a dangerous European situation. Describing the general election campaign of 1747, Philip Yorke, 2nd Earl of Hardwicke, informed his wife, 'As to foreign Affairs, you may be sure like a true Electioneer I think more of the contest in Staffordshire, than the State of Genoa, and provided the English freeholders have beef and beer enough am little concerned how the countrymen fare in Flanders.'[60]

And yet contemporaries were sure that popular opinion was of crucial importance.[61] Much was a matter of perception. Britain in European eyes was, as Chavigny put it, 'un etat populaire', where ministries and the Crown itself were subject to the popular will.[62] Great attention was devoted by foreign diplomats to indications of discontent in Britain and it was claimed that these limited the capacity of the ministry to follow a chosen foreign policy.[63] Thus, in 1733, many diplomats saw the political weakness and popular tumults associated with the Excise Crisis as limiting Britain's ability to intervene in the War of the Polish Succession. As a result of such beliefs, foreign diplomats invested both time and money in printing pamphlets, placing newspaper reports and attempting to influence MPs.[64] It was also believed that public opinion could influence specific policies. For example, George I and several ministers wished to return Gibraltar to Spain in order to improve relations. However, fears of the public outcry in Britain were cited by ministers in letters written for private consumption by other ministers, as the reason why this scheme was abandoned, despite a specific promise by George I to Philip V of Spain.[65]

However, public opinion proves to be a very nebulous concept. It is difficult to isolate from the modes of expression: the press Instructions and Addresses, the exuberant London demonstrations of anti-Spanish sentiment in 1738–9. Occasionally it is possible to show that demonstrations were organised from above, such as the celebration of the victory of Cape Passaro, organised by the Earl of Lincoln at Peterborough. In general, the impact of public opinion can be questioned. It was widely agreed that anti-French feeling was very widespread,[66] and yet a French alliance was the central feature of British foreign policy for many years and was abandoned largely because of Anglo-French diplomatic differences in 1730, though fear of parliamentary criticism in the session of 1731 did play a part. There is no sign that neutrality in the War of the Polish Succession was in accordance with, or defiance of, any substantial body of public feeling. Walpole was not driven to war with Spain in 1739 by popular opinion. Instead he defied it successfully by carrying a settlement of Anglo-Spanish differences through Parliament. Rather, the campaign for war with Spain, as with the anti-excise campaign in 1733, had a major impact precisely because the ministry was divided over policy. It is true that Newcastle, the leading ministerial proponent of war, claimed to be influenced by the public clamour, but it could be suggested that he was more influenced by his wish to improve relations with Opposition figures such as Carteret. Popular opinion could only be effective if harnessed by powerful parliamentary or ministerial groups, and the absence of an effective representative system meant that these groups were not obliged to respond to popular campaigns.

VI

The relation which the affairs here in Parliament must have to those abroad.   Horace, Walpole, 1730[67]

Constitutionally Parliament's right to intervene in foreign policy was limited greatly by the royal prerogative. The king had the right of making peace and war, signing treaties, appointing and paying diplomats, giving them instructions and receiving their reports. Legally with limited rights – largely that of voting the funds necessary for the military forces, British and foreign, that were expected to give substance to foreign policy – Parliament had nevertheless acquired, during the recent wars with France, a position of considerable importance. As two pamphleteers put it in 1730,

> As to the right of making peace and war, the same is allowed and granted to be part of the King's high prerogative, tho' we find that the wisest of our monarchs have very rarely enter'd into any war without the approbation and consent of their parliaments: for who can give better and more wholesome advice and counsel in such arduous affairs?

> Tho' the making of peace is acknowledged to be within the prerogative of the Crown, yet it will most certainly be brought before you for your Approbation; which Ministers always esteem to be some kind of security to them.[68]

Parliamentary discussion of foreign policy was followed with great attention in Europe. Foreign envoys sent detailed and regular reports,[69] British envoys were instructed to publicise ministerial accounts of parliamentary events,[70] and politicians were aware of the great importance attached in Europe to parliamentary developments, and the consequent need to control them. Ministerial speakers claimed regularly that parliamentary opposition encouraged Britain's enemies and accused the Opposition of links with foreign envoys,[71] accusations that were substantiated by the excellent postal interception system that provided so much information about the activities of these envoys. Eighteenth-century ministries rarely lost parliamentary divisions, but it was believed that a small majority presaged a change either of ministers or measures.[72] It was certainly the case that troublesome sessions, as in 1718, 1730, 1733 and 1739, were often linked with ministerial weakness and divisions, whilst opponents of the Walpole ministry believed that their influence would be increased if they could create parliamentary difficulties for the ministry. Writing about the session of 1726, the Jacobite agent in Vienna claimed, 'the more vigorously the King's [James III] friends there oppose the measures of the Court, the more weight his cause will have at Vienna, grant they are not able to hinder the Whiggs from carrying all before them'.

Four years later the Austrian Chancellor was told by the British envoy that Austrian views of British attitudes were based on mistaken sources.

and that this Court lets itself be misled by such a supposition is plain, from the credit a Protest in time of Parliament, and a Craftsman or any such impertinent libel has at Vienna all the year long, of which they are not sparing in their applications, when they are pleased to descant upon what they call the true interest and disposition of the people.[73]

Parliamentary deliberations were not only influential in Europe. In Britain they could be used by politicians, sometimes members of the ministry, who sought to discredit the administration. Creating difficulties in parliamentary management was an established method by which politicians out of place, such as Walpole in 1717–19 or Pulteney from 1725, sought to win admission to office. Foreign policy provided convenient issues, because the ministry, dependent on parliamentary grants, could not avoid their debate, whilst contentious religious legislation could be postponed, and because it was easier to arrange a concerted opposition, and, in particular, to win Tory support, on these issues than on other areas of controversy, such as Church matters. Thus, the ministry sought to conduct foreign policy in order to minimise its parliamentary consequences.

Contentious legislation, such as peacetime subsidies, was avoided if possible, although, as in the negotiations with the Wittelsbachs in 1729–30, this could have detrimental diplomatic effects. An annual rhythm of diplomatic activity can at times be discerned with British diplomats receiving from the late summer onwards instructions, more frenetic as the session approached, to settle potentially embarrassing issues, whether it be the Dutch accession to treaties to which Britain was a party, as in 1725 and 1731, repairs to Dunkirk or the issue of French recruiting in Ireland, as in 1730, or Anglo-Spanish negotiations, as in 1729 and 1738.[74] The ministry was fortunate if difficulties occurred when Parliament was not sitting, as with the Hanoverian–Prussian war panic of 1729 and the Hanoverian neutrality of 1741.

Attempts to use parliamentary disquiet over foreign policy to win power proved singularly unsuccessful. Though the Stanhope ministry was dangerously overcommitted in 1718 Walpole was unable to gain office as he had hoped, whilst the years of interminable, unsuccessful negotiations and expensive armaments that began in 1725 were exploited by the new Opposition of Pulteney and Bolingbroke without success. The Opposition, and many foreign envoys, claimed that this was because of the impact of corruption,[75] but other factors must be considered and, in particular, the capacity of a well-informed Parliament to consider matters, and the influence of the Crown.

Parliamentary debates on foreign policy were of a high standard. Benefiting from ministerial and diplomatic experience, travel, personal contacts and correspondence, and the press, parliamentarians were very well informed about European affairs, and the standard of debate on foreign policy was very high in both Houses. It was necessary for ministers to win parliamentary approval and the lengthy preparations devoted to preparing speeches and seeking to influence members of both Houses suggest that the statements made about corruption were glib and inaccurate. Recognising this fact Walpole was very concerned to win parliamentary approval. Foreign policy debates saw lengthy and detailed speeches by senior members of the ministry explaining the purposes of government policy. Well-argued pamphlets defending policy were distributed to parliamentarians.[76]

There is no doubt about the energy Walpole devoted to winning parliamentary support for British foreign policy: he played a major role in many of the debates. It would be a mistake however to claim that Britain followed a parliamentary foreign policy, one based on a consideration of what Parliament would accept. Doubtless Walpole would have sought such a policy. When he wrote in July 1730 'Horace cannot be spur'd too much upon the affair of Dunkirk', he was thinking of the parliamentary consequences, and such an attitude characterised his stance on foreign policy.[77] Policies associated with him, such as neutrality in the War of the Polish Succession and opposition to subsidising foreign states in peacetime, were sensible in terms of parliamentary attitudes. However, Walpole was not the sole director of foreign policy, he was only its paymaster and defender, and nobody needed to tell him of the need to win the support of two men whose sensitivity to parliamentary attitudes was irregular, George I and George II.[78]

VII

Had their ministry been united and enjoying parliamentary support Georges I and II would have had limited room for political manoeuvre, particularly for their frequent attempts to use British resources to serve what they regarded as Hanoverian interests. Clayton Roberts has revealed recently the limited royal powers enjoyed by William III and Anne when confronted with parties determined to monopolise power.[79] Some commentators, such as the Austrian Resident Palm at the end of George I's reign, described the royal position in these terms, but in fact this was rarely, if ever, the case. Georges I and II benefited from bitter policy divisions amongst their ministers and sought to exploit them for their own ends. Many of these divisions related to foreign policy, for example in 1723–4 between the pro-Austrian ministers, such as Carteret and Cadogan, and the group more ready to align with the French, such as Townshend, Newcastle and the Walpoles, in 1729–30 between Townshend and the Walpoles supported by Newcastle, in 1739 between Newcastle and Walpole, in 1743–4 between Carteret and the Pelhamites, supported by Walpole's influence.

Foreign policy was an obvious topic for ministers to disagree over: it was complex, important in parliamentary terms and could be used to gain the support of rivals or to damn them in the eyes of the monarch. The latter was particularly important. It was George I's growing estrangement in the 1720s from his traditional Austrian sympathies that helped to destroy Carteret and Cadogan's political position. One side-effect of the anti-Austrian Treaty of Hanover of 1725 was the political neutral-isation of these ministers. A major reason for the failure of Walpole's Opposition in 1717–19 and the Pulteney–Boling-broke Opposition from 1725 was that in order to discredit the ministry, and retain Tory support, they challenged the current foreign policy, and, by so doing, incurred royal displeasure. The Tories, whether through Jacobite sympathies or not is unclear, hardly bothered to seek royal approval. Tory politi-cians defended the Treaty of Utrecht by which Britain had ditched her allies, including Hanover, and frequently criticised the Hanoverian connection and what they held, often correctly, to be Hanoverian-inspired policies. Senior Tories made little attempt to disguise their close links with foreign envoys seeking to thwart British policy, whether it was the Earl of Strafford with the Prussian Reichenbach in 1729–30, or Sir William Wyndham and Bolingbroke with the French Chavigny in 1732–5.[80] These connections infuriated the king, and the Opposition Whigs similarly played with fire by co-operating with Austrian envoys such as Stahremberg in 1725, Palm in 1726–7 and Kinsky in 1730.[81]

Policy could be opposed without losing royal approval, but it had to be opposed cautiously, and without mentioning Hanover. It was the continual presence of rivals of Walpole within the court and ministry that weakened his position. Royal determination to dictate policy in those spheres of British diplomacy of most concern to the king was important, particu-larly when combined with the royal policy of seeking advice from whomever he wished,[82] with the presence of a separate Hanoverian diplomatic service and Chancellory, under direct royal control, and with the fact that diplomats, appointed and paid by the king, could receive instructions from him contrary to the policy of the ministry.[83] The impact of this situation can be gauged from the draft of a letter from Townshend to Horace Walpole,

'His Majesty's thoughts upon the points of Mecklenburg and Sleswig, on which he is very earnest and would not suffer the least delay to be made. . . . I never saw the King more displeased in his life than he was upon reading what was said in this project and your despatches upon those two articles . . . for God's sake, Dear Horace, do your best, both your reputation and mine are at stake.[84]

VIII

In 1787 the Spanish prime minister, Count Floridablanca, told the British envoy in Madrid that though Carlos III of Spain 'had not literally a House of Lords and Commons to satisfy, and a professed opposition to encounter, yet he had also a species of Parliament, a publick, and a discontented party to manage, and that it was not in his power to do in every respect what his inclination might dictate'. The same was true for much of Europe for most of the eighteenth century.[85] British foreign policy appears different, appears akin to the other states with representative assemblies – Sweden, Poland, the United Provinces – because there was public discussion of policy, and active debate, in both Parliament and print. Both were important, but to concentrate on both would be a mistake. Parliament was a constant factor, but its active role was episodic; the impact of the press and of public opinion has probably been exaggerated. The centre of foreign policy formulation was the court, or, to be more specific, the meetings between king and principal ministers. In this respect Britain was no different from France, Spain or Austria, just as its diplomacy shared the common problems of eighteenth-century diplomacy: poor communications, untrained, ill-informed and disobedient diplomats, inadequate central supervision. British foreign policy in the age of Walpole lacked the spectacular aspects of the antecedent and subsequent periods, but in many respects, particularly in the period 1732–8, it was better matched to British capabilities and to the international situation than in other periods of the century. This was because policy whilst not guided by parliamentary and popular considerations was, through Walpole, influenced by it, because of a fortuitous international situation, because of a ministry strong enough to dominate Parliament, and because George II and Walpole were more perceptive in their conduct of and influence over foreign policy than men who knew more, argued more persuasively and satisfied that intellectual snobbery present in most historians.

7.   Walpole, 'the Poet's Foe'

J. A. DOWNIE

FOR twenty years, until his fall in 1742 and beyond, the immense figure of Sir Robert Walpole dominated English literature. The 'Great Man' made his presence felt in the best-known works of the age, and he was celebrated and condemned under a variety of disguises. He was the man with many names – 'Robin of Bagshot, alias Gorgon, alias Bluff Bob, alias Carbuncle, alias Bob Booty' – not only was he recognisable in John Gay's *The Beggar's Opera* as the 'fellow with a brown coat with a narrow gold binding', he was 'the favourite child-getter' as well.[1] Other counterparts included Flimnap, Lord High Treasurer of Lilliput in Swift's *Gulliver's Travels*, and Palinurus nodding at the helm of state in Pope's *The Dunciad*. In fact, Walpole was the real 'hero' of Pope's mock-heroic poem, the image of Peachum in Gay's burlesque masterpiece, and the antitype of the thief-taker and racketeer in Fielding's *The Life of Mr. Jonathan Wild the Great*.

It is paradoxical that Walpole should figure so prominently in the literature of the period, because he was constantly being accused of presiding over a decline in English letters. Throughout his long tenure of royal favour, his reputation amongst the *cognoscenti* was depressingly low. Far from being eulogised as the writer's friend, the 'Great Man' was satirised as 'the Poet's Foe'.[2] 'Perhaps no minister in English history would be so virulently and consistently assaulted by intellectuals as Walpole was in the years 1726–1728', Isaac Kramnick writes with justice of the days that witnessed the publication of *Gulliver's Travels*, *The Beggar's Opera* and *The Dunciad*, as well as the launching of that pre-eminent Opposition journal *The Craftsman*.[3] Censure of the prime minister was not restricted to a couple of years, however, and he was subjected to withering criticism from the aftermath of the South Sea Bubble onwards, as a powerful literary opposition indicted Walpole not merely of personal corruption, but the corruption of a nation.

The impression handed down to posterity by writers such as Swift, Pope and Gay – the founders of the celebrated Scriblerus Club – is of a kingdom in the process of rapid decay. Under the regime of Walpole, Swift claimed to recognise 'the worst times and Peoples, and Oppressions that History can shew'.[4] On the contrary, history would seem to show that the fears of the opposition to Walpole's ministry were groundless, and should be discounted. Instead of Britain declining under the Hanoverians, its real growth was staggering. Nor does evidence of the nation's moral degeneracy appear overwhelming. The conflict between the myth spun by the opposition writers about the age of Walpole and hard historical fact can lead to a distorted view which has been called the 'Tory Interpretation of Literary History'. Indeed it has been suggested that the assumption that 'the Scriblerians won a total victory in their war with the Dunces, and that the Scriblerian cause was just' is as misleading and oversimplified a perspective as the equally pervasive Whig interpretation of history.[5]

The attitude of the opposition writers to Walpole and his administration therefore presents a problem. Given that, with the benefit of hindsight, their fears, as outlined in their many and varied attacks on the government, can largely be discounted, how should their motives be viewed? Were the Scriblerians and their allies genuinely concerned for the nation's manners, and did they really anticipate the subversion of the constitution, or were more personal considerations at the root of their violent antipathy towards Walpole? For in a way the relationship of the *cognoscenti* and the court could be seen as a literary version of Sir Lewis Namier's description of the realities of practical politics as a struggle between those who were in and those who were out of power. All the time the literary opposition was condemning the official disregard of the state of English letters, perhaps it was actually bemoaning its own failure to secure royal and ministerial patronage. Hence Pope's lament that in the reign of 'Th' Augustus born to bring Saturnian times'.

Gay dies un-pensioned with a hundred friends,
Hibernian politics, O Swift, thy doom,
And Pope's, translating three whole years with Broome.[6]

It has been noted that by 1737 'opposition to the administration was . . . obviously the course which any self-respecting
writer would take, at least if he were at all susceptible to the
influence of literary fashion'.[7] And yet most of the opposition
writers had, at some time or other, courted government
patronage. Nor is there any question that writers *were* patronised by the court during Walpole's tenure of office, however
much the circle surrounding Swift and Pope disapproved of
those who received official recognition. It is equally evident
that 'much of their work was more clever and effective than has
sometimes been admitted'.[8] One of the first things Walpole did
on assuming the premiership was to gain control 'of all but a
few of the valuable mediums of publicity', either through
'purchase or subsidy'.[9] True, he preferred to use less well-
known writers than previous administrations. During the four
last years of Queen Anne's reign both government and
Opposition had enlisted the support of the best writers of the
day – Swift, Defoe, Maynwaring, Addison and Steele. In
contrast, Walpole's propagandists were, in the main, anonymous hacks. No wonder that the *cognoscenti* were both offended
and angry when the court, far from patronising those whom
they considered to be the legitimate men of letters, seemed to
'want no better writers than [Colley] Cibber and [William
Arnall,] the British Journalist'.[10]

One of the main points of *The Dunciad* was to highlight the
way in which the 'Smithfield Muses' had been legitimised at
the expense of their authentic counterparts and brought 'to the
ear of Kings'. The Whig ministers – the 'great Patricians' of
Pope's poem – were blamed for this state of affairs: 'since your
selves inspire / These wond'rous works'.[11] Numerous minor
writers or 'dunces' were ridiculed by name, and notes were
added to *The Dunciad Variorum* of 1729 'to give some account' of
these hacks and poetasters, 'since it is only in this monument
that they must expect to survive'.[12] Among other things, *The
Dunciad* chronicles the system of government patronage under

Walpole, as in one form or another the vast majority of the dunces were its beneficiaries.

Three broad categories of patronised writer can be discerned: the man of substance who readily supported the regime and, as a result, received marks of favour; the would-be poet or man of letters who, for whatever reason, managed to secure reward and advancement; and the out-and-out hackney scribbler who simply wrote government propaganda for money. Similarly, there were three principal kinds of patronage: appointment to an office of power or profit; endowment of a regular pension or salary; and unambiguous remuneration in the form of hard cash. While distinctions between these categories are not always clear-cut, representative types of recipient can be found, all of whom were objects of derision to opposition writers like Pope.

Benjamin Hoadly is a prime example of a clergyman who made a career out of his political rather than his spiritual writings. Rewarded for his Whig propaganda during the reign of Queen Anne by being made Bishop of Bangor, he was transferred to the much more profitable diocese of Salisbury in October 1723 after publishing his 'Britannicus' letters in *The London Journal*. His ultimate reward was even more valuable. In 1734 he was preferred to Winchester, the third richest see in England with an annual income of some £5000 – more than the archbishopric of York. If Hoadly, in Pope's terms, was one of 'Heaven's Swiss, who fight for any god, or man' who would pay them, John, Lord Hervey, son of the Earl of Bristol, was his secular equivalent, a 'painted child of dirt that stinks and stings'.[13] To a cynical observer, Hervey's career must have been the perfect illustration of the rhythm of service and reward which was the basis of the system of patronage under Walpole.

Both Walpole and William Pulteney were godfathers to Hervey's children before he threw in his lot with the ministry by publishing *An Answer to the Occasional Writer No. II* in February 1727. 'Hervey had performed a considerable service', his biographer, Robert Halsband, remarks, 'no doubt [he] expected to be rewarded. At some time before the summer of the following year he was awarded a pension of £1,000 by the Court. Since his pamphleteering on the Ministry's behalf was the only service he performed during this interval the pension must have been his reward as well as his incentive to continue to lend them his support.'[14] The ploy worked. Hervey's next publication was followed by his appointment as Vice-Chamberlain to the King's Household, with a salary of £1159 p.a. He was also made a member of the Privy Council. Further pro-government pamphleteering brought additional rewards. In 1733, in concert with Walpole, Hervey published *The Reply of a Member of Parliament to the Mayor of his Corporation* on the excise bill. He was raised to the peerage as Baron Hervey of Ickworth three months later. *The Conduct of the Opposition*, also revised by Walpole, was written at the instigation of the king and queen. George II added £1000 a year to Hervey's salary soon afterwards.[15]

Throughout this period Hervey had been a staunch supporter of Walpole in Parliament, as well as a close friend of the king and queen. His multifarious services to the court and the ministry preclude any conclusion that he was patronised purely on account of his propaganda, but the correlation between Hervey's political support and friendship and official literary sponsorship is clear. Other examples of this sort of arrangement might easily be adduced, such as the case of Walpole's political factotum, Sir William Yonge, whose literary aspirations were derided by the opposition wits. Yonge wrote political pamphlets as well as verse. Hervey penned the Dedication to his *Sedition and Defamation Displayed* (1731). Once again, such services brought a tangible reward. Under Walpole, Yonge was Commissioner of the Treasury (from 1724 to 1727, and again from 1730 to 1735), Commissioner of the Admiralty (from 1728 onwards), and Secretary at War (from 1735). He even managed to survive the Great Man's fall, and remain in office under the Pelhams.

Yonge was abused by the Scriblerians as a pretender to poetry. He was only one of a number of indifferent writers who none the less found favour during the reigns of George I and George II. On one level the quarrel was merely an aesthetic one. Laurence Eusden was Poet Laureate until his death in 1730. Despite his very mediocre talents, he was less objectionable than his successor, Colley Cibber, who gradually became the mark at which opposition barbs were levelled as not only the type of court poet, but 'as a kind of Minister of Culture for

Walpole'.[16] It was only appropriate that Cibber would assume his place as King Dunce in the *Dunciad* in the 1743 version, in which it was explained that the 'very *hero* of the poem hath been mistaken to this hour': Cibber it was 'who, above all other poets of his time, was the *peculiar delight* and *chosen companion* of the nobility of England; and wrote, as he himself tells us, certain of his works at the *earnest desire of persons of quality*'. It had, after all, been Cibber who had brought the 'Smithfield Muses to the ear of Kings' as Poet Laureate.[17]

However, Cibber had not been favourite before his appointment. According to Gay, Stephen Duck, the 'thresher poet', was most highly regarded by the court, and Swift expected him 'to succeed Eusden in the laurel'.[18] At the instigation of Queen Caroline, Duck was given a house in Richmond Park, a pension and, subsequently, the Keepership of Merlin's Cave. Swift expressed his indignation in verse:

> From *threshing* corn, he turns to *thresh* his brains;
> For which Her Majesty allows him grains.
> Though 'tis confessed that those who ever saw
> His poems, think them all not worth a *straw*.[19]

Under Walpole, Swift suggested, the question of aesthetics was shelved, as the court tried to discover 'who can reach to worst of all?'

> For, though in nature depth and height
> Are equally held infinite,
> In poetry the height we know;
> 'Tis only infinite below.
> For instance: when you rashly think,
> No rhymer can like Welsted sink:
> His merits balanced you shall find,
> The laureate leaves him far behind.

Leonard Welsted had to be satisfied with the appointment of Commissioner of Lotteries in 1731. Cibber merited the Poet Laureateship not because he was the better poet but, paradoxically, because he was worse. In this topsy-turvy society, Swift insinuated, in order to receive recognition, poets strove to be 'worst of all'.[20]

Not even Cibber reached such depths in Swift's poetic treatment of the bathos, though, as 'Concanen, more aspiring bard, / Climbs downwards, deeper by a yard'. Laurence Hanson notes that Matthew Concanen 'provides a typical example of the talent employed and rewarded by Walpole'.[21] He successfully bridged the division between those who sought patronage more or less on account of their literary endeavours, and those who, not satisfied with 'thrumming the venal lyre' and turning out sycophantic verses on George II and his court, were prepared to write to the ministry's order for profit. As one of the editors of *The British Journal*, Concanen was to be located in 'the common sink of all such writers, a political newspaper'. According to Pope, he was also 'a hired scribbler in the *Daily Courant* . . . after which this man was surprisingly promoted to administer justice and law in Jamaica', becoming Attorney General of the island in 1732. Concanen's element was mud-slinging journalism, Pope claimed, as he excelled in 'love of dirt'.[22]

Concanen's associates in *The British Journal* and other political newspapers such as *The London Journal*, the *Daily Courant*, the *Free Briton*, the *Hyp-Doctor* and the *Corn-Cutter's Journal* were men bought by Walpole to defend his administration against the opposition press. Many of them are mentioned by name in *The Dunciad*. As well as Daniel Defoe, we find William Arnall, Thomas Burnet, George Duckett, Barnham Goode, John Henley, Philip Horneck, James Pitt, James Ralph and Edward Roome. To be fair, Pope also names several opposition journalists. But the overall thrust of his satire is anti-ministerial. Walpole countered the threat to his public image by funding an expensive press campaign. Over £50,000 was spent to that purpose in the ten years between 1732 and 1742. In an attempt to economise, the various government journals were combined in 1735 to form the *Daily Gazetteer*, which from then onwards was Walpole's only organ of propaganda. Although the printer, John Walthoe, received well over £4000 during the first 18 months of the paper's existence, 'Walpole's subsidies to the government press [slumped], and . . . they never returned to the level of the early 1730s',[23] when the opposition campaign to discredit the ministry was at its height.

The *Grub Street Journal* suggested in 1731 that, 'generally speaking, 8 or 9 papers were published in defence of the ministry' each week. There was some justification, then, in *The Craftsman's* complaint about 'the great encouragement which hath been lately given to these writers by a certain gentleman, at the public expense'. Proceeding to consider what a writer should or should not do, the pseudonymous editor, Caleb D'Anvers, pointed out that:

> He should not, for instance, charge his adversary with mercenary views when he hath owned that he writes himself for a reward, or the expectation of a reward, nor talk of freedom and independency whilst he is known to be under the restraint of a place or pensionary stipend from the Treasury.[24]

Walpole's writers were retained in just this way. On the death of John Trenchard, his collaborator in the stridently anti-ministerial *Cato's Letters*, Thomas Gordon was taken into the ministry's pay and made First Commissioner of the Wine Licences. Contemporaries dryly observed that this 'much diminished his patriotism'. The previously outspoken *British Journal* became a compliant government organ, Gordon's translation of Tacitus (1727) was dedicated to Walpole, and apparently he was directed to supervise the whole of the government press.[25]

Gordon's case was not unique. One of the authors of the pro-Walpole journal *Pasquin*, George Duckett, was Commissioner of the Excise, while the other, Edward Roome, was Solicitor to the Treasury, a position also held by Philip Horneck, another of Walpole's journalists. 'Orator' Henley, on the other hand, was paid a salary of £100 p.a. to write the *Hyp-Doctor*. And whereas the *London Journal* was bought by Walpole in September 1722 to silence criticism, other papers were launched to support his cause. The Treasury paid out over £1000 over 18 months to underwrite the costs of the

Corn-Cutter's Journal, and it was distributed through the Post Office, a service previously granted to only the *London Journal*, the *Daily Courant* and the *Free Briton*. When the vigour of the *Craftsman's* attacks on his policies subsided around 1735, Walpole was ready to cut his sponsorship of the government press, and he did not greatly increase it even when challenged by new opposition journals like *Common Sense* and *The Champion*.

If Matthew Concanen was a typical Walpolean writer, the case of William Arnall best illustrates the character of the Great Man's patronage. Although Joseph Mitchell was known as Walpole's poet as a result of the many verses he addressed to him, Arnall claimed to be his closest supporter. According to James Ralph, Arnall was 'taken from the engrossing desk to defend the minister, of whose favour he seemed, on many occasions to enjoy a greater share than any other mercenary'. Arnall himself admitted that he had been 'vouchsafed' Walpole's 'protection' before he had 'attained [his] twentieth year', and in 1734 he reminded him that he had 'laboured for seven years past' on his behalf, and ascribed himself: 'Me who am so truly your own'.[26]

It has been suggested that Arnall was paid a pension of £400 p.a., and that he received in all almost £11,000 from the ministry.[27] However, it is likely that this sum was to defray production costs of the *Free Briton*, and to distribute amongst those involved in writing Walpole's newspapers. Writing to the Great Man on 26 March 1730 'concerning the money that is due on account of the *Free Briton*', Arnall advised 'the most easy course of payment as various parties have a dependence on it'. Far from Arnall pocketing the disbursement himself, he was forced to petition Walpole on his own behalf. 'I must add that my private occasions do at this time very much need your generous assistance', he concluded, 'and if you can favour me with thirty pounds it will be the greatest obligation and of the utmost service to me.' This does not sound like a man with a regular pension, although Arnall certainly sought more security through 'a provision . . . during life'. In 1732 he asked for the offices of either Clerk of the Pipe in the court of the Exchequer in Ireland or Auditor of the Imprest, but received neither. By 1734 he was lamenting the 'astonishing change of

[his] fortune', but Walpole displayed no great desire to reward him for his services. During his ministry, the writer appears to have been employed out of necessity, rather than choice.[28]

The Great Man managed to do without the immense talent of Swift as propagandist, just as the court saw fit to appoint Cibber Poet Laureate in the teeth of Pope and Gay. There is little to indicate that these choices were regretted. But the fruits of Scriblerian antagonism were reaped by monarch and minister alike. We have suggested that there were indeed aesthetic grounds upon which the system of patronage under Walpole might be censured. However, government writers questioned the sincerity of opposition complaints, and charged the critics of the ministry with 'mercenary views'. Certainly Swift, Pope and Gay all had disappointments to nurse with regard to Walpole. Other talented writers who eventually turned against the Great Man, James Thomson, for instance, or Henry Fielding, originally sought his favour. Among the journalists, it was noted that essayists like Thomas Gordon were in effect rewarded for their anti-government propaganda by being bought off by the ministry. 'Have I been the man', William Arnall asked Walpole, 'who after having listed myself to asperse and injure you entered into your service when the cause of abusing you would no longer support me?'[29] Opposition writers accused ministerial propagandists of mercenary motives only to have the accusation thrown back in their faces.

Swift visited England in 1726, and had a number of audiences with Walpole. He claimed to have 'no other design . . . than to represent the affairs of Ireland to him in a true light', but contemporaries were quick to discern ulterior motives, and rumours spread that the two men had reached an accommodation, involving the preferment of Swift to an Irish bishopric. Subsequently Swift promised to 'study revenge' unless Walpole used him 'better next summer than he did last'. On the death of George I, Swift hoped that his interest with the court of George II would lead to the replacement of Walpole by his friends, and he persuaded a dozen Tories to go in line to kiss the hands of the new king and queen in anticipation of a brave new world. When Walpole held on to office, Swift resigned himself to his fate, aware that his ambitions would come to nothing, 'unless I would have been a greater rascal than happened to suit with my temper'.[30]

Pope's affairs with the Great Man are even more complicated. He was on dining terms with Walpole in the late 1720s, which is suggestive of some intimacy. Only with the publication of *The Dunciad* in 1728 did he begin to criticise the regime openly. E. P. Thompson wonders whether this was because Walpole 'had two hostages to hold against' him, on account of the involvement in Black activity in Windsor Forest of his brother-in-law, Charles Rackett, and his son, Michael Rackett, which meant 'Pope had to tread very warily . . . for several years'.[31] (Charles Rackett died in 1728 and Michael Rackett had already fled the country.) However, there are indications, strange as it may seem given Pope's Roman Catholicism, that he coveted the Poet Laureateship, and it was really only after Cibber's appointment in 1730 that Pope's real offensive on the Robinocracy began.[32]

Gay's pursuit of patronage was more open. He had been Commissioner of the Lottery under George I, and expected a suitable position to be added by the new queen to the one he held. But when the list of Queen Caroline's household was announced in the autumn of 1727, he found, to his chagrin, that he had been appointed Gentleman Usher to the youngest princess, Louisa. Gay refused the position and looked on it as a calculated insult on Walpole's part. Swift called it 'one of the cruellest actions I ever knew, even in a minister of state', but Pope looked upon Gay as 'a free man' without obligations to the court, and wrote him 'a long congratulatory letter upon it'. His 'expectations' having 'vanished', Gay turned his back on Walpole. Just over three months later *The Beggar's Opera* began its record-breaking run on the London stage. 'Does Walpole think you intended an affront to him in your opera', Swift asked, 'Pray God he may, for he has held the longest hand at hazard that ever fell to any sharper's share'.[33]

The failure of the Scriblerians to gain any sort of satisfaction from Walpole is interesting. James Thomson's conduct follows a similar pattern. Arriving in London in 1726, he dedicated *Winter*, the first published poem of *The Seasons*, to Sir Spencer Compton, *Summer* to George Bubb Dodington, and *On the Death of Sir Isaac Newton* to Walpole as the 'most illustrious patriot'. He gained a reluctant present of 20 guineas from Compton and a mention in the first edition of *The Dunciad* for his pains. Turning to the opposition, Thomson attacked Walpole's foreign policy in *Britannia* (1729). He continued to seek patronage, and was given the post of Secretary of Briefs in the Court of Chancery by his tutee's father, Charles, Lord Talbot, the Lord Chancellor. However, after the publication of his celebration of the British constitution, *Liberty* (1735–36), he was awarded a pension, not from the king, but from his son, Frederick, the Prince of Wales. It would not be stretching the facts to interpret Thomson's conduct as mercenary; he turned away from the court after failing to secure patronage, and proceeded to attack it instead.

The career of Henry Fielding perhaps best displays this seemingly equivocal attitude towards Walpole. Given the antagonistic stance he took up in his plays of the 1730s, his contributions to opposition journals like *Common Sense* and *The Champion*, if not to *The Craftsman* itself,[34] and, above all, his attack on Great Men in *Jonathan Wild*, it is hard to come to terms with his intermittent courtship of the Prime Minister. Like Thomson, he celebrated Walpole early on in his career as the 'bulwark of liberty against Jacobitism and Popery', and in 1732 he dedicated his play, *The Modern Husband*, to him. 'Nobody has ever satisfactorily explained this circumstance', Pat Rogers remarks, 'it is scarcely possible to believe it a piece of ironic effrontery.'[35] Indeed Fielding was capable of fulsome flattery of Walpole. *The Journal of a Voyage to Lisbon*, Fielding's last completed work, refers to the Great Man as 'one of the best of men and of ministers'. This time Fielding can scarcely be accused of pursuing his own interest, for by 1754 Walpole was dead. And yet there are no ironic pointers accompanying this straightforward compliment.

How, then, should Fielding's conduct be interpreted? Initially he tried to gain Walpole's patronage, for which he was included among the dunces in the original London edition of *On Poetry: A Rapsody*. Swift changed his mind, apparently, because Fielding adopted the pseudonym H. Scriblerus Secundus in the 1730s. Recently, however, Brian McCrea has questioned whether Fielding was trying to continue 'the traditions and values of the Scriblerus Club'. Arguing that his anti-Walpole writings do not reflect his 'true personal sentiments', McCrea attempts to show that Fielding and Walpole shared a common Whig ideology, and that when he satirised the Great Man, it was purely on account of his corruption. On the other hand, Pat Rogers feels 'he changed sides, it appears, less on account of ideology than in order to pay his bills', which supports the contemporary view that the writers of the opposition were motivated by self-interest.[36]

Fielding's conduct is a perfect illustration of the problem facing anyone who tries to justify the Scriblerian campaign to discredit Walpole. But we need to examine the ideological basis of their opposition before writing it off merely as factious and self-interested. In indicting Walpole of corruption, Fielding was doing more than question the Prime Minister's personal integrity – he was attacking his policies *tout court*. Walpole was the poet's foe not just because he failed to patronise poets, or because he patronised the wrong poets.' He was condemned by the opposition wits on religious, moral and political grounds. In the eyes of Swift, Pope and Gay, the aesthetic question was symptomatic of a much deeper malaise in British society, and they felt that Walpole was at the root of all the trouble.

It is customary to call the Scriblerians 'Tory satirists', and to insinuate that their politics, and those of their allies, were soundly Tory. Clearly this causes problems when trying to equate their views with Whig writers like Fielding. However in 1730 Pope reminded Swift: 'you are a Whig, as I am'; and on a number of occasions Swift drew his correspondents' attention to the fact that he was 'of the old whig principles, without the modern articles and refinements'.[37] To call theirs the 'Tory Interpretation of Literary History', therefore, is a misnomer. It distorts the ideological basis of their opposition to Walpole, insinuates that their motives were unprincipled (which was just what ministerial propagandists intended), and obscures the common ground between their views and those of writers like Henry Fielding. The conviction with which men like Swift propounded old-fashioned political ideals is remarkable, and should not be dismissed purely on account of its apparent anachronism.

When trying to construct a platform upon which Tories and

dissident Whigs could unite and oppose Walpole, Bolingbroke and Pulteney fell back on a rhetoric of 'Country' ideology which predated the emergence of the Whig and Tory parties. Although his own background was solidly Tory, Bolingbroke was prepared to acknowledge the common ground between himself and those 'old' Whigs who did not share Walpole's 'modern' Whig tenets. The sincerity of Bolingbroke's enunciation of Country views is open to question.[38] Similarly the coherence of the opposition attacks on the system of Walpole is still being debated by historians. None the less, certain key features can be isolated and their implications examined. At the heart of the conflict between 'old' and 'modern' Whigs was interpretation of the Glorious Revolution and the significance of the events of 1688–9, and the key word in Opposition circles was *corruption*.

While 'modern' Whig writers like Defoe preferred not to resort to tradition to explain contemporary politics,[39] Swift and Bolingbroke constantly harked back to antiquity. They believed (or claimed to believe) in an ancient constitution which was the basis of their political system. The monarchy was 'an empire of laws, and not of men', in which 'the King enjoys all the prerogatives necessary to the support of his dignity, and the protection of his people, and is only abridged from the power of injuring his own subjects'.[40] Walpole claimed that the Revolution established, for the first time, the limited or mixed English monarchy, but the opposition theorists saw it merely as a return to the original model, from which the Stuarts, and James II in particular, had diverged. Further, under the Hanoverians, they asserted, 'all things [were] tending towards absolute power'[41] once again, as the constitution was being systematically undermined or *corrupted* by Walpole.

In his poem *Liberty* James Thomson celebrated

The full, the perfect plan
Of Britain's matchless constitution, mixt
Of mutual checking and supporting powers,
King, Lords, and Commons.[42]

But this system of checks and balances was threatened by an

encroaching prerogative. In the 1730s it was said in Parliament that 'the power of the crown is now infinitely greater than it was for some years after the Revolution'.[43] Country ideology maintained that it was vital that the executive should remain quite separate from the legislature in order to protect the rights and privileges of the individual, and that ' "corruption" would follow if the Crown discovered any means at all of attaching members of Parliament to it in the pursuit of its business'.[44] For this reason, opposition writers like Swift advocated annual Parliaments. 'For, who sees not', he explained, 'that while such assemblies are permitted to have a longer duration, there grows up a commerce of corruption between the ministry and the deputies, wherein they both find their accounts to the manifest danger of liberty, which traffic would neither answer the design nor expense, if Parliaments met once a year.'[45]

The traditional remedy for the *corruption* of Parliament was the introduction of triennial bills to prevent standing Parliaments, and place bills to prevent pensioner Parliaments, thus minimising the risk posed by bribery of one sort or another to the free proceedings of the House of Commons. Instead, the Whigs had passed the Septennial Act to provide stability in the face of the supposed Jacobite threat. This was seen by the Opposition as an attempt by the Whigs to perpetuate themselves in power. With the growth of royal prerogative, the existence of a standing army, and more or less open interference in elections and in parliamentary proceedings on the part of the executive, Swift believed that the ancient constitution was in a 'desperate' condition, and he feared that he 'might outlive liberty in England'.[46] Personal integrity was being assaulted, and found wanting. In *Glubbdubdrib*, Gulliver summons 'some English yeomen of the old stamp' and compares them with their descendants in contemporary Britain. While the former were 'so famous for the simplicity of their manners, diet and dress; for justice in their dealings; for the true spirit of liberty; for their valour and love of their country', their grandchildren, through 'selling their votes and managing at elections, have acquired every vice and *corruption* that can possibly be learned in a Court'.[47]

The corruption of the constitution went hand in hand with the corruption of the nation's morals. 'Liberty cannot be preserved', Algernon Sidney had warned, 'if the manners of the people are *corrupted*.'[48] The writings of the opposition wits tied in the decline in liberty with the decay of personal probity. In *The Dunciad*, Pope envisaged a society akin to that portrayed in Orwell's *1984*, in which a stupefied populace has willingly surrendered its rights and privileges, not to Big Brother, but to the Goddess Dulness. Dulness, having 'poured her spirit o'er the land and deep', 'bade Britannia sleep'. In the eyes of the Scriblerians, dulness leads to moral blindness – the inability to distinguish between right and wrong. This would inevitably have severe political and social repercussions, for Dulness 'ruled, in native anarchy, the mind'. In this way, the concern for the state of letters can be seen as only part of a much wider concern for the state of the nation. Dulness was urged by her votaries to proceed 'till learning fly the shore'. The perversion of literary and artistic taste was only one way in which the morals of the people were being corrupted under the Robinocracy.[49]

It is in this sense that Walpole, the poet's foe, is the 'true hero' of the *Dunciad*. When Pope added a fourth book to the poem in 1742, there was this crucial difference: the restoration of the Empire of Dulness was an established fact. Walpole had presided over this return to the Dark Ages – Pope's 'Saturnian age of lead'. In contrast, the opposition looked back to a golden age when the old ways and the old-fashioned virtues were maintained. As W. A. Speck observes:

> They placed the pristine era in a time when the country had been ruled by a natural aristocracy composed of peers and gentry, whose power was based on land. These had governed in the national interest, and under them government was a simple and practical art. They had been usurped by upstart monied men who, led by Walpole himself, had ousted the traditional rulers and governed entirely for their own self-interest.

Again, Swift is the spokesman for those who held these views, as he sadly contemplated the decline in the leaders of the nation since the Civil War. 'We have seen a great part of the nation's money got into the hands of those', he wrote, 'who by their birth, education and merit, could pretend no higher than to wear our liveries.'[51]

Their traditional position in society threatened, it was little wonder that the Opposition yearned nostalgically for a paternalistic past, in which the lower orders knew their place and were content with their lot. In return for their loyalty, masters protected their dependents, and governed simply, in the interests of all. Clearly self-interest has its place in their outspoken condemnation of the situation under Walpole, but it was based, at bottom, on an ideology which was totally at odds with that of the Great Man and his supporters. The golden age was of course a myth. However, its potency should not be underestimated. The opposition theorists believed that 'freedom consists in a people being governed by laws made with their own consent; and slavery in the contrary'.[52] Under Walpole, they professed to see all things moving toward that negation of freedom, absolutism. We do not have to assume that the Scriblerian view was the right one, much less that their cause was just. Nor did they succeed in winning the war of words they waged with the apologists of Walpole's ministry. Patently, they were defeated.

The decline in literary patronage was another manifestation of the degeneration of the nation. Queen Anne's reign 'was something of a golden age for patronage', but the Hanoverians were less concerned with the state of English letters than their predecessors. They preferred opera, Walpole painting. The 'great patricians' of the age inspired the Smithfield Muses, although a few wealthy men patronised writers of merit. Walpole, on the other hand, paid only for services rendered or anticipated, and was quick to cut back if and when the opportunity arose.[53] For this reason, more than any other, the writers who were patronised by the court and the ministry during the age of Walpole were no match, on aesthetic grounds, for those who derided the Great Man and decried his governance. Lord Hervey, that staunchest of government supporters, admitted that *The Craftsman* was 'a much better written paper than any of that sort that were published on the side of the Court', and perhaps he should have the last word. Instead of the reign of George II being a Dark Age for English letters, he believed that they were never

> at a higher pitch, either for learning, strength of diction, or elegance of style, than in this reign. All the good writing, too, was confined to political topics, either of civil, military, or ecclesiastical government, and all the tracts on these subjects printed in pamphlets. It might very properly be called the Augustan age of England for this kind of writing.[54]

8. Print and Politics in the Age of Walpole

MICHAEL HARRIS

THE implicit relationship between print and politics had received long-term acknowledgement in England through two centuries of state control. Occasional dislocations of the system during the seventeenth century revealed the substance of official fears and in the early 1680s a temporary lapse in the licensing arrangements was followed by a volley of new periodicals carrying vigorous comment, the bulk of it hostile to the government. At the same time print had become the accepted vehicle for the national dissemination of ideas and information of all kinds. The demand that existed for London-based material during the later seventeenth century was most fully demonstrated by the massive sale of the Stationers' Company almanacs. Between 1664 and 1687 the total annual printing of these items only once fell below 300,000 copies and was usually well over this figure.[1] At the same time, in the sophisticated urban environment of the capital itself, with its high level of literacy and range of commercial interests, information in print was generated on a very large scale. The appearance of miscellaneous periodical publications, broadsides, ballads and a variety of other forms of ephemeral output reflected an appetite for print which was almost insatiable.

It was against this background that the licensing system was finally allowed to lapse in 1695.[2] The sudden disappearance of pre-publication censorship and the end of geographical restrictions on printing was followed by a chain reaction of newspaper publication. Commercially this form of output was particularly valuable as it catered for an immense latent demand and also offered a means by which the press, in an increasingly competitive market, could be kept regularly employed. Politically the possibilities were immediately clear. In a period of intense party controversy no other medium offered such ease of dispersal and range of regular access within the community. These advantages, which also gave the newspaper its force as an advertising medium, remained crucial to the intimate relationship between politics and the press and led to the gradual dominance of the newspaper as an instrument of political propaganda.

The means by which London-based publications carried information and comment through the nation were complex but highly effective and offered the politicians, like the booksellers in a commercial context, channels of communication with rich possibilities. Different forms of publication fitted into the distribution pattern in different ways. Some papers, particularly those published daily or consisting mainly of essay material, were focused in London and the adjacent areas. Others, though also selling in the capital, were directed mainly towards a provincial readership. The consistently successful thrice-weekly newspapers were invariably published on Tuesday, Thursday and Saturday to synchronise with the posts coming into and leaving London, the titles themselves underlining their provincial orientation. As the author of a new paper remarked in 1715, 'The Words *Flying-Post*, *Post-Man*, *Post-Master*, *Post-Boy*, *London Post*, and *St James's Post* are already taken up; so that there is no Post left for me but the *Penny-Post*'.[3] The weekly journals which developed in response to the tax legislation of 1712 and which, combining essay material and news, became one of the main vehicles of political propaganda were distributed very widely. In 1715 the author of the *British Mercury* announced that among the advantages of advertising in his paper was '*its spreading so far, there being near 4,000 printed every Time, and those carefully distributed into all Parts not only of this City, but of the whole Nation*'.[4] Most of the journals were published on one or other of the three post days, usually Saturday to allow for inclusion of the week's news, although Thursday publication enabled copies to reach provincial centres by the weekend. Some of the proprietors of the Saturday weeklies attempted to get the best of both worlds by issuing copies of their papers the preceding Thursday. In the mid 1740s the arrangements for publication were spelled out by the author of the *Westminster*

Journal in a notice to a contributor which stated that 'ATTICUS' *Letter came too late, the Journal being always at the Press on Thursday Morning, by reason many are sent into the Country by Post, Coaches, Waggons and reach 50 or 60 Miles by the same Morning they are published here.*'[5]

The distribution of copies in the vicinity of the capital itself involved a combination of printer and bookseller-based delivery services, the penny post and a range of retail outlets extending to the 'indigent *Poor* and miserable *Blind Hawkers*' who sold copies through the street.[6] However, although a variety of alternative methods were also employed, most copies of the London papers reached provincial purchasers through the Post Office. The value of this outlet depended partly on the efficiency of the service which, under the direction of Ralph Allen, was improving rapidly through the middle decades of the century.[7] Greater regularity and wider geographical cover undoubtedly helped to extend national access to the London press. None the less distribution through the post depended less on these reforms than on the intervention of groups with free access to the system. The routine charges remained high and would have been prohibitive for the general supply of newspapers, without the intermediate access provided by the personnel of government offices, the six Post Office clerks of the roads and individual Members of Parliament. By providing a cut-price supply, based on established franking privileges, these groups became involved in freelance newspaper distribution on a very large scale. The balance between the activity of the groups shifted during the century and is hard to pin down in detail. In the case of the Under-Secretary of State Charles Delafaye, the random survival of his personal newspaper ledger provides a brief view of the potential involvement of a government official in the distribution process.[8] During the period 1703 to 1714 Delafaye supplied 70 individual customers through the Post Office with a cross-section of London newspapers. Drawn entirely from the middle and upper ranks of society they were scattered through the British Isles as far afield as Dublin and Guernsey. Although an assessment of Delafaye's weekly distribution is problematic it seems likely that during the parliamentary session he was sending out between 300–400 copies a week. He was also involved in the supply of French and Dutch gazettes, through a continental agent, to 18 London coffee-houses. His personal efforts in this area may have been partly a by-product of his Huguenot connections and were also perhaps linked to his spell as compiler of the *London Gazette*. Even so, the limited evidence suggests that his activity was paralleled by colleagues in the same and other government departments.

However, the main boost to the use of the Post Office as a channel for the supply of London newspapers during the Walpole administration came through the personnel of the office itself. Using their free access to the service on an increasing scale the Clerks of Roads were described in the *Craftsman* in 1728 as 'a sort of licensed Hawkers over the whole Kingdom'.[9] The scale of their involvement and that of the other privileged groups was brought to light during a parliamentary inquiry in 1764 which revealed that a total of something over 35,000 copies of London newspapers were passing through the Post Office every week under frank.[10] Purchasers relying on this means of supply still had to pay something in the region of 2*d.* per copy extra and it was this differential that gave the local press its commercial opportunity. At the same time the activities of the semi-official groups could lead to some distortion of the service on either commercial or political grounds and, during the 1730s in particular, the Post Office provided a vital adjunct to Walpole's propaganda programme.

While the Post Office underpinned the national supply of copies of London newspapers, the material which they carried reached a much wider audience through the wholesale process of republication. In this area the local papers which relied almost entirely on the selective redeployment of information and comment from the London press were of major importance. The post-1695 diaspora of printers from London led to the setting-up of newspapers in a widening circle of urban centres.[11] The process of growth was erratic as the tax laws and pressure of competition picked off under-financed publications but the upward trend was clear enough. At the high points reached in the early 1720s and the mid 1740s, 24 and 41 provincial newspapers were in publication.[12] The distribution of these papers, carrying their heavy load of London material, was based on increasingly far-flung networks of newsmen and agents of the sort established in the neighbourhood of the capital and it has been suggested that the overlapping circuits provided access by the middle of the century to 'the most remote and isolated hamlets and farm-houses'.[13] Certainly secondary access through the local press broadened the range of London papers and a further considerable boost was given by the new and highly successful magazines of the 1730s. Achieving massive national circulations, the *Gentleman's* and the *London*, during the first decade of publication at least, leaned very heavily on the London newspapers. Their voluminous extracts were drawn entirely from the leading essay papers in which the political disputes were focused and it was in this way that many readers must have obtained cut-price access to the content of the London press. The ebb and flow of material across various forms of publications gave newspaper propaganda a peculiarly pervasive force and provided one of the major spin-offs of a political stake in the London newspapers.

The access which the London newspapers offered to a national readership at first or second hand was given its sharpest focus in the context of the public house. It was through the coffee-houses and respectable taverns that a large proportion of readers were most consistently exposed to the content of the London papers. In the capital itself a striking concentration of public houses existed. It was estimated in 1739 that there was a total of 551 coffee-houses, 207 inns and 447 taverns, as well as a vast number of beer and brandy houses in the central area.[14] The proportion of these which supplied their customers with newspapers cannot be established but it is clear that at the upper levels the provision of a cross-section of publications was being made on quite a large scale. During the late 1720s one writer complained that the newspapers were costing individual coffee-house proprietors at least £20 p.a. and that they were providing 'some two, some three, some four of a Sort of the Leading Papers, every Day, besides Duplicates of most of the others'.[15]

By the 1730s some of the main coffee-houses had established a general library facility, taking in magazines and pamphlets which were made available to their customers, while a few apparently hired out newspapers on demand. The same writer suggested that through the London coffee-houses alone an edition of a single paper could pass through 20,000 hands a day, and the public house undoubtedly formed an important link in the infrastructure of urban communication. In the provinces, inns and taverns were drawn into some level of newspaper provision. However it was the expanding circle of provincial coffee-houses, themselves a symbol of a developing cultural and political identity, that became the focus for the supply of London publications. By mid century most substantial market towns probably had at least one coffee-house, while a variable number were established in a wide circle of urban communities, particularly those which were identified as local centres of commerce and politics. Bristol and Liverpool contained nine and six respectively and most county towns probably offered two or more by the 1740s.[16]

It was through the range of public houses that the press and politics were brought into their closest physical conjunction. The presence of the newspapers became in itself the basis of a generalised political atmosphere in which discussion circled around the issues and events of the day. The coffee-house politician as a satirical type, often a shopkeeper or tradesman, pontificating on public affairs solely on the strength of a reading in the London newspapers, appeared early in the century and recurred in the hostile writings of ministerial journalists. As a contributor to the *Daily Gazetteer* remarked in 1737, 'There's scarce an Alley in City and Suburbs but has a Coffee-house in it, which may be called the School of Public Spirit, where every Man over Daily and Weekly Journals, a Mug, or a Dram, perhaps – notwithstanding the Gin Act – learns the most hearty Contempt of his own Personal, Sordid Interest, to which he owes his Bread only and devotes himself to that glorious one, his Country.'[17]

At the same time the role of the public house could take on a harder political form. Since the beginning of the century they had provided the location for meetings of a broad range of interest groups, clubs and societies and it was almost inevitable that the shareholding proprietors of the London newspapers should have chosen to hold their regular meetings in selected coffee-houses and taverns in the Temple Bar area.[18] Many of the semi-formal organisations had some sort of political interest but it was through the activities of the shifting groups of politicians themselves that the public house became locked into low profile, party organisation. Under the Walpole administration the Cocoa Tree Chocolate House in Pall Mall assumed considerable importance as the regular meeting place for groups of leading Tory politicians. Although the association with the Tory party dated back to the beginning of the century, the political connection took on a more formal character when Edward Harley's 'Board' established itself on the premises in 1727.[19] Meeting weekly during each parliamentary session the 'Board' provided a stable forum for discussion as well as the machinery for co-ordinating party strategy. During the initial stages of publication, the major Opposition newspaper, the *Craftsman*, was linked to the Cocoa Tree which provided poste restante facilities for correspondence and although the link was soon broken it provides a further pointer to the close relationship between press, politics and the public house.[20] In the provinces a similar sort of interconnection existed and the coffee-houses, often split by party affiliation, provided a natural base for local political activity, particularly during the general elections.[21]

Within the community at large access to the newspapers and the materials they contained was extended through a battery of more or less casual circumstances. Loan arrangements in families or within neighbourhoods, group purchase or public readings, provision through barbers' and chandlers' shops and ultimately through the random use of newspapers for packaging or in the 'bog-house', made such publications a routine feature of the lives of a very broad cross-section of the community. None the less, both in London and the provinces, the newspaper remained a medium of an intractably middling sort.

This social character, which arose partly from the structure of ownership and finance, was emphasised in the limited appeal of the content as well as in the pattern of distribution. It has been suggested that there was a qualitative shift in the position of the press during the 1760s.[22] This seems rather speculative. Certainly the aggregate number of copies had risen by this time and continued to rise. However, what this meant in terms of readership development is not at all clear. In the 1730s it was estimated that each issue of the *Craftsman* was read by at least 40 people, a figure not far above other speculative estimates of the period, and this, allowing for a maximum print-run of 13,000, would have given the paper *de facto* readership in the region of half a million.[23] Even allowing for exaggeration, this figure suggests a volume of potential newspaper purchasers at a middling social level which could easily have mopped up the expanded output of the 1750s and 1760s. It is certainly clear enough that the London newspapers of the later period showed no more inclination to broaden their general appeal than those published 20 or 30 years before.[24] The rising tide of newspapers, sold at rising prices, continued to spill into other sections of the community. However, growth seems to have been primarily within the ill-defined middling levels of society where the expansion in general literature was also based and where political battles were increasingly lost or won. At the same time the increase in titles, the greater interest among provincial papers in local affairs, and the move away from politics in general, and newspaper content in particular, among the established magazines and the new literary reviews, probably served to dissipate the national impact of the London papers. Much more detailed work needs to be done on the English press before the full picture of the relationship of the newspaper and society and politics can be drawn, and one of the purposes of this essay is to suggest that more attention may need to be paid to continuity than to change.

Few politicians of the early eighteenth century, engaged in the struggle for power, felt able to neglect the open line of communication represented by the London press. After 1695 the possibility of breaking the connection faded rapidly. Although the lapse of the Licensing Act appeared to be the result of some sort of political absence of mind, it acknowledged an emerging ideological consensus. Whatever the sharp and divergent views on the practical limits, a level of agreement existed between Whigs and Tories on the virtues of a 'free press' and the legitimate involvement of 'public opinion' within the political system. Consequently, while the idea of the reintroduction of some form of prepublication censorship lingered on under the Walpole administration, and was given a sharp nudge by an introduction of stage licensing in 1737, the newspapers were not seriously threatened. The Stamp Tax introduced in 1712 and tightened up in 1725 and 1742 can be seen either as a gesture towards an alternative system of control or primarily as a revenue-raising measure.[25] In either case its long-term impact was limited to denying access by purchase to the lower-income groups. The main instrument of restraint available to those in power, as to any private individual, lay in the law of libel.[26] This ambiguous device could be highly effective when mobilised against extremist, usually Jacobite, material or against under-financed papers pursuing an opposition line. Its general value as a means of financial harassment was fully demonstrated in 1737 when a series of prosecutions caused considerable dislocation to the Opposition propaganda effort. The commercial splits within the leading weeklies, the *Craftsman* and *Common Sense*, served to underline the fragmentation of the Opposition itself.[27] None the less, the well-known difficulties of obtaining a conviction and the associated increase in public interest made the regular application of the law alone largely unproductive.

Given the limitations of direct control, the production of counter-propaganda became a regular part of political strategy. Robert Harley had been one of the first to see the value of a consistent campaign in print to secure as well as to gain access to power.[28] His personal involvement in the area led to the construction of a complex organisation which came to be centred on the newspaper press and which was concerned with both the production and distribution of materials and with the oversight of his opponents. As his influence declined prior to 1714 the system he had established lost its shape and was not fully reconstructed until Sir Robert Walpole took office and moved into the same area. Walpole's personal interest in the propaganda process is hard to pin down. To some extent he was forced into taking action by the alarming success of the newspaper opposition in the mid 1720s and as a result ministerial propaganda was always implicitly reluctant and self-justifying. His employment of a range of authors conspicuously short of reputation and literary talent itself suggests a limited priority.[29] On the other hand Walpole developed quite close relationships with some of his political writers including the archetypal hack William Arnall, and was still showing a concern for printed propaganda in the months after his resignation in 1742.[30] As a practical politician of immense skill his interest may have shifted and wavered over his long period in office but his involvement, if only through financial commitment, was maintained throughout.

Walpole's concern with the press, perhaps even more than Harley's, was characterised by his deployment of the machinery of government in its support. The Treasury which formed Walpole's power base underpinned his propaganda campaigns. According to the findings of the Committee of Secrecy set up in 1742 to inquire into his misuse of public finds, Walpole spent over £50,000 on the production and distribution of newspapers and pamphlets in the decade up to February 1741.[31] His actual expenditure must have been rather higher than this. Characteristically Walpole chose his principal intermediary with the press from among the Treasury person- nel and from the 1720s the Treasury Solicitor, Nicholas Paxton, a sinister and elusive figure, was deeply involved in the oversight of Opposition publications and in directing pro- secutions. This activity was linked to Paxton's less visible but equally important work in the payment and direction of ministerial journalists, a subterranean political interest that emerges most clearly from the literary output of his opponents.[32] From early on in the Walpole administration large sums of public money were deployed within the London press. Established papers, including the influential *London Journal*, were bought in, new papers were set up and a range of authors were added to the pay-roll. William Arnall in par- ticular received increasing sums of money for his political services and was said at his premature death in 1735 to have been in receipt of a pension of £400 p.a.[33] Walpole occasionally used his control of state patronage to reward his writers, but this benefit was certainly much less prevalent than his opponents suggested.

One of the main areas of expenditure from Treasury funds lay in the subsidised distribution of propaganda materials. This had played a major part in the development of Harley's campaigns at the beginning of the century though the mechanics of the process remain very obscure. Under Walpole, involvement with the distribution of free copies of pro- ministerial publications was at least as extensive and perhaps more systematic. The precise nature of the arrangements emerge from five detailed accounts preserved among Walpole's personal papers. These are concerned with a sequence of pamphlets which may have been, in part at least, put together under Walpole's personal supervision.[34] The first three, covered by accounts submitted at the end of the financial year in 1735, were (1) *Opposition No Proof of Patriotism*, (2) *Considerations on the Publick Funds* and (3) *The Grand Accuser of Ye greatest Griminal*. The other two, dispersed simultaneously early in 1739, were (4) *The Convention Vindicated* and (5) *The Grand Question*. The distribution in all five cases was virtually identical at or around the very high figure of 10,000 copies. The bill for pamphlet (1) selling at 6*d*. amounted to £250, the charge for pamphlets (2) and (3) selling at 1*s*. came to a total of £980. 14*s*. Publication of all the pamphlets was apparently organised either by John Peele or Samuel Buckley, though only the accounts for the first three items carry one or other of their names.[35] Peele was a wholesale pamphlet publisher who seems to have begun his profitable association with the Walpole administration at the time of the *London Journal* take-over in 1722. He continued as part-owner and publisher of this paper as well as of the *Free Briton* and became a proprietor of the *Daily Gazetteer* when the paper was set up in 1735 to consolidate ministerial interests.[36] An even more fully developed link between the administration and the booktrade can be found in the career of Samuel Buckley. As a bookseller and proprietor of the *Daily Courant*, a paper widely distributed by the administration from at least as early as the 1720s, he combined his commercial activities with the official post of Gazetteer. This meant that he was on the strength of the Secretary of State's office and as a Justice of Peace for Westminster he was erratically involved in the prosecutions directed at Opposition publications.[37] Peele and Buckley were evidently responsible for organising the primary distribution of materials, although the process may also have involved other members of the trade.

The post provided the main channel through which the national resources of government could be most effectively mobilised for propaganda purposes. All five statements show the largest number of copies were delivered to the Clerks of the Roads by way of the Comptroller Joseph Bell. In every case, between 3000 and 3500 pamphlets were supplied for redirection, mainly perhaps through the country post-masters who formed a far-reaching network for local redistribution. According to the opposition papers some attempt was made to mobilise the local Post Office officials to supply political information but it was as the wholesale distributors of ministerial propaganda that they were most regularly attacked. Referring to publications defending the ministerial position on the excise, the author of *A Review of the Excise-Scheme* claimed that they had been sent out in such numbers that,

> *the poor hackney beasts of the* Post Office *have couched under their Bruthen.* Circular Letters have been sent in the name of Mr JOS. BELL to all the *Post-masters* in the Kingdom, with Orders *to make* these Papers *as public as they can*; to send up the Names of all Persons within their Delivery, who keep Coffee-houses, where Gentlemen resort to read the NEWS, that They may likewise be furnished with them GRATIS, and even most private families have them crouded in upon Them by the same Hands.[38]

There seems to have been a good deal of substance in such ironic comments. A similar process of redistribution through the post probably underlay the large-scale supply of the personnel at the principal government offices who could be expected to pass on copies to their established customers and other contacts. About 1500 copies of each of pamphlets (2) and (3) were directed to this group and in the 1739 lists 400 copies of each item was delivered to the offices of the two Secretaries of State, Lord Harrington and the Duke of Newcastle. Although not specified, the post was probably used to provide the direct supply to the Collectors of the Customs and of the Excise who also received a very large number of copies. About 2000 copies of each of the pamphlets (3), (4) and (5) were sent to both these strikingly unpopular but geographically effective groups of government officials. Their presence in every substantial community, particularly around the coasts, was regularly exploited during the parliamentary elections and their controversial involvement in local politics seems to have taken in the quite large-scale distribution of propaganda in various forms. A close eye was apparently kept on the political orthodoxy of even quite minor employees in this area. In Hereford in 1728, for example, an innkeeper who was also the local exciseman was dismissed for rashly attempting to supply his customers with the *Craftsman* and *Fog's Journal*.[39]

The publishers also used the post to send copies direct to individual members of major interest groups in both London and the provinces. In 1739 lists show that the usual 740 copies were 'Sealed up and sent to the Post-Office for the Country Clergy', while 745 members of the Lords and Commons were sent copies of each item 'Singly by penny post'. Whatever the method of delivery used in London itself few of those in office or with some sort of political interest were left without copies either for their own use or for personal redistribution. Lord Harrington and the Duke of Newcastle received, like Horatio Walpole, a dozen of each. The Lords of the Admiralty, the Sub-Governor and Directors of the Bank of England, the Commissioners of Excise, Trade and Customs, the Archbishops and Bishops, the Judges and the Lords Commissioners of the Treasury and their clerks were all targeted in the lists.

The effort was impressive and suggests the value placed on printed propaganda as well as the effort that was thought to be necessary to combat the superior selling power and general appeal of the Opposition publications. It may also indicate the way in which the sponsored newspapers of the Walpole period were projected into the community, again mainly through the Post Office. From the take-over of the *London Journal* in the early 1720s a regular and growing number of free copies of the London newspapers, paid for out of Treasury funds, were delivered by the publishers. From 650 a week the total had risen by 1731 to 3700, reaching a peak early in 1734 of 12,500 copies per week at the cost of over £100.[40] The daily papers which were subsidised by the administration, the *Daily Courant* and, from 1735, the *Daily Gazetteer*, were produced in a special double format to facilitate their regular, free distribution through the post. The consolidation of the ministry's newspaper interest in the *Gazetteer* seems to have resulted more from a drive for efficiency than from an attempt at long-term retrenchment. In 1741, 10,800 copies of this newspaper alone were sent to the

Post Office every week for dispersal.[41] How subsequent redistribution was organised does not emerge from the fragmented sources but it seems likely that the pattern established for the pamphlets was extended to the newspaper press.

The Opposition had no such resources, though individual Members of Parliament were in a position to exploit their franking privilege. However, even the routine distribution of materials through the post could not be relied on. According to one Opposition writer an open warrant was kept to hand in the Post Office for the interception of any politically doubtful items and the clerks were sometimes sent explicit instructions not to circulate such major anti-ministerial papers as the *Craftsman*, the *London Evening Post* and the *Champion*.

However, it was crucial to the Opposition to get their publications into as many hands as possible and during the late 1720s at least a considerable effort was made to boost the circulation of the *Craftsman*. This appears from four undated lists which survive among the papers seized by the authorities during the prosecution of its publisher, Richard Franklin, in 1730.[42] The lists may refer to the reprinted version of the *Craftsman* essays in pamphlet form rather than the journal itself though this is a matter of speculation. Three, containing 30, 58 and 59 overlapping names respectively, indicate a total distribution of up to 766 copies. The list with the fewest names shows the highest subscription rate and may therefore represent an early stage in the process of distribution building. In it Lord Gower and Sir William Wyndham were each credited with 48 copies while the two Pulteneys, Daniel and William, Lord Coventry and Sir John Rushout each took 40, 'Mrs Pulteney' received 6. Even the author and front-man Nicholas Amhurst who is not included elsewhere was put down for 4 copies. A note against the name of Samuel Sandys in the list suggests the way in which individual support was canvassed, 'at Chippenham near Newmarket, Cambridgeshire', it stated, 'if not in Town to thither and as many as He will take into the Country, when He comes to Town'. The fourth list contains 17 names and addresses mostly of peers and baronets, with the instruction, '10 To each'. The majority of the names on all the lists were of Members of the Houses of Lords and Commons representing a very broad spectrum of opinion, including high

Tories and moderate Opposition Whigs. Where delivery arrangements were given they either referred to instructions for copies to be sent to a London house for forwarding or to the use of the carriers. In the list with 30 names, Wyndham's 48 copies were to be sent on from Warminster by the Froome carrier while Rushout's 40 copies were to be delivered 'To Lady Northhamptons'. This sort of dispersal may reflect problems at the Post Office or simply an attempt to cut costs. The Opposition efforts to boost distribution received occasional notice in the ministerial press. 'Orator' Henley in the first number of his pro-ministerial *Hyp-Doctor*, a crazily written but surprisingly well-informed publication, claimed that if the public failed to buy his papers he would be forced to become a pensionary writer for the Opposition and as a slave to '*H——B—— W* – Windy – *W—— P——* Sir *J Rushlight*, get my *ministerial Papers* subscribed off at 50 a Head of each of them; and pack them like *B——ds*, *in Carts and Caravans to debauch the Country*'.[43]

What practical objectives did the politicians aim at through their consistent use of the newspaper press? This is not easy to answer but indications emerge partly from the special character of the newspaper which set it apart from other forms of publication. As an essentially reactive medium, reflecting the interests and concerns of its readers in a peculiarly direct way, the newspaper offered a considerable political opportunity. Under Walpole the Opposition consistently attempted to use the press as a link in what can be described as a circuit of political communication. Areas of traditional public concern were identified and associated with parliamentary or related political activity. These developments were flagged in the newspapers and the response in the community at large redeployed in attacks on the administration. In this circular process the Opposition made all the running, attempting, for whatever reason, to push back the frontiers of political involvement, while the ministry doggedly attempted to hold the line, sometimes counter-attacking but more often remaining on the defensive. The application of this technique by the Opposition was not at all clear-cut and was used in a variety of circumstances. However, one of its most consistent and pragmatic applications appeared in the attempt on the Opposition side to maintain a direct link between constituency opinion and the parliamentary behaviour of individual MPs. This strategy, which had been employed in a desultory way since the 1690s, was of particular importance to the hybrid and loose-knit Opposition to Walpole, newspaper content sometimes merging with other elements of low-level party organisation. The continued existence of a legitimist-Tory group whose structure and personnel have been brought out of the shadows and whose activity in the period continued to be of some importance, gives the use of the press in this area an added sense of reality.[44]

The party element in the political propaganda deployed through the newspapers worked at various intellectual levels. The campaigns of the Queen Anne period had been vigorous but fragmented. During Walpole's term in office the consistent and long-drawn-out confrontation between politicians in and out of power allowed for the development of a more sophisticated debate. On both political sides the newspapers offered the most fully worked-out statement of ideology available to contemporaries and the elaborate critique of national history and politics offered in the press conceptualised the Opposition and ministry division and provided the setting for the more detailed and parliament-centred strategy.[45] As well as carrying material which contributed to the general sense of unity the *Craftsman* itself provided, at least until the mid 1730s, a focus for the idea of group solidarity – the medium, to a certain extent, becoming the message. The presentation of argument through a single putative author, Caleb D'Anvers, provided readers with a focus of interest and the close identification in the public mind between D'Anvers and the Opposition appeared in the use of the name in a vast range of output in verse and prose.[46] Both Pulteney and Bolingbroke made use of the name outside the context of the *Craftsman* and the identification helped, however superficially, to cover over some of the underlying fissures in the Opposition. Political material published in the London newspapers was not sharply differentiated and the content of the sponsored papers often had a considerable overlap with that of commercial publications. On the opposition side, for example, much valuable propaganda material appeared in the *London Evening Post*, a paper under the direction of the Tory printer Richard Nutt and owned collectively by a group of booksellers, many with links with other Opposition papers.[47] From the outside the London press gave a clear impression of an established two-party system and this image was itself of some political importance.

In the Opposition newspapers the emphasis on the legitimate constitutional role of public opinion was linked to the demand that 'the people', a term never very closely defined, should be given a sufficient range of information on which to base political judgement. This led the *Craftsman* and associated papers to place some emphasis on the supply of current material which itself had high potential as propaganda. As a ministerial writer stated, 'Those who would make any considerable and lasting Impressions on the Minds of the Generality of Mankind, must do it by Relation of Facts.'[48] The *Craftsman* was continuously involved during the late 1720s in providing the details of a series of sensitive, international negotiations, an area in which it developed a solid reputation and for which its publisher was successfully prosecuted.[49] The ministerial papers consistently denounced the publication of such semi-privileged information not least on the grounds of the complexities of the issues. In one characteristic reply, a contributor to the *Craftsman* remarked that even a cobbler or porter could handle the details if they were explained and that 'as the *Common People* is affected by the Conduct of foreign Affairs as much as it is by *domestick Administration* so they have an equal right to be informed about it'.[50] The right to know was also linked to the efforts in the press to open up Parliament and display at least some of the workings of government. The proceedings were protected by privilege and during the late 1720s effective action was taken against a number of newsletter writers and the publishers of several provincial papers.[51] However, there was little reason subsequently for newspapers to become directly involved in the publication of debates. From the early 1730s the *Gentleman's* and *London* magazines printed a version during the recess and through these publications an outline of proceedings was made widely available. During the session the writers of the *Craftsman* and other Opposition papers contented themselves with providing, amongst a mass of other materials, an oblique commentary on events in

Parliament highlighting the issues under consideration and rehearsing the arguments.

Although the debates themselves were outside the scope of the newspaper press, other forms of hard parliamentary information were occasionally introduced as part of the process by which the circuit between constituency and representative could be completed. The current division list which very rarely reached publication was associated in various ways with the Opposition papers. Lists already in print and detailing the vote on such crucial issues as septennial Parliaments occasionally reappeared in the London papers as part of a campaign.[52] Equally, some historical material in this form was fitted into the general pattern of propaganda and used to point-up contemporary issues. In the *Champion*, for example, in May 1741 the author remarked that 'The Necessity of the Pension Bill, which was rejected by the ***** of *******, cannot be more clearly demonstrated, than by the following Extract from the *Black List of Court Creatures* in King Charles IIs *Pension Parliament*',[53] filling several columns with this obsolete material. However, the major propaganda opportunity lay in the publication of current lists. The only one to appear in its original form in an Opposition paper was the division on the Excise Bill which generated more separate lists than any other issue of the period. The risk involved in publication was considerable and the author of the *Craftsman* may have been influenced by the dangers in withdrawing his original offer of publication.[54] In the event it appeared at length in two issues of *Fog's Weekly Journal* during the summer recess with the routine apparatus of places and pensions against each name on the ministerial side and a list of absentees.[55] It was linked in *Fog's* with the Lords vote on the South Sea Company and followed up with a parliamentary list of 1647. Subsequently, an edition of the excise list in red and black was advertised in the *Craftsman* but perhaps more as a threat than a promise.[56]

At the end of the decade the printers of the main Opposition essay papers, the *Craftsman* and *Common Sense*, both published separate lists of the vote on the Spanish Convention, items which were said to be widely distributed by Opposition supporters.[57] Justification of this sort of material recurred in the Opposition papers and following the election of 1741 a conventional list of Members of Parliament was published in the *Craftsman* in which roman and italic type was used to distinguish generally between supporters of ministry and Opposition.[58] These items, loudly condemned in the ministerial papers but popular with readers, served a dual purpose. As well as bringing local pressure to bear on Members of Parliament on the basis of their parliamentary behaviour, they helped to emphasise Opposition solidarity.[59] The way in which this form of propaganda could operate locally was indicated in some ironic comments in the *Craftsman* about the return home of pro-ministerial Members of Parliament following the defeat of the Excise Bill. 'I am afraid that many of them', it stated, 'at first, congratulated their Neighbours on the Defeat of the Scheme, and gave themselves, an Air of being against it; but the Lists, that are now spread through most Parts of the Kingdom, have undeceived the People as to that Point and reduc'd those Gentlemen to several little Shifts.'[60]

The attempt to close the political circuit through use of the press was perhaps most clearly evident in the publication of constituency addresses or instructions. These had been used for propaganda purposes since the seventeenth century but during the 1730s became a staple of the Opposition campaigns. By flagging issues which were pending or already before Parliament the Opposition papers attempted to stimulate local action leading to the preparation of instructions. These items, which invariably contained some general political comment, were intended to direct representatives on the line of parliamentary action to be followed on specific issues. Reports of the preparation of instructions and the finished texts were then published in the Opposition papers subsequently moving through a range of related publications and occasionally reappearing as collections in book form.[61] The involvement of the press helped to extend their impact and could serve to stimulate further local activity. The process was fully demonstrated during the excise crisis when the *Craftsman* in December 1732, after reporting the preparation of instructions in the City, remarked '*This is a laudable Precedent for reviving the ancient Practice of the People in giving their Representatives Instructions upon all great Occasions, and We hope will be followed by every County and Borough in England.*'[62] In the event 49 constituencies sent up instructions against the excise, most appearing simultaneously across the Opposition press. The Spanish Convention provided a similar focus for this form of integrated propaganda but the device was also employed in relation to a range of issues in the Opposition parliamentary programme. Support for triennial parliaments, place bills and the prosecution of Walpole was deployed in the press through constituency instructions and in the early 1740s the London newspapers were filled with blocks of material of this kind.[63] In the ministerial press and in Parliament the instructions were both satirised as absurd and condemned as the product of local sharp practice. However, while consistently denouncing the principle, the Walpole newspapers did not hesitate to publish sympathetic items of the same sort.

The circuit was also employed by the Opposition in the crucial area of the prompt and regular attendance of MPs. The independent country gentlemen and squires, to whom the Opposition looked for support in Parliament, were traditionally reluctant to come to town before Christmas or to stay on until the recess. Yet in general the level of attendance among these groups under the Walpole administration was better than might have been expected and during the final assault on the Prime Minister has been described as superb.[64] How was this achieved? Both ministry and Opposition sent out circular letters to their supporters urging prompt attendance.[65] At the same time it appears that the newspaper press had a part to play in the process of whipping-in and a good deal of attention was paid to attendance in the main Opposition papers. The issue was given almost definitive treatment in the *Craftsman* shortly before the opening of the 1729 session.[66] 'By not coming to town', it was stated, 'you are daily insulting your Electors', and the writer went on to make the recurring threat that on any occasion, 'Lists may be made showing how every individual Member *voted* in the Question, and who were the Absentees; They whose Names shall be found in the *last List*, will I am persuaded be laid aside with *Contempt* and *Ignominy* to whatever Place they may pretend to offer their Services again.' The *Craftsman* on attendance, as on pensions, was reprinted as a separate item on various occasions. In January 1731 it was advertised 'On a Broad Sheet of Imperial Paper, fit to be fram'd', and reappeared in October 1741 as a 6*d*. pamphlet.[67]

The absentees were identified on the excise list and exhortation and threats built up in the press from 1740. Before the sessions of 1741 and 1742 the *Craftsman*, *Common Sense* and the *London Evening Post* carried a variety of material in which the obligation of attendance and the political reaction of the electors was given some prominence. In the home news section of the *Champion*, for example, in 1741 it was stated that 'The Public may be assur'd that the most exact Minutes are taken of all *Neuters*, and *Absentees*, and Apostates, which will be printed, when Time shall serve, in Terrorem; and in which those who *lately* fell off from the *Truth*, will be set forth in their *proper Colours*.'[68] Later in the decade matters were taken a stage further and it was claimed in the *London Evening Post* 'that an Association will be propos'd for opposing all those at any future Election who shall be absent at this extraordinary Crisis'.[69] In this sort of newspaper involvement it may be possible to identify one strand of the subterranean 'party' organisation of the hard-pressed and fragmented Opposition groupings.

Although the volume of this sort of pragmatic material was not very great in relation to other elements in the propaganda process it represents an important and identifiable strand of interest. The attempt to use the newspapers as a political conductor continued erratically throughout the campaigns against the Walpole administration and was evident in the context of each parliamentary session. None the less a focus was provided in the sequence of general elections within which local pressures on MPs was given its most direct and tangible form. In this setting the electors were themselves encouraged to investigate the parliamentary behaviour of individual candidates through the application of sets of queries. This device, pioneered in the 1690s, brought together in convenient and punchy form the elements of constituency/representative propaganda and provided a useful adjunct to the more measured addresses which filled the papers during the elections. The ministerial response to all such items was uniformly hostile. In the subsidised papers the independence of MPs and the mystery of Parliament were consistently pointed up, while all forms of Opposition propaganda were condemned as ludicrous and unconstitutional.[70]

The outcome of all this activity through the press is

impossible to assess in detail given the range of overlapping influences, local circumstances and the generally cloudy relationship between any form of propaganda and the individual. None the less, under the Walpole administration the London newspapers were established as a consistent element in the political life of the nation. These publications have not been taken very seriously outside the grand crises of the 1730s. This is partly because of the emphasis placed by historians on the increasingly static character of the political system, dominated by a single party and controlled at every level by the manipulation of patronage. In this setting the scope for effective propaganda is limited and consequently the press has been represented as a marginal device with little importance when set against the realities of the closet. However, a recent shift in the accepted analysis of national politics, particularly through Linda Colley's valuable study of the Tory party, has opened up new areas of political organisation and activity and this in turn has important implications for the evaluation of the press. The sponsored newspapers of this period were not only concerned with stirring up or exploiting popular feeling on suitable issues, nor even with influencing the actions of individual voters during the general elections, though both formed part of an overall objective. The involvement of the press with political activity was more subtle and pervasive, taking in the relationship between individual politicians, between politicians and their supporters, between constituents and their representatives, and between the political nation at large and their rulers. Most contemporary politicians had a firm belief in the power of the press and their continuous interest combined with the comprehensive availability of the newspapers and their content helped to establish a view of politics in which the emphasis was on responsibility and participation. Although the political system was becoming increasingly fossilised during the middle decades of the century, whatever residual flexibility remained was expressed through the London press.

List of Abbreviations

Add. MSS	Additional Manuscripts
AE Paris	Quai d'Orsay, Archives du Ministère des Affaires Etrangères
AHR	*American Historical Review*
Ang.	Angleterre
AN Paris AM B⁷	Archives Nationales, Archives de la Marine, Pays Etrangères
ASG	Archivio di Stato, Genoa
AST	Archivio di Stato, Turin
BIHR	*Bulletin of the Institute of Historical Research*
BL	British Library, London
Bodl.	Department of Western Manuscripts, Bodleian Library, Oxford
Bradfer–Lawrence	Norfolk and Norwich Record Office, Bradfer–Lawrence Collection, Townshend State Papers and Letters
C(H)	Cholmondeley Houghton papers
Chewton	Chewton Mendip, Chewton House, papers of James, 1st Earl Waldegrave
CJ	*Journal of the House of Commons*
Cobbett	W. Cobbett, *Parliamentary History of England* (36 vols, 1806–20)
CP	Correspondance Politique
CUL	Cambridge University Library
DNB	*Dictionary of National Biography*
Dresden	Sächsisches Hauptstaatsarchiv, Geheimes Kabinett, Gesandschaften, Dresden
Eg.	Egerton MSS
EHR	*English Historical Review*
Fonseca	Haus-, Hof-, und Staatsarchiv, Nachlass Fonseca, Vienna
HHStA	Haus-, Hof-, und Staatsarchiv, Vienna
HJ	*Historical Journal*
HL	Huntington Library, San Marino, California
HMC	Historical Manuscripts Commission Reports
Hull	Hotham papers
JEH	*Journal of Economic History*
JHI	*Journal of the History of Ideas*
LM Ing.	Lettere Ministri, Inghilterra
Marburg	Marburg, Staatsarchiv, Bestand 4
Merseburg	Merseburg, Deutsches Zentralarchiv, Rep. XI (England)

NLI	National Library of Ireland
P & P	*Past & Present*
PRO	Public Record Office, London
RA	Windsor Royal Archive, Stuart Papers
Rawl.	Rawlinson Letters
RO	Record Office
SHR	*Scottish Historical Review*
SPD	State Papers, Domestic
SPF	State Papers, Foreign
SRO	Scottish Record Office
sup.	supplement
TRHS	*Transactions of the Royal Historical Society*
UL	University Library

Bibliography

The place of publication is London unless otherwise stated.

INTRODUCTION

For reasons of space I have not referred to key works mentioned in the notes to this essay or the bibliographies of other essays. The best introductory survey, though not all would accept his account of party development, is W. Speck, *Stability and Strife: England 1714–1760* (1977). Essential background is provided by G. Holmes (ed.), *Britain after the Glorious Revolution* (1969). An important, though outdated, bibliography is S. Pargellis and D. J. Medley (eds), *Bibliography of British History: The Eighteenth Century 1714–1789* (Oxford, 1951). The Oxford Histories of England are to be replaced by new volumes. Two provocative recent works are J. C. D. Clark, 'A General Theory of Party, Opposition and Government, 1688–1832', *HJ*, 23 (1980) 295–325, and R. Porter, *English Society in the Eighteenth Century* (1982). Important work on social topics include R. W. Malcolmson, *Life and Labour in England 1700–1780* (1981); R. B. Rose, 'Eighteenth-century Price Riots and Public Policy in England', *International Review of Social History*, 6 (1961); E. P. Thompson, 'Eighteenth-century English Society: Class Struggle without Class?', *Social History*, 3 (1978). An interesting recent work is J. and M. Jacob (eds), *The Origins of Anglo-American Radicalism* (1984). Valuable discussions of the social structure include D. Marshall, *The English Poor in the Eighteenth Century* (1956), and G. E. Mingay, *The Gentry* (1976). A valuable recent survey of religious and intellectual developments is J. Redwood, *Reason, Ridicule and Religion: The Age of Enlightenment in England 1660–1750* (1976). Possibly the best approach to the period is by a careful reading of sources: D. B. Horn and M. Ransome (eds), *English Historical Documents, 1714–1783* (1957); L. W. Hanson (ed.), *Contemporary Printed Sources for British and Irish Economic History, 1701–1750* (Cambridge, 1963); the accounts of travellers to Britain such as C. de Saussure, *A Foreign View of England in the Reign of George II* (1902); printed correspondence, particularly volumes 2 and 3 of W. Coxe, *Memoirs of the Life and Administration of Sir Robert Walpole, Earl of Orford* (3 vols, 1798), and the relevant volumes of the Historical Manuscript Commission reports; newspapers, both London and provincial, a large number of the latter being accessible in several major provincial libraries; and contemporary literature: pamphlets, plays, poetry and novels, the works of Defoe, Fielding, Gay, Johnson, Pope and Swift.

1. THE POLITICAL MANAGEMENT OF ROBERT WALPOLE

W. Coxe's *Memoirs of the Life and Administration of Sir Robert Walpole, Earl of Orford* (3 vols, 1798) was a landmark in the Whig interpretation of history as well as a work of massive scholarship, on which all subsequent historians have drawn. The best modern biography by J. H. Plumb (1956–60) is unfinished as yet. There is a good concise biography by H. T. Dickinson, *Walpole and the Whig Supremacy* (1973). Betty Kemp's *Sir Robert Walpole* (1976) has little to say. For a short account of Walpole's constitutional position as Prime Minister see G. Holmes, 'Sir Robert Walpole', in H. Van Thal (ed.), *The Prime Ministers*, vol. I (1974) Ch. 1.

The biographies of Members of Parliament and the history of constituencies are covered in *The House of Commons 1715–54*, ed. R. Sedgwick (1970) 2 vols. There is a good account of contemporary politics in B. W. Hill, *The Growth of Parliamentary Parties 1689–1742* (1976) Pt III. The best first-hand accounts of debates are to be found in *The Parliamentary Diary of Sir Edward Knatchbull 1722–30*, ed. A. N. Newman (Camden Society, 3rd ser. XCIV, 1963) and from 1730 onwards in HMC, Egmont Diary. Richard Chandler, *The Debates of the House of Commons*, vols VI–XIV (1742–4), gives contemporary reports, many MPs having sent in their speeches to him. For collected debates from newspapers and other sources see W. Cobbett, *Parliamentary History of England*, vols VIII–XII (1811–2).

For the role of the Opposition, mainly from the Whig side, see C. B. Realey, *The Early Opposition to Sir Robert Walpole* (Philadelphia, 1931) and A. Foord, *His Majesty's Opposition* (Oxford, 1964). For a good account of the agitation against Walpole's excise scheme see P. Langford, *The Excise Crisis: Society and Politics in the Age of Walpole* (Oxford, 1975). For Tory politics treated from different standpoints, consult E. Cruickshanks, *Political Untouchables: The Tories and the '45* (1979), and L. Colley, *In Defiance of Oligarchy: The Tory Party 1714–60* (Cambridge, 1982). For a court–country approach, with which the present author disagrees, see H. T. Dickinson, *Liberty and Property: Ideology in Eighteenth-Century Britain* (1977), and W. A. Speck, 'Whigs and Tories Dim their Glories: English Political Parties under the First Two Georges' in *The Whig Ascendancy*, ed. J. Cannon (1981) Ch. 3.

2. POPULAR POLITICS IN THE AGE OF WALPOLE

A great deal about elections and constituency politics can be gleaned from Romney Sedgwick (ed.), *The House of Commons 1715–54*, 2 vols (1970). For the links between parliamentary and extra-parliamentary politics see Paul Langford, *The Excise Crisis: Society and Politics in the Age of Walpole* (Oxford, 1975); Linda Colley, *In Defiance of Oligarchy: The Tory Party 1714–60* (Cambridge, 1982); and Linda Colley, 'Eighteenth-Century English Radicals before Wilkes', *TRHS*, 5th series, XXXI (1981) 1–19. The best studies of the roles of London and Westminster in the opposition to Walpole are Nicholas Rogers, 'Resistance to Oligarchy: the City Opposition to Walpole and his Successors, 1725–47', in *London in the Age of Reform*, ed. John Stevenson

(Oxford, 1977) pp. 1–29; Nicholas Rogers, 'Aristocratic Clientage, Trade and Independency: Popular Politics in Pre-Radical Westminster', *P & P*, no. 63 (1973) 70–106; Alfred James Henderson, *London and the National Government 1721–1742* (Durham, N.C., 1945); Lucy Sutherland, 'The City of London in Eighteenth-Century Politics', in *Essays Presented to Sir Lewis Namier*, ed. Richard Pares and A. J. P. Taylor (London, 1956) pp. 49–74; and I. G. Doolittle, 'Walpole's City Elections Act (1725)', *EHR*, xcvii (1982) 504–29. For pressure groups organised by those outside the ruling oligarchy see N. C. Hunt, *Two Early Political Associations* (Oxford, 1961); Lillian M. Penson, 'The London West India Interest in the Eighteenth Century', *EHR*, xxxvi (1921) 373–92; and Richard B. Sheridan, 'The Molasses Act and the Market Strategy of the British Sugar Planters', *JEH*, xvii (1957) 62–83. there are a growing number of works on popular disturbances in the eighteenth century. For the age of Walpole, in particular, the most useful are D. G. D. Isaac, 'A Study of Popular Disturbances in Britain 1714–1754' (University of Edinburgh, unpublished PhD thesis, 1953); Nicholas Rogers, 'Popular Protest in Early Hanoverian England', *P & P*, no. 79 (1978) pp. 70–100; Nicholas Rogers, 'Riot and Popular Jacobitism in Early Hanoverian England', in *Ideology and Conspiracy: Aspects of Jacobitism, 1689–1759*, ed. Eveline Cruickshanks (Edinburgh, 1982) pp. 70–88; J. De L. Mann, 'Clothiers and Weavers in Wiltshire during the Eighteenth Century', in *Studies in the Industrial Revolution*, ed. L. S. Pressnell (London, 1960) pp. 66–96; E. P. Thompson, *Whigs and Hunters* (London, 1975); George Rudé, *Paris and London in the Eighteenth Century* (London, 1970); and John Stevenson, *Popular Disturbances in England 1700–1870* (London, 1979). The main sources for ideology and the press are H. T. Dickinson, *Liberty and Property: Political Ideology in Eighteenth-Century Britain* (London, 1977) esp. Ch. 5; G. A. Cranfield, *The Development of the Provincial Press 1700–1760* (Oxford, 1962); G. A. Cranfield, 'The *London Evening Post*, 1727–1744: a Study in the Development of the Political Press', *HJ*, vi (1963) 20–37; and Laurence Hanson, *Government and the Press 1695–1763* (Oxford, 1936).

3. A CLIENT SOCIETY: SCOTLAND BETWEEN THE '15 AND THE '45

For the economic and social background there are relevant sections in T. C. Smout, *A History of the Scottish People 1560–1830* (1969); B. P. Lenman, *An Economic History of Modern Scotland* (1977); and Henry Hamilton, *An Economic History of Scotland in the Eighteenth Century* (1963). R. H. Campbell's *Scotland Since 1707: The Rise of an Industrial Society* (1965) is another sound general survey and its author edited, with J. B. A. Dow, a *Source Book of Scottish Economic and Social History* (1968), which reprints several relevant documents. At present the most up-to-date published work on demographic developments in this period will be found in the early sections of M. Flinn (ed.), *Scottish Population History* (Cambridge, 1977).

There are several convenient brief studies of the Act of Union. P. H. Scott, *1707: The Union of Scotland and England* (1979) is recent and sound. The development of post-Union political activity in North Britain may be followed in P. W. J. Riley, *The English Ministers and Scotland 1707–1727* (1964); Alexander Murdoch, *The People Above: Politics and Administration in Mid-Eighteenth Century Scotland* (1980); and in J. S. Shaw, *The Management of Scottish Society 1707–1764* (Edinburgh, 1983). There is important material on Ilay in John M. Simpson, 'Who Steered the Gravy Train, 1707–1766?', in N. T. Phillipson and Rosalind Mitchison, *Scotland in the Age of Improvement* (1970) pp. 47–72.

The structure of the Jacobite movement is examined in B. P. Lenman, *The Jacobite Risings in Britain 1689–1746* (1980). The same author examines 'The Scottish Episcopal Clergy and the Ideology of Jacobitism', in Eveline Cruickshanks (ed.), *Ideology and Conspiracy: Aspects of Jacobitism, 1689–1759* (Edinburgh, 1982) pp. 36–48. The patriotic theme in Jacobite ideology is brought out in Ian Ross and Stephen Scobie, 'Patriotic Publishing as a Response to the Union', in T. I. Rae (ed.), *The Union of 1707* (1974) pp. 94–119.

4.   WALPOLE AND IRELAND

Until the appearance of the long-awaited eighteenth-century volume (IV) of *A New History of Ireland*, ed. T. W. Moody, F. X. Martin and F. J. Byrne (Oxford, 1976–), the starting-point must still be W. E. H. Lecky's classic *A History of Ireland in the Eighteenth Century*, 5 vols (2nd edn, 1982), of which the University of Chicago Press has published a one-volume abridgement (1972). Lecky's contemporary, J. A. Froude, though inferior as an historian, shares the advantage of having written his *The English in Ireland in the Eighteenth Century*, 3 vols (1881), before the destruction of so many of the Irish public records in 1922. The biases of the two men, Liberal and Tory, counterpoint nicely. Neither, however, pays the first half of the century the close attention they give the final hectic decades, a criticism equally applicable to many modern general histories, of which the most reliable and most generous to the earlier period are J. C. Beckett, *The Making of Modern Ireland 1603–1923* (2nd edn, 1981), and Edith Mary Johnston, *Ireland in the Eighteenth Century* (Gill History of Ireland no. 8, Dublin, 1974). One valiant attempt to right the chronological imbalance enshrined by Lecky is Francis Godwin James, *Ireland in the Empire 1688–1770* (Cambridge, Mass., 1973), which also endeavours to set the early eighteenth-century 'Irish question' in a British and imperial perspective. This would be a signal service, but unfortunately the results are patchy and the book's merits offset by inaccuracy in points of detail.

Otherwise little has been written on politics in Walpolean Ireland. J. L. McCracken's essay, 'From Swift to Grattan', in *The Irish Parliamentary Tradition*, ed. Brian Farrell (Dublin, 1973), is a whistlestop tour with little opportunity to examine the terrain, and the same author's pamphlet, *The Irish Parliament in the Eighteenth Century* (Irish Historical Association, Irish History Series no. 9, Dundalk, 1971), travels even more rapidly. David Hayton has sketched in the changing pattern of parties and factions in the period 1692–c.

1735, and has sought to explain developments in management, in 'The Beginnings of the "Undertaker System" ', in *Penal Era and Golden Age: Essays in Irish History 1690–1800*, ed. Thomas Bartlett and David Hayton (Belfast, 1979). Two articles on particular aspects, F. G. James, 'The Irish Lobby in the Eighteenth Century', *EHR*, LXXXI(1966) 543–57, and J. L. McCracken, 'Irish Parliamentary Elections 1727–68', *Irish Historical Studies*, V (1946–7) 209–30, are useful if rather superficial surveys of important topics which have yet to be replaced by more systematic investigation. Political ideas have fared slightly better. A chapter in Caroline Robbins, *The Eighteenth-Century Commonwealthman* (Cambridge, Mass., 1959) pp. 134–76, follows the progression from Molyneux to Grattan. Since her pioneering journey, however, our understanding of the context of early eighteenth-century political thought has been deepened by the writings of J. G. A. Pocock, H. T. Dickinson and others, and a ray or two of this new light has recently permeated the Irish scene. Michael Ryder's examination of the debate over the proposal for an Irish national bank, 'The Bank of Ireland 1721: Land, Credit and Dependency', *HJ*, XXV (1982), reassesses Protestant Irish political thought in English terms, a valuable corrective to the traditional emphasis on precursory nationalism, though perhaps erring on the other side in its underestimate of the strength and pervasiveness of 'patriotic' sentiment.

Too often in Irish historiography the age of Walpole has been viewed instead as 'the age of Swift', but this concentration on Swiftian scholarship has produced some fine achievements, most notably by Americans. Oliver W. Ferguson's *Jonathan Swift and Ireland* (Urbana, Ill., 1962), has, as might be expected, a lot to say on the Drapier, during which he takes issue with the predominantly economic explanation of the furies aroused by Wood's patent that was offered in Albert Goodwin, 'Wood's Halfpence', *EHR*, LI (1936) 647–74 (rprt. in *Essays in Eighteenth-Century History*, arranged by Rosalind Mitchison [1966]), a careful piece that in other respects has stood the test of time. For information, nothing on the dean compares with the masterly biography by Irvin Ehrenpreis, *Swift: The Man, His Works and the Age*, 3 vols (1962–83). On a related theme Robert Munter's *The History of the Irish Newspaper 1685–1760* (Cambridge, 1967), is another excellent study, revealing much more about Irish politics and society than its title would suggest.

Formerly, the standard economic history was George O'Brien, *The Economic History of Ireland in the Eighteenth Century* (Dublin, 1918), but this field is being thoroughly ploughed by revisionists, especially L. M. Cullen, in whose books the process is best followed: *Anglo-Irish Trade 1660–1800* (Manchester, 1968); *An Economic History of Ireland since 1660* (1972); and the very wide-ranging *Emergence of Modern Ireland 1600–1900* (1981), probably the most stimulating but certainly unsuitable for a beginner. Constantia Maxwell's panoramic social histories, *Country and Town in Ireland under the Georges* (2nd edn, Dundalk, 1949), and *Dublin under the Georges* (2nd edn, 1956), while old-fashioned, still convey vividly the flavour of the period.

Finally, for those eager to sample primary source material a good deal of high political correspondence is preserved in William Coxe, *Memoirs of the Life and Administration of Sir Robert Walpole*, 3 vols (1789), and *Letters Written by . . . Hugh Boulter*, 2 vols (Dublin, 1770), to be taken with Swift's *Correspondence*, ed.

Harold Williams, 5 vols (Oxford, 1963–5), and *Drapier's Letters*, ed. Herbert Davis (Oxford, 1935; rprt. 1965), as the essential relish.

5. ECONOMIC POLICY AND ECONOMIC DEVELOPMENT

Large numbers of economic history textbooks deal with this period. For the more traditional approach the best examples are D. C. Coleman, *The Economy of England 1450–1750* (Oxford, 1977) and Charles Wilson, *England's Apprenticeship 1603–1763* (1965). For more recent attempts at quantification and model-building see Roderick Floud and Donald McCloskey, *The Economic History of Britain since 1700*, vol. 1: *1700–1860* (Cambridge, 1981), especially the chapters by N. C. R. Crafts, W. A. Cole and E. L. Jones. All three books contain detailed bibliographies with details of the many monographs and articles (too numerous to cite here) which deal with specific trades and industries. The definitive discussion of population is E. A. Wrigley and R. S. Schofield, *The Population History of England 1541–1871: A Reconstruction* (1981). The social history of this period has received increasing attention in recent years after a long period of neglect. Roy Porter, *English Society in the Eighteenth Century* (Harmondsworth, 1982) is a brilliant synthesis of what has so far been achieved. For the important developments in urban society see P. J. Corfield, *The Impact of English Towns 1700–1800* (Oxford, 1982). Both Porter and Corfield include extensive bibliographies. J. G. Rule, *The Experience of Labour in Eighteenth-Century Industry* (1981) is a stimulating study of a rather neglected field; on attitudes to labour Edgar Furniss, *The Position of the Labourer in a System of Nationalism* (Boston and New York, 1920) is a work of high quality, unjustly overlooked. There is a masterly review of recent additions to the extensive historiography of mercantilism by D. C. Coleman, 'Mercantilism Revisited', *HJ*, 23, no. 4 (1980).

Financial administration is brilliantly dealt with by P. G. M. Dickson, *The Financial Revolution in England* (1967). The administration of the land tax is dealt with by W. R. Ward, *The English Land Tax in the Eighteenth Century* (Oxford, 1953), but we know little in detail about the administration of other taxes. P. Mathias, *The Brewing Industry in England 1700–1830* (Cambridge, 1959) deals, however, with the administration of the beer excise. W. Kennedy, *English Taxation 1640–1799: An Essay on Policy and Opinion* (1913) is a study which has not been superseded of the major trends in thought relating to taxation. The most recent study of the excise crisis is P. Langford, *The Excise Crisis: Society and Politics in the Age of Walpole* (Oxford, 1975); some further information about the background to the excise scheme is in Jacob M. Price, 'The Excise Affair Revisited: the Administrative and Colonial Dimensions of a Parliamentary Crisis', in Stephen Baxter (ed.), *England's Rise to Greatness* (Berkeley, Calif., 1983).

6. FOREIGN POLICY

The best introductions to eighteenth-century foreign policy are P. Langford, *The Eighteenth Century* (1976) and J. R. Jones, *Britain and the World 1649–1815*

(1980). D. B. Horn, *Great Britain and Europe in the Eighteenth Century* (Oxford, 1967) is difficult to use; his *British Diplomatic Service 1689–1789* (Oxford, 1961) is excellent. J. S. Bromley, 'Britain and Europe in the Eighteenth Century', *History* (1981) is very good. G. C. Gibbs has written some very important pieces on the Walpole period, all characterised by a very high level of scholarship, and important insights: 'The Revolution in Foreign Policy', *Britain after the Glorious Revolution*, ed. G. Holmes (1969); 'Parliament and Foreign Policy in the Age of Stanhope and Walpole', *EHR* (1962); 'Britain and the Alliance of Hanover', *EHR* (1958); 'Laying Treaties before Parliament in the Eighteenth Century', *Studies in Diplomatic History*, ed. R. Hatton and M. S. Anderson (1970); 'Parliament and the Treaty of Quadruple Alliance', *William III and Louis XIV*, ed. R. Hatton and J. S. Bromley (Liverpool, 1968). A superb introduction to the European situation is D. McKay and H. Scott, *The Rise of the Great Powers* (1983). Sir R. Lodge, 'English Neutrality in the War of the Polish Succession', *TRHS* (1931) and 'The Treaty of Seville', *TRHS* (1932) are weak. Important for Anglo-French relations are J. Dureng, *Le Duc de Bourbon et L'Angleterre* (Paris, 1911); P. Vaucher, *Robert Walpole et la Politique de Fleury* (Paris, 1724); and A. Wilson, *French Foreign Policy during the Administration of Cardinal Fleury* (Cambridge, Mass., 1936; rprt. 1972). On British Mediterranean policy, G. H. Jones, 'La Gran Bretagna e la destinazione di Don Carlos al trono di Toscana', *Archivio Storico Italiano* (1982); M. Martin, 'The Secret Clause, Britain and Spanish Ambitions in Italy 1712–31', *European Studies Review* (1976); E. Armstrong, *Elisabeth Farnese* (London, 1892); G. Quazza, *Il Problema Italiano e l'equilibrio europes 1720–38* (Turin, 1965); J. Black, 'The Development of Anglo-Sardinian Relations in the First Half of the Eighteenth Century', *Studi Piemontesi* (1983). For the late 1710s: B. Williams, *Stanhope* (Oxford, 1932); R. Hatton, *Diplomatic Relations between Great Britain and the Dutch Republic* (1950); D. McKay, 'The Struggle for Control of George I's Northern Policy, 1718–19', *Journal of Modern History* (1973). For the 1720s: J. Chance, *Alliance of Hanover* (1923); A. Goslinga, *Slingelandt's Efforts towards European Peace* (The Hague, 1915). For the 1730s: J. Black, '1733 – Failure of British Diplomacy?', *Durham University Journal* (1982). There are large gaps, in the literature particularly for 1721–4 and 1736–9. There are no scholarly biographies of George II, Townshend or Harrington. Hatton's excellent *George I* (London, 1978) is weak after 1721. J. Black, 'George II Reconsidered: a Consideration of George's Influence in the Conduct of Foreign Policy, in the First Years of his reign', *Mitteilungen des Osterreichischen Staatsarchivs* (1983) stops in 1735. R. Browning, *The Duke of Newcastle* (New Haven, Conn., 1975) and J. Black, 'An "Ignoramus" in European affairs?' (on Walpole), *British Journal for Eighteenth-Century Studies* (1983) for the ministers. There are no studies for the 1730s of the Hanoverian connection nor of parliamentary debates on foreign policy. On commercial factors see: P. Dickson, 'English Commercial Negotiations with Austria, 1737–52', *Statesmen, Scholars and Merchants*, ed. A. Whiteman, J. S. Bromley and P. Dickson (Oxford, 1973); E. Holdner, 'The Role of the South Sea Company in the Diplomacy Leading to the War of Jenkins' Ear, 1729–1739', *Hispanic American Review* (1938); G. Walker, *Spanish Politics and Imperial Trade* (1979); C. Andrews, 'Anglo-French Commercial

Rivalry, 1700–1750', *American Historical Review* (1914–15); G. B. Hertz, 'England and the Ostend Company', *EHR* (1907); J. McLachlan, *Trade and Peace with Old Spain 1667–1750* (Cambridge, 1940). The best introductions to Jacobitism are G. H. Jones, *The Mainstream of Jacobitism* (Cambridge, Mass., 1954); P. Fritz, *The English Ministers and Jacobitism* (Toronto, 1975). On the press see: G. C. Gibbs, 'Newspapers, Parliament and Foreign Policy in the Age of Stanhope and Walpole', *Mélange offerts à G. Jacquemyns* (Brussels, 1968); J. Black, 'The British Press and European News in the 1730s: the Case of the *Newcastle Courant*', *Durham County Local History Society Bulletin* (1981); J. Black, 'The Press, Party and Foreign Policy in the Reign of George I', *Publishing History* (1984).

There is a large amount of printed primary material. Cobbett's *Parliamentary History* is very useful, but see M. Ransome, 'The Reliability of Contemporary Reporting of the Debates of the House of Commons, 1727–1741', *BIHR* (1942–3). For diplomatic correspondence see: the many volumes of *British Diplomatic Instructions* (Camden, 3rd series); Chesterfield's letters, ed. B. Dobree (1932); *Annals and Correspondence of the Viscount and the First and Second Earls of Stair*, ed. J. Graham (1875); and several volumes of the HMC reports: Egmont diary, Polwarth, Townshend, Weston, Trevor papers, and, for the Jacobites, the Stuart papers; Sir R. Lodge, *Private correspondence of Benjamin Keene* (Cambridge, 1933). Reports from and Instructions to British envoys can be found in several volumes of *Sbornik Imperatorskogo Russkogo Istoricheskogo Obschchestva* (St Petersburg, 1867–1916). A very important source for Council meetings in Lord Chancellor King's Notes, appendix to P. King, *Life of John Locke* (1830); for court developments, *Some Materials towards Memoirs of the Reign of King George II by John Lord Hervey*, ed. R. Sedgwick (1931) needs to be handled with care. For contrasting ministerial and Opposition views on foreign policy in the last years of the ministry see: Philip Yorke, *The Life and Correspondence of Philip Yorke, Earl of Hardwicke* (3 vols, 1913); G. H. Rose, *A Selection from the Papers of the Earls of Marchmont* (3 vols, 1831).

7. WALPOLE, 'THE POET'S FOE'

No adequate study of the press in the age of Walpole has yet been written, but three largely out-of-date studies offer some coverage: D. H. Stevens, *Party Politics and English Journalism 1702–1742* (1916); W. T. Laprade, *Public Opinion and Politics in Eighteenth-Century England to the Fall of Walpole* (1936); and L. Hanson, *Government and the Press 1695–1763* (1936). Nor has Walpole's organisation of propaganda been examined at all closely, although the standard biography, J. H. Plumb, *Sir Robert Walpole* (2 vols so far published, 1957, 1960), contains a few details, and might be supplemented by H. T. Dickinson, *Walpole and the Whig Supremacy* (1973).

A lucid account of the literary opposition is to be found in B. A. Goldgar, *Walpole and the Wits* (Lincoln, Nebr., 1977). A comprehensive account of Swift's politics is attempted in J. A. Downie, *Jonathan Swift, Political Writer* (1984), while Pope is dealt with in M. Mack, *The Garden and the City* (1969). B.

McCrea, *Henry Fielding and the Politics of Mid-Eighteenth-Century England* (Athens, Ga., 1981) is valuable as a guide to Fielding's political career, but is out of touch on the historical context and unreliable on Fielding's ideological position. The *Craftsman* is most easily approached through S. Varey (ed.), *Lord Bolingbroke: Contributions to the Craftsman* (Oxford, 1982). The Scriblerian response to the duces is investigated in P. Rogers, *Grub Street* (1972).

The ideology of the Opposition can be studied in I. Kramnick, *Bolingbroke and his Circle* (1968; Cambridge, Mass, 1968); J. G. A. Pocock, *Politics, Language and Time* (1972); and H. T. Dickinson, *Liberty and Property* (1977; paperback edn, 1979). The best introduction to the subject, however, is the excellent chapter on the opposition to Walpole in W. A. Speck, *Stability and Strife* (1977) pp 219–38.

8. PRINT AND POLITICS IN THE AGE OF WALPOLE

The newspapers of the eighteenth century have not received much detailed attention in their own right. There is no comprehensive bibliography, the best list appears in George Watson (ed.), *New Cambridge Bibliography of English Literature*, vol. 2: *1660–1800* (Cambridge, 1971), and no general view of the development of the newspapers which takes account of modern research. The London press of the middle decades of the century is particularly neglected. The only recent investigation of its overall structure, which includes a view of political associations, appears in Michael Harris, 'The London Newspaper Press, 1725–1746' (London University, PhD dissertation, 1973). R. L. Haig, *The Gazetteer* (Carbondale, Ill., 1960) contains a full-length study of a single London paper but this is mainly concerned with internal organisation and with the second half of the century. Two important but very different studies on either side of the Walpole period offer an analysis of the press as a medium of political communication. Alan Downie, *Robert Harley and the Press* (1979) looks at the use made of various forms of propaganda up to 1714, while John Brewer in *Party Ideology and Popular Politics at the Accession of George III* (Cambridge, 1976) is concerned to show the pervasive character of the national press at the time of the Wilkes crisis. In the Walpole period itself the political content of the London papers provides a major source for the investigation of ideology in Isaac Kremnick, *Bolingbroke and his Circle* (Cambridge, Mass., 1968) and forms an element in Paul Langford, *The Excise Crisis* (Oxford, 1975). The most effective investigation of the national press in the context of a political uproar appears in Thomas W. Perry, *Public Opinion, Propaganda and Politics in Eighteenth-Century England* (Cambridge, Mass., 1962) although this is concerned entirely with the Jew Bill of the mid 1750s. More attention has been paid to the control of the political press in the Walpole period than to its content and the best treatment of this specialist area remains Laurence Hanson, *Government and the Press 1695–1763* (Oxford, rprt. 1967). A number of political essays and some related material from the London press has been reprinted as part of the output of such major writers as Lord Bolingbroke and Henry Fielding. This can provide useful access to the material and Simon Varey (ed.), *Lord Bolingbroke's Contributions to the Craftsman*

(Oxford, 1982), and W. B. Coley (ed.), *The Jacobites Journal* (Oxford, 1975) and *The True Patriot* (Oxford, 1982) are among the most effective publications of this sort.

The English provincial press is rather better served than its London counterpart. Two good studies of the newspapers published outside the capital during the first half of the eighteenth century appear in G. A. Cranfield, *The Development of the Provincial Newspaper 1700–1760* (Oxford, 1962) and R. M. Wiles, *Freshest Advices* (Columbus, Ohio, 1965). Although both include some political material much more needs to be done to investigate political attitudes expressed through individual publications. A number of valuable studies of this sort have already been completed including Jeremy Black, 'The *Cirencester Flying-Post* and *Weekly Miscellany*', *Cirencester Archaeological and Historical Society Annual Report and Newsletter*, 25 (1983); Black, 'Manchester's First Newspaper: the *Manchester Weekly* Journal', *Transactions of the Historical Society of Lancashire and Cheshire*, 130 (1981).

Notes and References

INTRODUCTION: AN AGE OF POLITICAL STABILITY?
Jeremy Black

Place of publication is London unless otherwise stated.

1. John Childs, *The Army, James II and the Glorious Revolution* (Manchester, 1981).

2. PRO SPD 54/19: Wade to the Duke of Newcastle, Secretary of State for the Southern Department, 29 Aug. 1729.

3. Black, 'The British Navy and British Foreign Policy in the First Half of the Eighteenth Century', *Studies in History and Politics* (forthcoming).

4. AE Paris, CP Ang. 350: Chammorel to Morville, French Foreign Minister, 16 Apr. (ns) 1725.

5. J. H. Plumb, *The Growth of Political Stability in England, 1675–1725* (1967).

6. F. McLynn, *France and the Jacobite Rising of 1745* (Edinburgh, 1981).

7. E. Cruikshanks, *Political Untouchables: The Tories and the '45* (1979); L. Colley, *In Defiance of Oligarchy: The Tory Party 1714–60* (Cambridge, 1982).

8. K. Ellis, *The Post Office in the Eighteenth Century* (Oxford, 1958); K. Ellis, 'British Communications and Diplomacy in the Eighteenth Century', *BIHR*, XXXI (Nov. 1958) 158–67.

9. BL Add. MSS 51390: Hanbury-Williams to Lord Holland, 28 Oct. 1739.

10. Black, 'Parliament and the Political and Diplomatic Crisis of 1717–18', *Parliamentary History Yearbook*, 3 (1984).

11. Dresden 2676: Le Coq to Augustus II of Saxony-Poland, 5 Aug. (ns) 1727; AST LM Ing. 40, 48: Ossorio to Charles Emmanuel III of Sardinia, 1 June (ns) 1733, 2 Apr. (ns) 1742; BL Add. MSS 32686: Newcastle to ——, 18 July 1721.

12. G. V. Bennett, *The Tory Crisis in Church and State 1688–1730: The Career of Francis Atterbury, Bishop of Rochester* (Oxford, 1975).

13. I. Krammick, *Bolingbroke and his Circle* (Cambridge, Mass., 1968); H. T. Dickinson, *Liberty and Property* (1977) Ch. 3.

14. *London Journal*, 11 Apr. 1730.

15. RO Hertford, Panshanger MSS D/EP F55: Hutcheson to Earl Cowper, 21 Mar. 1722.

16. P. G. M. Dickson, *The Financial Revolution in England* (1967).

17. M. Raeff, *The Well-Ordered Police State: Social and Institutional Change through Law in the Germanies and Russia, 1600–1800* (New Haven, Conn., 1983).

18. D. Baugh, 'Poverty, Protestantism and Political Economy: English Attitudes towards the Poor, 1660–1800', in S. Baxter (ed.), *England's Rise to*

Greatness, 1660–1763 (Berkeley, Calif., 1983) Ch. 3. I should like to thank Joanna Innes for letting me read her paper 'English Houses of Correction and "Labour discipline" c. 1600–1780: a Critical Examination'.

19. Valuable administrative studies include Ellis, *Post Office*; D. Baugh, *British Naval Administration in the Age of Walpole* (Princeton, N.J., 1965); Dickson, *Financial Revolution*; M. A. Thomson, *The Secretaries of State, 1681–1782* (Oxford, 1932); H. Roseveare, *The Treasury: The Evolution of a British Institution* (1969); W. R. Ward, *The English Land Tax in the Eighteenth Century* (1953).

20. R. Browning, *Political and Constitutional Ideas of the Court Whigs* (Baton Rouge, La., 1982) Ch. 1.

21. Bodl. MS A.269: Gibson to Bishop Nicolson, 3 Dec. 1717. I have benefited in this section from the chapter synopsis produced by W. R. Ward.

22. Black, 'The Catholic Threat and the British Press in the 1720s and 1730s', *Journal of Religious History* (1984); *London Journal*, 17 Sept. 1720; *Daily Courant*, 3 Jan., 2 Apr., 1734; *Flying Post, or Post Master*, 3 Sept. 1717; *Norwich Mercury*, 24 Dec. 1730.

23. G. F. Nuttall (ed.), *Calendar of the Correspondence of Philip Doddridge 1702–51* (1979) p. 76: Doddridge, a leading nonconformist, to Samuel Clark, 17 Jan. 1735; *Read's Weekly Journal, or British Gazetteer*, 9 June 1733; *Northampton Mercury*, 14 May 1739.

24. *Fog's Weekly Journal*, 13 Oct. 1733.

25. N. Sykes, *William Wake, Archbishop of Canterbury*, 2 vols (Cambridge, 1957).

26. BL Add. MSS 37394: Charles Delafaye, Undersecretary of State in the Southern Department, to Charles Whitworth, Plenipotentiary at the Congress of Cambray, 7 May 1724.

27. N. Sykes, *Edmund Gibson, Bishop of London* (Oxford, 1926); N. C. Hunt, *Two Early Political Associations: The Quakers and the Dissenting Deputies in the Age of Sir Robert Walpole* (Oxford, 1961); R. F. J. Kendrick, 'Sir Robert Walpole, the Old Whigs and the Bishops, 1733–36: a Study in Eighteenth-century Parliamentary Politics', *HJ*, xi (1968) 421–45. I should like to thank Stephen Taylor for letting me read his forthcoming *HJ* article on the Quakers' tithe bill of 1736.

28. W. Marshall, 'Episcopal Activity in the Hereford and Oxford Dioceses, 1660–1760', *Midland History*, 8 (1983) 106–120; D. R. Hirschberg, 'Episcopal Incomes and Expenses, 1660–c. 1760', in R. O'Day and F. Heal (eds), *Princes and Paupers in the English Church 1500–1800* (Leicester, 1981) p. 227.

29. R. Davies and E. G. Rupp, *A History of the Methodist Church of Great Britain* (1965) i; F. Baker, *John Wesley and the Church of England* (1970); A. Armstrong *The Church in England, the Methodists and Society, 1700–1850* (1973); J. D. Walsh, 'Origins of the Evangelical Revival', in G. V. Bennett and J. D. Walsh (eds), *Essays in Modern Church History in Memory of Norman Sykes* (1966).

30. *The Englishman*, 21 Oct. 1715. I have benefited from discussing this point with Colin Haydon. On the unimportance of church issues in Kent elections see A. N. Newman 'Elections in Kent and its Parliamentary Representation 1715–54' (Oxford University D.Phil. dissertation, 1957) pp. 35–6.

31. BL Add. MSS 62558 f.80: diary of Mrs Caesar, wife of a Tory MP.

32. *A Letter on a Proposed Alteration of the 39 Articles by Lord Walpole written 1751* (1863) 5–6: Horace Walpole to Nockold Tompson, later Mayor of Norwich, 12 Dec. 1751; Chewton: Delafaye to Earl Waldegrave, Ambassador in France, 18 Mar. 1731; BL Add. MSS 47028 f.257: Lord Percival to Charles Dering, Dec. 1718.

33. BL Add. MSS 28156: Wager to Admiral Norris, 17 Aug. 1734.

34. Newspapers such as the *Thistle* of Edinburgh carried a lot of material from the London press.

35. Several important theses on local politics are unfortunately unpublished. See Newman, 'Elections in Kent'; J. F. Quinn, 'Political Activity in Yorkshire, c. 1700–1742' (University of Lancaster, M.Litt. dissertation, 1980); D. S. O'Sullivan 'Politics in Norwich, 1701–1835' (University of East Anglia, M.Phil. dissertation, 1975); K. von den Steinen, 'The Fabric of an Interest: the First Duke of Dorset and Kentish and Sussex Politics, 1705–65 (University of California, Los Angeles, Ph.D. dissertation, 1969).

36. P. Borsay, 'The English Urban Renaissance: the Development of Provincial Urban Culture c. 1680–c. 1760', *Social History*, 5 (1977) 581–603; P. Borsay, 'Culture, Status, and the English Urban Landscape', *History*, 67 (1982) 1–12; P. J. Corfield, *The Impact of English Towns 1700–1800* (Oxford, 1982); P. Clark (ed.), *The Transformation of English Towns 1600–1800* (1984); G. Jackson, *Hull in the Eighteenth Century* (1972). I should like to thank Jonathan Barry for letting me read some of his forthcoming work on Bristol.

37. The 'eyes of the whole nation are constantly fixed on the conduct and proceedings of this city, as the Primum Mobile of Great Britain', *Craftsman*, 7 Oct. 1727, *London Journal* 22 July 1727; RA 93/96: Hay, Jacobite Secretary of State, to Daniel O'Brien, Jacobite agent in Paris, 8 May (ns) 1726; BL Add. MSS 62558 f.34: Mrs Caesar's diary; N. Rogers, "London Politics from Walpole to Pitt' (University of Toronto, Ph.D. dissertation, 1975); N. Rogers, 'Money, Land and Lineage: the Big Bourgeoisie of Hanoverian London', *Social History*, IV (1979) 437–54; A. J. Henderson, *London and the National Government 1721–42* (Durham, N.C., 1945).

38. For ministerial opposition to 'overloading the landed interest' with taxation, see Cobbett, vol. x, col. 31, 7 Mar. 1737.

39. J. H. Plumb, *The Commercialization of Leisure in Eighteenth-Century England* (Reading, 1973); N. McKendrick, J. Brewer and J. H. Plumb, *The Birth of a Consumer Society* (1982).

40. An interesting recent study is D. Rollison, 'Property, Ideology and Popular Culture in a Gloucestershire village 1660–1740', *P & P*, 93 (1981) 70–97.

41. E. P. Thompson, *Whigs and Hunters: The Origin of the Black Act* (1975); D. Hay, P. Linebaugh and E. P. Thompson, *Albions's Fatal Tree: Crime and Society in Eighteenth-Century England* (1975); J. Brewer and J. Styles (eds), *An Ungovernable People: The English and Their Law in the Seventeenth and Eighteenth Centuries* (1980); J. Beattie, 'The Pattern of Crime in England 1660–1800', *P & P*, 62 (1974) 47–95; J. H. Langbein, 'Albion's Fatal Flaws', *P & P*, 98 (1983) 96–120.

42. G. Holmes, 'The Achievement of Stability: the Social Context of

Politics from the 1680s to the Age of Walpole', in J. Cannon (ed.), *The Whig Ascendancy* (1981) Ch. 1, pp. 1–22; G. Holmes, *Augustan England: Professions, State and Society 1680–1730* (1982).

43. Important recent works on ideological developments after 1688 include J. P. Kenyon, *Revolution Principles: The Politics of Party 1689–1720* (Cambridge, 1977); H. T. Dickinson, 'The Eighteenth-Century Debate on the "Glorious Revolution" ', *History*, 61 (1976) 28–45; J. Dunn, 'The Politics of Locke in England and America in the Eighteenth Century', in J. W. Yolton (ed.), *John Locke: Problems and Perspectives* (Cambridge, 1969); M. P. Thompson, 'The Idea of Conquest in Controversies over the 1688 Revolution', *JHI*, 38 (1977) 33–46; M. Goldie, 'Edmund Bohun and *Jus Gentium* in the Revolution Debate 1689–1693', 20 (1977) 569–86.

44. Kenyon, *Revolution Principles*, p. 204.

45. *Flying Post or Post Master*, 6 Feb. 1733.

46. Cobbett, vol. IX, col. 1288, 10 Feb. 1737.

47. A. Charlesworth (ed.), *An Atlas of Rural Protest in Britain 1548–1900* 1983) pp. 44–8, 82–5, 119–21. I have benefited from Professor Malcolmson's advice on this topic. AE Paris, CP Ang. 404: Cambis to Amelot, French Foreign Minister, 2 Apr. (ns) 1739.

48. ·John Hervey, 1st Earl of Bristol, *Letter-Books*, ed. S. H. A. Hervey, 23 Oct. 1738; AE Paris, CP Ang. 324: Chammorel to Dubois, French Foreign Minster, 15, 26 June (ns) 1719; AN Paris AM. B^7 145: Maurepas, French Naval Minister, to Mandel, agent in London, 5 Sept. (ns) 1733; ASG LM Ing. 11: Gastaldi, Genoese envoy, to the Senate of Genoa, 25 May (ns) 1733.

49. *Mist's Weekly Journal*, 14 Jan. 1727.

50. This is shown in forthcoming work by Dr Cruickshanks.

51. B. Lenman, *The Jacobite Risings in Britain 1689–1746* (1980); F. McLynn, *The Jacobite Army in England 1745* (Edinburgh, 1983).

52. BL ADD MSS 37388: Whitworth to Cadogan, 28 Feb. (ns) 1722.

53. Cobbett, vol. XI, col. 224, 21 Nov. 1739.

54. *Northampton Mercury*, 28 Oct. 1723.

55. Earl Stanhope (ed.), *Miscellanies* (1863) pp. 68–9: memorandum by Sir Robert Peel, Dec. 1833.

1. THE POLITICAL MANAGEMENT OF SIR ROBERT WALPOLE,
1720–42   *Eveline Cruickshanks*

1. *The House of Commons 1715–54*, ed. R. Sedgwick (1970) (thereafter *HC*) vol. I, pp. 30–1. This was one of the most important discoveries Sedgwick made while writing his survey, but historians have ignored it.

2. J. H. Plumb, *Sir Robert Walpole* (1956–60) vol. I, p. 358.

3. Blenheim MSS (in BL), box 8, Sunderland's plans for a new Parliament. This box does not seem to have reached the BL.

4. There are no full secret-service accounts for Walpole. He spent £77,450 on it in 1723 and £105,350 in 1725 (Plumb, *Walpole*, vol. II, p. 106n).

5. E. A. Reitan, 'The Civil List in Eighteenth-Century British Politics', *HJ*, IX (1966) 318–37.

6. P. C. Yorke, *The Life and Correspondence of Philip Yorke, Earl of Hardwicke* (Cambridge, 1913) vol. II, pp. 206–8.

7. H. Roseveare, *The Treasury 1600–1870* (1973) p. 18.

8. *HC*, vol. I, pp. 407–8, 591–2.

9. R. Browning, *The Duke of Newcastle* (1975) p. 61.

10. E. Gregg and C. Jones, 'Hanover, Pensions and the "Poor Lords" ', *Parliamentary History*, I (1982) 173–80; Sir L. Namier, *The Structure of Politics at the Accession of George III* (2nd edn, 1957) pp. 221–5.

11. HMC, *Egmont Diary*, vol. I, p. 153; C. B. Realey, *The Early Opposition to Sir Robert Walpole* (Philadelphia, 1931) p. 94.

12. P. C. Yorke, 2nd Earl of Hardwicke, *Walpoliana* (1781) p. 17.

13. John, Lord Hervey, *Some Materials towards Memoirs of the Reign of George II*, ed. R. Sedgwick (1931) vol. I, pp. 177–8.

14. P. D. Stanhope, Earl of Chesterfield, *Characters* (1778) p. 31.

15. HMC, *Egmont Diary*, vol. I, pp. 31–2.

16. P. D. G. Thomas, *The House of Commons in the Eighteenth Century* (Oxford, 1971) pp. 16–17, 351, 357.

17. *The Craftsman*, 3 Aug. 1728. I owe this reference to Professor James Woolley of Lafayette College, Pennsylvania.

18. Chesterfield, *Characters*, p. 31; Hardwicke, *Walpoliana*, p. 9.

19. Chatsworth MSS, Edward Walpole to the Duke of Devonshire, 16 Feb. 1738 (History of Parliament transcripts).

20. CUL, C(H) MSS: William Selby to Josiah Burchett, 2 Oct, 1740; John Hedworth to Sir Robert Walpole, 12 Oct. 1740; Sir Humphrey Howorth to Sir Robert Walpole, 3 Feb. 1740 (History of Parliament transcripts).

21. Hardwicke, *Walpoliana*, p. 7.

22. Plumb, *Walpole*, vol. II, p. 91.

23. W. Coxe, *Memoirs of the Life and Administration of Sir Robert Walpole, Earl of Orford* (1798) vol. I, p. 757; *A Selection from the Papers of the Earls of Marchmont*, ed. Sir G. H. Rose (1831) vol. II, pp. 76–7.

24. BL Add. MSS 32, 955, f.94.

25. *HC*, vol. II, pp. 550–2, 567–8.

26. Ibid., vol. I, p. 14; Hardwicke, *Walpoliana*, p. 9.

27. *HC*, vol. I, pp. 484–5; CUL, C(H) MSS, Thomas Brereton to Sir Robert Walpole, 26 July 1734.

28. *HC*, vol. I, p. 20.

29. Ibid., p. 214.

30. Ibid., p. 282.

31. Ibid., pp. 19, 34, 62; E. Cruickshanks, *Political Untouchables: The Tories and the '45* (1979).

32. L. Colley, *In Defiance of Oligarchy: The Tory Party 1714–60* (Cambridge, 1982) Ch. 4. On Addison, see F. P. Lock, *Swift's Tory Politics* (1983) p. 99.

33. Robert Molesworth, *An Account of Denmark, As It Was in the Year 1692* (1694); *HC*, vol. II, p. 402.

34. Ibid., vol. I, p. 68; Chatsworth MSS, Henry Pelham to the Duke of Devonshire, 17 Nov. 1739.

35. Diary of Sir Dudley Ryder, 18 Oct. 1739 (History of Parliament transcript).

36. Hardwicke, *Walpoliana*, p. 9. For Walpole's intelligence system see P. Fritz, 'The Anti-Jacobite Intelligence System of the English Ministers, 1715–43', *HJ*, xiv (1973) 271–80, and *The English Ministers and Jacobitism between the Rebellions of 1715 and 1745* (Toronto, 1975); and Cruickshanks, *Political Untouchables*, pp. 15–6, 23–4, 42, 57–8.

37. N. C. Hunt, *Sir Robert Walpole, Samuel Holden, and the Dissenting Deputies*, Dr Williams Lecture, no. 11 (Oxford, 1957), and his *Two Early Political Associations: The Quakers and the Dissenting Deputies in the Age of Sir R. Walpole* (Oxford, 1961); Cobbett, vol. viii, col. 1046; HMC, *Egmont Diary*, vol. ii, p. 244.

38. T. F. J. Kendrick, 'Sir Robert Walpole, the Old Whigs and the Bishops, 1733–36', *HJ*, ii (1968) 421–45; A. Foord, *His Majesty's Opposition 1714–1830* (Oxford, 1964) pp. 109–10, 140n.

39. Yorke, *Hardwicke*, vol. i, p. 186; HMC, *Egmont Diary*, vol. i, p. 315; Hardwicke, *Walpoliana*, p. 16; Coxe, *Walpole*, vol. ii, p. 644. For a good account of the 'country' party and its Tory links, see David Hayton 'The "Country" Interest and the Party System, 1689–c. 1720', *Party and Management in Parliament, 1660–1784*, ed. C. Jones (Leicester, 1984) pp. 37–85.

40. HMC, *Carlisle MSS*, p. 150.

41. Hardwicke, *Walpoliana*, p. 7.

42. A. N. Newman, 'The Political Patronage of Frederick, Prince of Wales', *HJ*, i (1958) 68–74.

43. W. A. Speck, *Stability and Strife: England 1714–1760* (1977) pp. 222–6; H. T. Dickinson, *Bolingbroke* (1970) Ch. 11, and his *Liberty and Property: Political Ideology in Eighteenth-Century Britain* (1977) pp. 163–92.

44. B. W. Hill, *The Growth of Parliamentary Parties 1689–1742* (1976) Pt iii; J. C. D. Clark, 'The Decline of Party, 1740–1760', *EHR*, xciii (1978) 499–527, and his *The Dynamics of Change: The Crisis of the 1750s and English Party Systems* (Cambridge, 1982) Introduction.

45. *HC*, vol. ii, p. 407; Coxe, *Walpole*, vol. i, pp. 411–2; Colley, *In Defiance*, pp. 76, 79–81, and her 'The Loyal Brotherhood and the Cocoa Tree: the London Organization of the Tory Party, 1727–1760', *HJ*, xx (1977) 77–95.

46. J. B. Owen, *The Rise of the Pelhams* (1957) p. 42.

47. HMC, *Egmont Diary*, vol. i, p. 2; *The Parliamentary Diary of Sir Edward Knatchbull 1722–30*, ed. A. N. Newman (Camden Society, 3rd series, xciv, 1963) pp. 27–8, 30.

48. J. Beckett, 'A Back-Bench M.P. in the Eighteenth Century: Sir John Lowther of Whitehaven', *Parliamentary History*, i (1982) 79–97.

49. Coxe, *Walpole*, vol. ii, p. 520.

50. Chesterfield, *Characters*, p. 31.

51. Sheila Lambert, *Bills and Acts: Legislative Procedure in Eighteenth-Century England* (Cambridge, 1971) pp. 29–51; Thomas, *House of Commons*, pp. 46, 51.

52. *CJ*, vol. xxii, pp. 54, 56; *HC*, vol. i, pp. 465–6; vol. ii, pp. 441–2; Hardwicke, *Walpoliana*, p. 6.

53. Hervey, *Memoirs*, p. 364.

54. Plumb, *Walpole*, vol. ii, p. 253.

55. HMC, *Egmont Diary*, vol. i, pp. 356–9; for a good account of popular

agitation and the press controversy, see P. Langford, *The Excise Crisis* (Oxford, 1975).

56. HMC, *Egmont Diary*, vol. I, p. 46; Cobbett, vol. VIII, cols 706–52, 803–26, 1026–38; *HC*, vol. I, pp. 470–1; vol. II, pp. 21, 77–8, 456–8.

57. Cobbett, vol. VIII, cols 861–3, 936–9, 1124–5, 1142–8; RA 140/203, 153/80, 153/82; BL Add. MSS 32, 779 ff.352–6; HMC, *Egmont Diary*, vol. I, pp. 131, 244–68. For the disappearance of the papers of the South Sea Company see John Carswell, *The South Sea Bubble* (1960) pp. 216–65.

58. *HC*, vol. I, pp. 67–8.

59. HMC, *Egmont Diary*, vol. I, pp. 35–44, 53–4, 56–7; Plumb, *Walpole*, vol. II, pp. 210–17; HMC, *Carlisle MSS*, pp. 68–9.

60. *HC*, vol. I, pp. 37, 43; HMC, *Egmont Diary*, vol. II, p. 150.

61. N. Rogers, 'Resistance to Oligarchy: the City Opposition to Walpole and his Successors, 1725–47', in *London in the Age of Reform*, ed. J. Stevenson (Oxford, 1977) pp. 1–29; I. G. Doolittle, 'Walpole's City Elections Act (1725)', *EHR*, XCVII (1982) 504–29.

62. *HC*, vol. I, p. 45, vol. II, p. 342; HMC, *Egmont Diary*, vol. II, pp. 16, 18, 31–2.

63. Chatsworth MSS, Henry Pelham to the Duke of Devonshire, 16 Oct. 1739.

64. *HC*, vol. II, pp. 497–8; Yorke, *Hardwicke*, vol. I, p. 250; Hardwicke, *Walpoliana*, p. 7; H. T. Dickinson, *Walpole and the Whig Supremacy* (1973) p. 181; Owen, *Rise of the Pelhams*, p. 2.

65. Yorke, *Hardwicke*, vol. I, p. 253.

66. Cruickshanks, *Political Untouchables*, pp. 25–6; Thomas, *House of Commons*, pp. 2, 246.

67. Dickinson, *Bolingbroke*, p. 269; Colley, *In Defiance*, pp. 228, 230.

68. Yale University, Beinecke Library, Osborn Collection, Duchess of Marlborough to Lord Stair, 21 Feb. 1741. I am grateful to Stephen Parks for providing me with a photocopy of this letter.

69. National Library of Scotland MSS 7044, ff.158–9, William Pulteney to Lord Tweeddale, 1 Mar. 1741.

70. *HC*, vol. I, p. 46; Horace Walpole, *Correspondence*, ed. W. S. Lewis (Yale edn, New Haven, Conn., 1937–83) vol. XVII, p. 220; W. A. Speck, ' "The Most Corrupt Council in Christendom": Decisions in Controverted Elections, 1702–42', in *Party and Management in Parliament*, ed. C. Jones, pp. 107–21; *CJ*, vol. XXIV, p. 297; Chatsworth MSS, Lord Hartington to the Duke of Devonshire, 27 Dec. 1741, and Edward Walpole to same, 9 Jan. 1742.

71. *HC*, vol. II, pp. 1–2, 204–5; Lewis (ed.), *Walpole Correspondence*, vol. XVII, pp. 242, 298; Owen, *Rise of the Pelhams*, pp. 3, 13–4, 18–33.

72. Coxe, *Walpole*, vol. III, p. 592.

2. POPULAR POLITICS IN THE AGE OF WALPOLE   H. T. Dickinson

1. See especially J. H. Plumb, *The Growth of Political Stability in England 1675–1725* (London, 1967) Ch. 6, and John Cannon, *Parliamentary Reform 1640–1832* (Cambridge, 1973) Ch. 2.

2. Romney Sedgwick, *The House of Commons 1715–1754*, 2 vols (London, 1970) vol. I.

3. J. G. A. Pocock, 'The Classical Theory of Deference', *AHR*, LXXXI (1976) 516–23.

4. BL Add. MS 32689, f.7; W. Hay to Newcastle, 3 Nov. 1733. Cf. William Ferguson, 'Dingwall Burgh Politics and the Parliamentary Franchise in the Eighteenth Century', *SHR*, XXXVIII (1959) 100–7.

5. Sedgwick, *House of Commons*, vol. I, p. 203.

6. Linda Colley, *In Defiance of Oligarchy: The Tory Party 1714–60* (Cambridge, 1982) pp. 162–6.

7. Paul Langford, *The Excise Crisis: Society and Politics in the Age of Walpole* (Oxford, 1975) pp. 113, 130.

8. Ibid., pp. 124–30.

9. I. G. Doolittle, 'The Half Moon Tavern, Cheapside and City Politics', *Trans. London and Middlesex Archaeological Soc.*, XXVIII (1977) 328–32; and Nicholas Rogers, 'Resistance to Oligarchy: the City Opposition to Walpole and his Successors, 1725–47', in *London in the Age of Reform*, ed. John Stevenson (Oxford, 1977) p. 13.

10. Nicholas Rogers, 'Aristocratic Clientage, Trade and Independency: Popular Politics in Pre-Radical Westminster', *P & P*, 63 (1973) 75, 94–6.

11. Sedgwick, *House of Commons*, vol. I, pp. 244–5.

12. Linda Colley, 'Eighteenth-Century English Radicalism before Wilkes', *TRHS*, 5th series, XXXI (1981) 7–9; Colley, *In Defiance of Oligarchy*, p. 138.

13. Sedgwick, *House of Commons*, vol. I, p. 340.

14. Colley, *In Defiance of Oligarchy*, p. 163.

15. Sheila Lambert (ed.), *House of Commons Sessional Papers of the Eighteenth Century*, 2 vols (Wilmington, Delaware, 1975–6) vol. I, pp. 31–2.

16. Lucy Sutherland, *The East India Company in Eighteenth-Century Politics* (Oxford, 1952) pp. 17–30; Lucy Sutherland, 'The City of London in Eighteenth-Century Politics', in *Essays Presented to Sir Lewis Namier*, ed. Richard Pares and A. J. P. Taylor (London, 1956) pp. 49–74; Gerald B. Hertz, 'England and the Ostend Company', *EHR* XXII (1907) 255–79; and N. C. Hunt, 'The Russia Company and the Government, 1730–42', *Oxford Slavonic Papers*, VII (1957) 27–65.

17. Lillian M. Penson, 'The London West India Interest in the Eighteenth Century', *EHR*, XXXVI (1921) 373–92; and Richard B. Sheridan, 'The Molasses Act and the Market Strategy of the British Sugar Planters', *JEH*, XVII (1957) 62–83.

18. For the dissenting pressure groups in the age of Walpole see N. C. Hunt, *Two Early Political Associations* (Oxford, 1961).

19. Ibid., p. 159.

20. Cobbett, vol. VIII, col. 1305–6.

21. See especially Lucy Sutherland, 'Edmund Burke and the Relations between Members of Parliament and their Constituents', *Studies in Burke and His Times* (1968) vol. X, pp. 1005–8. This view has been challenged by Langford, *Excise Crisis*, Ch. 4; Linda Colley, 'The Tory Party, 1727–1760' (Cambridge University, unpublished Ph.D. dissertation, 1976) pp. 110–11,

156–8, 163–4; Thomas Perry, *Public Opinion, Propaganda and Politics in Eighteenth-Century England* (Cambridge, Mass., 1962); and Marie Peters, *Pitt and Popularity* (Oxford, 1980) pp. 46–57.

22. Langford, *Excise Crisis*, Appendix A.

23. Ibid., Ch. 4; and Rogers, 'Resistance to Oligarchy', p. 6.

24. These details are from Langford, *Excise Crisis*, Ch. 8 and especially pp. 52–3.

25. Rogers, 'Resistance to Oligarchy', pp. 7–13.

26. Ibid., p. 12.

27. Colley, *In Defiance of Oligarchy*, p. 166.

28. Ibid., p. 168.

29. *Gentleman's Magazine*, XII (1742) 159–61, 217, 274.

30. *The Several Addresses of the Merchant Company and Corporations of Edinburgh, to the Magistrates and Town Council thereof* (Edinburgh, 1739).

31. *Common Sense*, 20 Oct. 1739.

32. BL Add. MS 35406, f.159; quoted by Rogers, 'Resistance to Oligarchy', p. 9.

33. Quoted by Sedgwick, *House of Commons*, vol. I, p. 282.

34. For this account of London politics see N. Rogers, 'Resistance to Oligarchy', pp. 2–7; and Alfred James Henderson, *London and the National Government, 1721–1742* (Durham, N.C., 1945), *passim*.

35. I. G. Doolittle, 'Walpole's City Elections Act (1725)', *EHR*, XCVII (1982) 504–29.

36. Rogers, 'Aristocratic Clientage', pp. 73–5, 78–83.

37. See the borough entries in Sedgwick, *House of Commons*, vol. I.

38. PRO SPD 35/32: S. Legge to Townshend, 30 Aug. 1722.

39. Sedgwick, *House of Commons*, vol. I, p. 203; and John Stevenson, *Popular Disturbances in England 1700–1870* (London, 1979) p. 24.

40. See especially D. G. D. Isaac, 'A Study of Popular Disturbances in Britain 1714–1754' (Edinburgh University, unpublished Ph.D. dissertation, 1953); John Stevenson, *Popular Disturbances*; and George Rudé, *Paris and London in the Eighteenth Century* (London, 1970).

41. Nicholas Rogers, 'Riot and Popular Jacobitism in Early Hanoverian England', in *Ideology and Conspiracy: Aspects of Jacobitism, 1689–1759*, ed. Eveline Cruickshanks (Edinburgh, 1982) p. 83.

42. PRO SPD 35/27: item 15.

43. Ibid., 35/54: items 54–8.

44. Nicholas Rogers, 'Popular Protest in Early Hanoverian England', *P & P*, 79 (1978) 70–100.

45. Rogers, 'Riot and Popular Jacobitism', pp. 81–5.

46. George Rudé, *Paris and London*, pp. 218–20.

47. BL Add. MS 32690, f.84: to Newcastle, 28 Sept. 1735.

48. Pat Rogers, 'The Waltham Blacks and the Black Act', *HJ*, XVII (1974) 465–86; and E. P. Thompson, *Whigs and Hunters* (London, 1975).

49. Isaac, 'Popular Disturbancies in Britain', pp. 104–21.

50. H. T. Dickinson and K. J. Logue, 'The Porteous Riot', *History Today*, XXII (1972) 272–81.

51. C. R. Dobson, *Masters and Journeymen* (London, 1980) pp. 61–2; Isaac, 'Popular Disturbances in Britain', pp. 51–78; and John Stevenson, *Popular Disturbances*, p. 114.

52. Isaac, 'Popular Disturbances in Britain', pp. 92–103; and John Stevenson, *Popular Disturbances*, pp. 120–1.

53. Isaac, 'Popular Disturbances in Britain', pp. 51–78; and J. De L. Mann, 'Clothiers and Weavers in Wiltshire during the Eighteenth Century', in *Studies in the Industrial Revolution*, ed. L. S. Pressnell (London, 1960) pp. 66–96.

54. G. A. Cranfield, *The Development of the Provincial Newspaper 1700–1760* (Oxford, 1962) Ch. 6.

55. Laurence Hanson, *Government and the Press 1695–1763* (Oxford, 1936) pp. 64, 67–9, 108–12; and F. S. Siebert, *Freedom of the Press in England 1476–1776* (Urbana, Il., 1865) pp. 318–20, 340–4, 382–3.

56. G. A. Cranfield, 'The *London Evening Post*, 1727–1744: a Study in the Development of the Political Press', *HJ*, vi (1963) 20–37.

57. For these details about the provincial press see Cranfield, *Provincial Newspaper*, Chs 6 and 7.

58. BL Add. MS 32695, vol. ii, f.391: 11 Nov. 1740.

59. J. Trenchard and T. Gordon, *Cato's Letters*, 4 vols (5th edn, London, 1748). Some of the best of their essays are reprinted in David L. Jacobson (ed.), *The English Libertarian Heritage* (New York, 1965).

60. Thomas Carte, *A Full Answer to the Letter from a Bystander* (London, 1742) p. 206; The *Craftsman* quoted in the *Gentleman's Magazine*, iv (1734) 281, and, xi (1741) 378; and *Common Sense*, 15 Apr. 1739, 6 Oct. 1739 and 10 Jan. 1741.

61. *London Journal*, 9 Sept. 1732.

62. *The Livery-Man: Or Plain Thoughts on Public Affairs* (London, 1740) pp. 7, 56, quoted by Colley, *In Defiance of Oligarchy*, p. 169.

63. [John Campbell], *The Case of the Opposition Impartially Stated* (London, 1742) pp. 51–2.

3. A CLIENT SOCIETY: SCOTLAND BETWEEN THE '15 AND THE
'45   *Bruce P. Lenman*

1. J. H. Plumb, *Sir Robert Walpole*, vol. i: *The Making of a Statesman* (1956) p. 127.

2. There are several printed versions of the Treaty of Union and of the Act for securing the Protestant Religion and Presbyterian Church Government. Two of the handiest will be found in G. S. Pryde, *The Treaty of Union of Scotland and England, 1707* (Edinburgh, 1950) pp. 81–107, and G. Donaldson, *Scottish Historical Documents* (Edinburgh, 1970) pp. 268–77. (This latter, as the pagination suggests, contains an abbreviated version of the Articles of Union.)

3. T. C. Smout, *Scottish Trade on the Eve of Union, 1660–1707* (Edinburgh, 1963) pp. 244–53.

4. Carstares to Harley, 24 Oct. 1706, cited in A. I. Dunlop, *William Carstares and the Kirk by Law Established* (Edinburgh, 1967) p. 115.

5. N. T. Phillipson, 'The Social Structure of the Faculty of Advocates', in A. Harding (ed.), *Law-Making and Law-Makers in British History* (1980) pp. 146–56.

6. J. S. Shaw, *The Management of Scottish Society 1707–1764* (Edinburgh, 1983) pp. 21–35.

7. Sir Andrew Agnew of Lochnaw, *The Hereditary Sheriffs of Galloway* (2nd edn, Edinburgh, 1893) vol. II, p. 332.

8. For a survey of Scottish franchise courts and their extant records see P. Rayner, B. Lenman and G. Parker, *Handlist of Records for the Study of Crime in Early Modern Scotland (to 1747)*, List and Index Society, Special Series (1982) vol. 16, pp. 113–43.

9. The view is T. C. Smout's in M. Flinn *et al.* (ed.), *Scottish Population History from the 17th Century to the 1930s* (Cambridge, 1977) p. 200. For Webster's survey see J. G. Kyd (ed.), *Scottish Population Statistics including Webster's Analysis of Population 1755*, Scottish History Society, 3rd series, vol. XLIV (Edinburgh, 1952).

10. E. A. Wrigley and R. S. Schofield, *The Population History of England 1541–1871: A Reconstruction* (1981) pp. 173–4.

11. For a survey of the physical setting and developments to c. 1730 see B. Lenman, *An Economic History of Modern Scotland* (1977) Chs 1–3.

12. R. A. Dodgshon, *Land and Society in Early Scotland* (Oxford, 1981), and I. Whyte, *Agriculture and Society in Seventeenth-Century Scotland* (Edinburgh, 1979). For Highland social structure see F. J. Shaw, *The Northern and Western Islands of Scotland: Their Economy and Society in the Seventeenth Century* (Edinburgh, 1980).

13. S. G. E. Lythe and J. Butt, *An Economic History of Scotland 1100–1939* (Glasgow, 1975) pp. 112–13.

14. R. Mitchison, 'The Movement of Scottish Corn Prices in the Seventeenth and Eighteenth Centuries', *Economic History Review*, 2nd Series, LVIII (1965) 278–91.

15. D. Defoe, *A Tour Through the Whole Island of Great Britain* (1 vol., Everyman edn, 1974) p. 386.

16. A. J. Durie, *The Scottish Linen Industry in the Eighteenth Century* (Edinburgh, 1979) Chs 1–4.

17. B. F. Duckham, *A History of the Scottish Coal Industry*, vol. I *1700–1815* (Newton Abbot, 1970) is still the best introduction, though the subsequent volume appears to have been jettisoned. For the tramways see C. J. A. Robertson, *The Origins of the Scottish Railway System 1722–1844* (Edinburgh, 1983) Ch. I.

18. H. Hamilton, *An Economic History of Scotland in the Eighteenth Century* (Oxford, 1963) pp. 17–36.

19. J. S. Shaw, *Management of Scottish Society*, Ch. 5.

20. I am extremely grateful to Dr Rab Houston for his kindness in allowing me to read the typescript of his forthcoming book on literacy in early modern Britain with particular reference to Scotland and the north of England. The origins and affiliations of Scottish MPs in this period are admirably set out in Romney Sedgwick, *The History of Parliament: The House of Commons 1715–1754*, 2

vols (1970). The Scottish contribution to the great speculative manias of the era may be traced in G. P. Insh, *The Company of Scotland* (1932); H. Montgomery Hyde, *John Law* (1969); John Carswell, *The South Sea Bubble* (1961); and J. N. M. Maclean, *Reward is Secondary* (1963). For the involvement of the Duke of Montrose in the South Sea Bubble and for his over-optimistic hopes, see Montrose to Mungo Graham of Gorthie, 2 June, 30 June, 13 Aug. 1720, SRO, GD220/5/833/1 and 14 resp., CD220/5/834/7a.

21. Viscount Primrose to 3rd Earl of Loudon, 22 July 1714, HL MS LO 12455, Loudon Papers.

22. Viscount Primrose to 3rd Earl of Loudon, 26 Nov. 1737, HL MS LO 9309.

23. 1st Earl of Rosebery to 3rd Earl of Loudon, 27 May and 24 June 1707, HL MS LO 9311 and LO 9310.

24. Viscount Primrose to 3rd Earl of Loudon, 1 Jan. 1724, HL MS LO 9303.

25. 2nd Earl of Rosebery to 4th Earl of Loudon, c. Feb. 1738, HL MS LO 7249.

26. 2nd Earl of Rosebery to 4th Earl of Loudon, 17 Feb. 1739, HL MS LO 7233, plus enclosed note, MS LO 7232, and petition to Sir Robert Walpole MS LO 7235.

27. Rosebery to Loudon, 3 Apr. 1739, HL MS LO 7236.

28. Rosebery to Loudon, 15 May 1739, HL MS LO 7238.

29. Rosebery to Loudon, 14 Feb. 1740, HL MS LO 7241; and Mar. 1740, HL MS LO 7242.

30. Rosebery to Loudon, 28 Nov. 1740, HL MS LO 12462; and 19 Mar. 1741, HL MS LO 7244.

31. 1st Duke of Montrose to Mungo Graham of Gorthie, 13 Mar. 1719, SRO GD220/5/828/23.

32. 'An Account of all I owe in England', Mar. 1727, shows his gaming debts, HL MS LO 9313, and Rosebery to Loudon, 11 Apr. 1741, shows his martial plans, MS LO 7245.

33. DNB, vol. xxxix, has a convenient biography of Mansfield. A less satisfactory account of John Snell will be found in *ibid*., vol. liii.

34. W. L. Burn, 'Memorandum on the 18th century MSS in the Loudon (Scotch) collection'. This typescript, dated 10 Oct. 1933 and preserved at the Huntington Library, California, is not only the best working guide to the papers but also contains Burns's preliminary conclusions on material he was working on with a view to submitting an application for financial support from the Huntington. The work was a generation ahead of the scholarship of its day. The application appears to have been unsuccessful.

35. Sir James Campbell to 3rd Earl of Loudon, 10 Aug. 1725, HL MS LO 8138.

36. Campbell to Loudon, 12 Aug. 1725, HL MS LO 8112.

37. Campbell to Loudon, 24 Aug. 1725, HL MS LO 8086.

38. Campbell to Loudon, 2 Sept. 1725, HL MS LO 8093.

39. Campbell to Loudon, 11 Sept. 1725, HL MS LO 8104.

40. Campbell to Loudon, 30 Aug. 1725, HL MS LO 8085.

41. There is no satisfactory modern biography of the 2nd Duke of Argyll

because of the unavailability of the Inverary Archives, but the *DNB*, vol. VIII gives the bare bones of his career succinctly.

42. For the background to, and motivation for, the Jacobite risings see B. P. Lenman, *The Jacobite Risings in Britain 1689–1746* (1980).

43. Lord Grange to 3rd Earl of Loudon, 2 Sept. 1715, HL MS LO 11428; and 10 Sept. 1715, MS LO 11429.

44. Grange to Loudon, 31 Jan. 1716, HL MS LO 8838; 25 Mar. 1725, MS LO 8837; and 9 Apr. 1717, MS LO 8842.

45. Grange to Loudon, 25 June 1717, HL MS LO 8843.

46. For a general introduction to Scots Law see *An Introductory Survey of the Sources and Literature of Scots Law*, Stair Society (Edinburgh, 1936) vol. I. The most convenient account of Grange is still *DNB*, vol. XVII.

47. B. Lenman, 'The Scottish Episcopal Clergy and the Ideology of Jacobitism', in E. Cruickshanks (ed.), *Ideology and Conspiracy: Aspects of Jacobitism* (Edinburgh, 1982) pp. 36–48.

48. Lord Grange to 3rd Earl of Loudon, 21 Mar. 1727, HL MS LO 8852.

49. Grange to Loudon, 12 July 1727, HL MS LO 8851.

50. P. W. J. Riley, *The English Ministers and Scotland 1707–1727* (1964) esp. Ch. XVI.

51. Lord Grange to 3rd Earl of Loudon, 26 Jan. 1727, HL MS LO 8845.

52. H. R. Sefton, 'Lord Ilay and Patrick Cumming: a Study in Eighteenth-Century Ecclesiastical Management', *Scottish Church History Society Records*, vol. XIX (1977) pp. 203–16.

53. Sir James Steuart of Goodtrees to Montrose, 10 Mar. 1715, SRO, GD220/5/475/2.

54. A. R. MacEwen, *The Erskines* (Edinburgh, 1900). For the early history of 'Moderate' views see the opening sections of I. D. L. Clark, 'Moderatism and the Moderate Party in the Church of Scotland 1752–1805' (King's College, Cambridge University, Ph.D., dissertation 1964).

55. John H. Simpson, 'Who Steered the Gravy Train, 1707–1766?', in N. T. Phillipson and R. Mitchison (eds), *Scotland in the Age of Improvement* (Edinburgh, 1970) pp. 56–7.

56. Henry Pelham to Robert Trevor, 21 Sept. 1745, quoted in J. T. Findlay, *Wolfe in Scotland* (1928) pp. 50–1.

4. WALPOLE AND IRELAND   *David Hayton*

1. Walpole to Grafton, 3 Oct. 1723, quoted in A. Goodwin, 'Wood's Halfpence', *EHR*, LI (1936) 656.

2. This interpretation is particularly associated with J. H. Plumb. See, for example, *Sir Robert Walpole: The King's Minister* (1960) p. 67; *The Growth of Political Stability in England 1675–1725* (1967) pp. 182–4.

3. For example, J. C. Beckett, *The Making of Modern Ireland 1603–1923*, 2nd edn (1981) pp. 188–91; F. G. James, *Ireland in the Empire 1688–1770* (Cambridge, Mass., 1973) pp. 131–3, 164–5. The inference of a causal connection between the crisis over Wood's Halfpence and the institution of an 'undertaker system' seems to have originated with J. L. McCracken, 'The

Undertakers in Ireland and their Relations with the Lords Lieutenant 1724–1771' (Queen's University, Belfast, MA thesis, 1941), the first full-length study of the subject. See Chs II–III, esp. pp. 52–4.

4. NLI MSS 8802/3: Edward Cooke to William Fownes, n.d. (1730?).

5. BL Add. MSS 21,122, f.15: Marmaduke Coghill to Edward Southwell, 18 Aug. 1724.

6. E. Gregg, *Queen Anne* (1980) p. 130.

7. F. G. James, 'The Irish Lobby in the Early Eighteenth Century', *EHR*, LXXXI (1966) 543–57; R. Sedgwick, *The House of Commons 1715–1754* (1970) vol. I, pp. 156–8.

8. For what follows, in this and the succeeding paragraph, see D. Hayton, 'The Beginnings of the "Undertaker System"', in T. Bartlett and D. Hayton (eds), *Penal Era and Golden Age: Essays in Irish History 1690–1800* (Belfast, 1979) pp. 41–50.

9. PRO SP63/375/208: Godwin to Charles Delafaye, 9 Oct. 1717.

10. W. Coxe, *Memoirs of the Life and Administration of Sir Robert Walpole* (1798) vol. II, p. 174.

11. Sedgwick, *House of Commons*, vol. I, p. 490; Coxe, *Walpole*, vol. II, pp. 175–80.

12. BL Add. MSS 47,029, ff. 16–18: Abercorn to Lord Perceval, 18 Feb. 1720.

13. PRO C108/421: Arthur St Leger to Lord Londonderry, 5 Aug. 1720.

14. Walpole MSS (Lord Walpole, Wolterton Hall, Norfolk): Sunderland and Stanhope to Craggs, n.d.; 'Minutes about Ireland 20/21 June 1720'; Sunderland to Walpole, 21 Sept. 1720; 'Memorial relating to schemes proposed for making ... savings upon the military ... establishment of Ireland ...'; PRO SP67/7/81: Craggs to Grafton, 4 Oct. 1720. I am very grateful to Lord Walpole for permission to consult his manuscripts.

15. Walpole MSS: Walpole to Sunderland, 11 Oct. 1720; Grafton to Craggs, 17 Oct. 1720.

16. Sedgwick, *House of Commons*, vol. I, p. 490; Public Record Office of Northern Ireland, T.2825/A/1/17: Conolly to Grafton, 11 May 1721; Surrey RO, Guildford Muniment Room, 1248/5, f.35: Thomas Brodrick to Midleton, 30 May 1721; Sir R. G. A. Levinge, *Jottings of the Levinge Family* (Dublin, 1877) p. 65. No notice is taken of these manoeuvres in J. H. Plumb, *Sir Robert Walpole: The Making of a Statesman* (1956), where St John Brodrick appears (p. 377) as a Tory. I must thank the Deputy Keeper, PRO Northern Ireland, for making available to me documents and transcripts in his care.

17. W. Philips, *St. Stephen's Green* ..., ed. C. Murray (Dublin, 1980) pp. 17–20.

18. BL Add. MSS 47,029, f.33: James Macartney *et al.* to Perceval, 2 June 1720; Add. MSS 34,778, f.33: Thomas Medlicott to Edward Southwell, 3 Apr. 1721.

19. BL Add. MSS 21,122, f.7: Coghill to Southwell, 31 Jan. 1722[–3].

20. *The Journals of the House of Commons of the Kingdom of Ireland 1613–1776* (1753–76) vol. V, pp. 60–1; R. Hatton, *George I, Elector and King* (1978) p. 369, n.23.

21. J. Swift, *The Drapier's Letters*, ed. H. Davis (Oxford, 1935) pp. xviii–xlii; Devonshire MSS (the Duke of Devonshire, Chatsworth House, Derbyshire):

Hale to Devonshire, 10 Sept. 1724 (I owe this reference to Dr A. P. W. Malcomson).

22. Goodwin, 'Wood's Halfpence', 656.

23. PRO SP63/381/141–3: Walpole to Grafton, 24 Sept. 1723.

24. Coxe, *Walpole*, vol. II, pp. 276–8; PRO SP63/381/145–6: Grafton to Walpole, 24 Sept. 1723.

25. Coxe, *Walpole*, vol. II, p. 350.

26. PRO SP63/381/141–3, 190–1: Walpole to Grafton, 24 Sept., 3 Oct. 1723.

27. BL Add. MSS 32,686, f.362: Walpole to Newcastle, 24 Oct. 1723; West Suffolk RO 423/885: Walpole to Grafton, 26 Oct. 1723; Coxe, *Walpole*, vol. II, p. 282.

28. BL Add. MSS 32,686, f.372: Newcastle to Walpole, 28 Oct. 1723; Coxe, *Walpole*, vol. II, p. 350; W. Suffolk RO 423/888: Grafton to Townshend, 19 Jan. 1724.

29. Plumb, *Walpole: The King's Minister*, pp. 68–9.

30. Christ Church, Oxford, Wake MSS, vol. XIV (unfoliated): Bishop Godwin to Archbishop Wake, 5 Oct. 1723; PRO SP63/381/135: Midleton to Walpole, 21 Sept. 1723; Coxe, *Walpole*, vol. II, pp. 354–6.

31. BL Add. MSS 32,686, f.357: Newcastle to Walpole, 22 Oct. 1723; W. Suffolk RO 423/887: Townshend to Grafton, 7 Jan. 1724; Coxe, *Walpole*, vol. II, p. 363.

32. Guildford Mun. Room 1248/5, ff. 324, 344–5: Midleton to Thomas Brodrick, 21 Oct., 28 Dec. 1723; BL Add. MSS 47,030, ff. 57–8, Philip Perceval to Lord Perceval, 30 Jan. 1724.

33. Coxe, *Walpole*, vol. II, pp. 286, 364; Guildford Mun. Room 1248/5, ff. 360–1: St John Brodrick to Midleton, 17 Jan. 1724.

34. BL Add. MSS 32,687, f.54: Walpole to Newcastle, 1 Sept. 1724.

35. PRO C110/46/313: O. Gallagher to Oliver St George, 9 Jan. 1725.

36. Guildford Mun. Room 1248/5, ff. 165–6, 213: Midleton to Thomas Brodrick, 12 Mar., 29 Apr. 1725; Christ Church, Wake MSS, vol. XIV: John Pocklington to Wake, 19 Aug. 1725; BL Add. MSS 21,122, ff. 24–5: Marmaduke Coghill to Edward Southwell, 30 Oct. 1725; *Letters Written by His Excellency Hugh Boulter* (Dublin, 1770) vol. I, p. 39.

37. BL Add. MSS 32,687, f.54: Walpole to Newcastle, 1 Sept. 1724.

38. *Drapier's Letters*, ed. Davis, pp. lvi, lx; James, *Ireland in the Empire*, pp. 122–3.

39. BL Add. MSS 38,016, f.7: Carteret to Edward Southwell, 1 Mar. 1726.

40. Coxe, *Walpole*, vol. II, p. 356.

41. McCracken, 'Undertakers and Lords Lieutenant', Ch III; J. Griffin, 'Parliamentary Politics in Ireland during the Reign of George I' (National University of Ireland, MA thesis, 1977) p. 168 *et seq.*

42. BL Add. MSS 21,123, f.32: Coghill to Southwell, 2 Apr. 1733; McCracken, 'Undertakers and Lords Lieutenant', Ch. III; *Boulter Letters*, vol. I, pp. 139–40, 164.

43. PRO Northern Ireland, T.2774: Thomas Tickell to Carteret, 23 June 1727; T.2534/2: Coghill to Southwell, 13 June 1728; *Boulter Letters*, vol. I, pp. 265, 267, 269.

44. PRO SP63/391/254: Carteret to Townshend, 14 Dec. 1729; BL Add. MSS 38,016, f.17: Carteret to ——, 26 Dec. 1729.

45. J. B. Owen, *The Rise of the Pelhams* (1957) pp. 12–14, 100; A. S. Foord, *His Majesty's Opposition 1714–1830* (Oxford, 1964) pp. 122–3.

46. NLI Wicklow MSS: Bishop Howard to Hugh Howard, 12 Oct., 2 Nov. 1731.

47. Ibid.: Bishop Howard to Hugh Howard, 12 Oct. 1731.

48. *Pue's Occurrences*, 14 Sept., 2, 20, 23 Nov., 11 Dec. 1731; 4 Jan., 5 Feb., 25 Mar. 1732.

49. Spencer MSS (Earl Spencer, Althorp, Northamptonshire), Burlington papers, box 1: Henry Boyle to Lord Burlington, 5, 10 Nov. 1731; NLI MSS 11478: Lord Palmerston to William Flower, 3 Mar. 1732. I am indebted to Professor E. Gregg for references to the Spencer MSS.

50. HMC, *Stopford–Sackville MSS*, vol. I, p. 147; D. Hayton, 'Divisions in the Whig Junto in 1709: Some Irish Evidence', *BIHR*, LV (1982) 209–12.

51. BL Add. MSS 28,123, f.44: Coghill to Southwell, 28 Jan. 1732; National Library of Wales, Add. MSS 3,582D: Lord Barrymore to Francis Price, 29 Jan. 1732.

52. HMC, *Stopford–Sackville MSS*, vol. I, p. 147.

53. BL Add. MSS 21,122, f.102: Coghill to Southwell, 25 Dec. 1729; Add. MSS 21,123, ff. 20, 32–4, 41–2, 53: Coghill to Southwell, 22 Feb., 5 Apr., 21 June, 26 Sept. 1733; Spencer MSS, Burlington papers, box 1: Boyle to Burlington, 29 Sept. 1733. Carter's friendship with Boyle is evinced by the letters from him which survive in Boyle's private papers: see PRO Northern Ireland, D.2707, *passim*.

54. HMC, *Egmont Diary*, vol. I, p. 463.

55. BL Add. MSS 21,123, ff. 62, 64: Coghill to Southwell, 20 Oct., 20 Nov. 1733; Add. MSS 46,984, ff. 214–16: William Taylor to Lord Egmont, 11 Dec. 1733.

56. BL Add. MSS 21,123, f.12: Coghill to Southwell, 4 Dec. 1732 [*recte* 1733].

57. HMC, *Various Collections*, vol. VI, pp. 61–2.

58. James, *Ireland in the Empire*, pp. 164–5.

59. PRO Northern Ireland, D.2707/A/1/7: Lords Justices to Dorset, 27 May 1735.

60. BL Add. MSS 21,123, f.27: Coghill to Southwell, 15 Mar. 1732[–3].

61. Ibid., ff.27,62: Coghill to Southwell, 15 Mar., 20 Oct. 1733. My reading of Boyle's character has benefited a great deal from discussions with Professor E. M. Johnston and Dr D. P. O'Donovan.

62. NLI Wicklow MSS: Bishop Howard to Hugh Howard, 20 Nov. 1735; HMC, *Various Collections*, vol. VI, pp. 64–7.

63. James, 'Irish Lobby', 555.

64. Sedgwick, *House of Commons*, vol. II, pp. 206–7, 474.

65. J. L. McCracken, 'The Conflict between the Irish Administration and Parliament, 1753–1756', *Irish Historical Studies*, III (1942–3) 160; BL Add. MSS 35,586, ff.174, 178: Robert Jocelyn to Hardwicke, 21 Aug. 1739, Devonshire to Hardwicke, 28 Aug. 1739; Add. MSS 47,008A, f.33: William

Taylor to Lord Egmont, 23 Nov. 1739; PRO SP63/404/240: Devonshire to Newcastle, 24 Nov. 1741.

5. ECONOMIC POLICY AND ECONOMIC DEVELOPMENT Michael Jubb

1. Phyllis Deane and W. A. Cole, *British Economic Growth, 1688–1959: Trends and Structure*, 2nd edn (Cambridge, 1967) p. 78.

2. J. D. Chambers, *The Vale of Trent, 1670–1800*, Economic History Review, Supplement 3 (1957); Charles Wilson, *England's Apprenticeship, 1603–1763* (London, 1965) pt III; Anthony J. Little *Deceleration in the Eighteenth-Century British Economy* (London, 1976).

3. E. A. Wrigley and R. S. Schofield, *The Population of England 1541–1871: A Reconstruction* (London, 1981).

4. Deane and Cole, *British Economic Growth*, Ch. II; Little, *Deceleration in 18th-Century British Economy*.

5. A. H. John, 'The Course of Agriculture Change, 1660–1760', in L. S. Pressnell (ed.), *Studies in the Industrial Revolution* (London, 1960); E. L. Jones (ed.), *Agriculture and Economic Growth in England 1650–1815* (London, 1967), and *Agriculture and the Industrial Revolution* (Oxford, 1974). See also articles by E. L. Jones, N. C. R. Crafts and W. A. Cole in Roderick Floud and Donald McCloskey (eds), *The Economic History of Britain since 1700*, vol. I (Cambridge, 1981).

6. W. A. Cole, 'Factors in Demand 1700–1800', in Floud and McCloskey (eds), *Economic History of Britain*.

7. Wrigley and Schofield, *Population of England*.

8. Cobbett, vol. VII, col. 911; 8 Geo I c. 15.

9. John Bennett, *The National Merchant; or Discourses on Commerce and Colonies* (1736) p. 6.

10. Phyllis Deane, 'The Output of the Woollen Industry in the Eighteenth Century', *JEH*, XVII, no. 2 (1957) 208–22.

11. PRO SP36/25 f.194.

12. *CJ*, XXIII, 70, 154–5.

13. See, for example, [Simon Smith], *The Golden Fleece* (1736); David Bindon, *Some Thoughts on the Woollen Manufacture of England* (1731).

14. Some of the manoeuvrings are recorded in HMC, *Egmont Diary*, vol. 2, pp. 150–69.

15. See, for example, John Smith, *Chronicon Rusticum-Commerciale: or Memoirs of Wool* (1747), which in addition to advancing wool growers' views reprints a large number of earlier pamphlets relating to the woollen industry. For the west country industry see J. de L. Mann, 'Clothiers and Weavers in Wiltshire in the Eighteenth Century', in L. S. Pressnell (ed.), *Studies in the Industrial Revolution* (1960).

16. MSS 89/54/2; PRO CO 389/29/72.

17. *CJ*, XX, 784.

18. HMC, *Portland MSS*, vol. v, p. 594; PRO CO 388/22 Q 142.

19. P. G. M. Dickson, 'English Commercial Negotiations with Austria, 1737–1750', in A. Whiteman *et al.* (eds), *Statesmen, Scholars and Merchants* (Oxford, 1972).

20. R. B. Sheridan, 'The Molasses Act and the Market Strategy of the British Sugar Planters', *JEH*, xvii, no. 1 (1957).

21. For the attempts to secure colonial timber supplies see R. G. Albion, *Forests and Sea Power* (1926). For attempts relating to other naval stores see the *Journal of the Commissioners for Trade and Plantations* (Cambridge, Mass., HMSO, 1920–38) vols. iv–vii, *passim*.

22. See R. A. Pelham, 'The West Midland Iron Industry and the American Market in the Eighteenth Century', *University of Birmingham Historical Journal*, ii (1950), and George Hammersley, 'The Charcoal Iron Industry and its Fuel, 1540–1750', *Economic History Review*, 2nd ser., xxvi (1973).

23. E. Furniss, *The Position of the Labourer in a System of Nationalism* (Boston and New York, 1920).

24. H. Heaton, *The Yorkshire Woollen and Worsted Industries* (1920).

25. J. de L. Mann, 'Clothiers and Weavers'; D. G. D. Isaac, 'A Study of Popular disturbances in Britain, 1714–1754' (Edinburgh University, Ph.D. dissertation, 1953) Ch. 2.

26. Cobbett, vol. x, col. 156.

27. Matthew Decker, *Essay on the Causes of the Decline of Foreign Trade* (1743) pp. 97–9.

28. John Smith, *Chronicon Rusticum-Commerciale*, vol. ii, p. 273.

29. W. R. Ward, *The English Land Tax in the Eighteenth Century* (1953); Colin Brookes, 'Public Finance and Political Stability: the Administration of the Land Tax 1688–1720', *HJ*, xvii, no. 2 (1974).

30. For full details of the scheme, see P. G. M. Dickson, *The Financial Revolution in England* (1967) pp. 84–8.

31. Ibid., Chs 5–6. Dickson's is by far the most authoritative discussion of the South Sea Bubble.

32. *CJ*, xxi, 392.

33. C(H) MSS Correspondence 1948, Josiah Colebrooke to Walpole, 26 Feb. 1733.

34. William Petty, *A Treatise of Taxes and Contributions*, reprinted in C. H. Hull (ed.), *The Economic Writings of Sir William Petty* (Cambridge, 1899) Ch. 15.

35. C(H) MSS 65/40.

36. Robert C. Nash, 'The English and Scottish Tobacco Trades in the Seventeenth and Eighteenth Centuries: Legal and Illegal Trade', *Economic History Review*, 2nd series, xxv, no. 3 (1982) is the most thorough assessment of the extent of tobacco frauds of all kinds.

37. Jacob M. Price, 'The Excise Affair Revisited: the Administrative and Colonial Dimensions of a Parliamentary Crisis', in Stephen Baxter (ed.), *England's Rise to Greatness* (Berkeley, Calif., 1983).

38. C(H) MSS 26/6/1 and Correspondence 1150–1, 24 and 26 July 1724.

39. See, for example, *Gentleman's Magazine*, 11, 1061.

40. HMC, 15th Report vi, Carlisle MSS 95, Lady Irwin to Carlisle, 9 Jan. 1733.

41. *Gentleman's Magazine*, 1, 148.

42. John Hervey, *Some Materials towards Memoirs of the Reign of George II*, ed. Romney Sedgwick (1931) vol. 1, pp. 100–1.

43. *The Craftsman*, no. 564; *Parliamentary History*, x, 91.

44. P. Mathias and P. K. O'Brien, 'Taxation in Britain 1715–1810', *Journal of European Economic History*, vol. 3 (1976).

45. Dickson, *Financial Revolution in England*, p. 210.

6. FOREIGN POLICY IN THE AGE OF WALPOLE *Jeremy Black*

1. 'As liberty has made us a kingdom of politicians; every man who converses with the world, finds himself necessarily engaged in debates of a publick nature: war and peace fill up the conversation of all societies' (*London Journal*, 21 Dec. 1728); *York Courant*, 1 July 1729.

2. There was also opposition in Russia to the role of Holstein influences, and in Spain to the Italian policies of Elizabeth Farnese. PRO SPF 90/19, 94/107: Du Bourgay, envoy in Berlin, to Lord Townshend, Secretary of State for the Northern Department, 3 Oct. (ns) 1725; Keene, envoy in Spain, to Duke of Newcastle, Secretary of State for the Southern Department, 9 Jan. (ns) 1731.

3. Ragnhild Hatton, *George I* (1978); Ragnhild Hatton, 'New Light on George I of Great Britain', in S. Baxter (ed.), *England's Rise to Greatness* (1983); AE Paris, CP Ang. 369: Broglie, French envoy in London, to Chauvelin, French Foreign Minister, 12, 16 Jan. (ns) 1730.

4. Attempts were made to develop trade through the Hanoverian port of Harburg. Import duties were greater on Hanoverian than on Russian lines, PRO SPD 36/10: memorandum about lessening the duties on Hanover linen, 16 Jan. 1729.

5. RO Aylesbury, Trevor MSS 10: Horace Walpole to Trevor, envoy at The Hague, 24 Oct. 1738; BL Add. MSS 9132,35586: 'Project of a Grand Allyance', 5 Oct., Horace Walpole to Lord Chancellor Hardwicke, 10 Oct. 1740.

6. Differences between George I and his British ministers over guaranteeing Julich–Berg to Prussia: Dresden 2673 III: Le Coq, Saxon envoy in London, to Lagnasc, Saxon diplomat, 4 Aug. (ns) 1724; CUL, C(H) correspondence 2349: Horace Walpole to Walpole, 11 Oct. (ns) 1734; RO Aylesbury, Trevor MSS 8, 10: Horace Walpole to Trevor, 26 Apr. 1737, 24 Oct. 1738; PRO SPF 90/49: Frederick the Great: 'family hatreds were generally more violent than others', Dickens, envoy in Berlin, to Harrington, Secretary of State for the Northern Department, 4 Feb. (ns) 1741.

7. Chewton: Tilson, Undersecretary in Northern Department, to Waldegrave, envoy in Vienna, 9 July 1728; HHStA, Vienna, Fonseca, Sinzendorf to Fonseca, Austrian envoy in Paris, 4 Feb. (ns) 1727; BL Add. MSS 37369: Hanoverian minister Bothmer to British diplomats Cadogan and Whitworth, 30 Aug. (ns) 1718.

8. Robinson, envoy in Vienna, complained, in a secret letter to Newcastle,

about George II's impact on Anglo-Austrian relations: BL Add. MSS 32778: 30 Sept. (ns) 1732.

9. AE Paris, CP Ang. 393: Chavigny, French envoy in London, to Chauvelin, 19 Jan. (ns) 1736.

10. Merseburg, 41: Bonet, Prussian envoy in London, to Frederick William I, 29 Mar. (ns) 1718.

11. BL Add. MSS 32686: Walpole to Newcastle, 25 July, 31 Aug. 1723. Walpole: 'by some gentlemen's way of talking, one would imagine that the ministers of England were the ministers of Europe' (Cobbett, vol. ix, col. 208, 19 Jan. 1734).

12. AE Paris, CP Ang. sup. 7, 393: Dubois, French Foreign Minister, to Chammorel, French envoy in London, 2 July (ns) 1723, Chavigny to Chauvelin, 3 May (ns) 1736. HHStA, Vienna, Varia 8: anon. memorandum, 16 Nov. (ns) 1734.

13. PRO SPD 36/19: Walpole to Newcastle, 24 June 1730; Chatsworth, Devonshire papers: Sir Robert Wilmot to Duke of Devonshire, 23 Jan. 1741.

14. PRO SPD 36/13, 36/18, 36/19: Delafaye, Under Secretary in Southern Department, to Newcastle, 31 July 1729, Newcastle to George II, 23 Apr., 25 June 1730, 'Walpole to Newcastle, 24 June 1730; BL Add. MSS 32787: Newcastle to Horace Walpole, 11 Apr. 1735.

15. PRO SPF 43/77: 'The substance of Count Kinsky's conversation with Sir Robert Walpole'; PRO SPD 36/31: Delafaye to Newcastle, 2 May 1734; CUL C(H) papers 26/66: minutes of conference on Austro-Spanish relations, 8 Nov. 1733; BL Add. MSS 32787: Newcastle to Keene, 12 Feb., 3 Apr. 1735; *London Evening Post*, 15 Feb., 21 June 1733.

16. BL Add. MSS 32795: Newcastle to Waldegrave, envoy in Paris 1730–40, 9 June 1737; PRO SPF 90/42, 82/59: Harrington to Dickens, 18 Jan. 1737, Wych, envoy in Hamburg, to Harrington, 4 Nov. (ns) 1738; RO Aylesbury, Trevor MSS 14: Horace Walpole to Trevor, 29 Sept. 1738.

17. BL Eg. 2684: Weston, Undersecretary in Northern Department, to Titley, envoy in Copenhagen, 25 Feb. 1737.

18. PRO SPF 84/301: Chesterfield, envoy in The Hague, to Townshend, 20 July (ns) 1728.

19. PRO SPF 78/187: draft to Horace Walpole, 8 Aug. 1727. For George's role in the drafting of instructions see: PRO SPF 78/189: draft to Horace Walpole, 21 May 1728; BL Add. MSS 32782: Delafaye to Newcastle, 31 July 1733; PRO SPD 36/4, 36/8, SPF 84/297 f. 233–4: George's comments on Newcastle to George, 18 Dec. 1727, 31 Oct. 1728, Harrington to George, no date; Dresden 2676: George told the Prussian envoy Wallenrodt that he was in favour of good relations with all powers but that he would not accept 'anyone treading on his toes' (Le Coq to Augustus II of Saxony–Poland, 25 July (ns) 1727, translated).

20. RO Aylesbury, Trevor MSS 5, 7: Horace Walpole to Trevor, 18 Nov. (ns) 1736, 22 Mar. 1737; BL Add. MSS 9132 f. 98: Mr Walpole's Apology. Horace never knew when to cease giving advice, and he encouraged envoys to maintain a secret correspondence: RO Aylesbury, Trevor MSS 4: Horace Walpole to Trevor, 7 Aug. (ns), 2 Sept. (ns) 1736.

21. BL Add. MSS 32758: Townshend to Horace Walpole, 15 Sept. 1728.

22. Newcastle attempted to keep Walpole in the dark: BL Add. MSS 32693: Newcastle to Harrington, 11 July 1740.

23. PRO SPF 84/368: On 'the clamour of the merchants' waking Newcastle up, Horace Walpole to ——, 8 Nov. (ns) 1737; PRO SPF 94/130: the Spanish first minister La Quadra, told Keene that the British ministry 'ought not to take the noise and clamours of our subjects for well-founded complaints' (Keene to Newcastle, 27 Jan. (ns) 1738); Wellcome Institute for the History of Medicine MSS 5006, diary of Dr Wilkes, p. 47: 'The whole nation was pleas'd' with the declaration of war; BL Add. MSS 9132 f. 99: Mr Walpole's Apology.

24. H. Temperley, 'The Causes of the War of Jenkins' Ear', *TRHS*, 3rd series, 3 (1909).

25. BL Add. MSS 35406: Newcastle to Hardwicke, c. 11 Aug. 1739.

26. In the 1730s British ministers were increasingly dissatisfied with the unwillingness of the Dutch to assist them. The financially weak Dutch were angry about the British failure to consult them. BL Add. MSS 32784: Newcastle to Waldegrave, 20 Apr. 1734; RO Aylesbury, Trevor MSS 24: Horace Walpole to Trevor, 13 Nov. 1740.

27. PRO SPF 84/359: 'our situation with Spain . . . is much like that we stand in to ye rest of the world . . . Good words and nothing else' (Trevor to Weston, 21 Sept. (ns) 1736). BL Add. MSS 23798: Weston to Robinson, 23 Apr. 1736. This was defended by ministerial newspapers, *Hyp-Doctor*, 23 Mar., 13 Apr. 1736.

28. Hardwicke, Cobbett, vol. xi, col. 677, 18 Nov. 1740.

29. PRO SPF 90/44, 90/48: Dickens to Harrington, 21 June (ns) 1738, 6 Dec. (ns) 1740; PRO SPF 90/25, 81/123: Du Bourgay to Townshend, 27 Aug. (ns) 1729, Townshend to Sutton, on mission to Copenhagen, 2 Sept. (ns) 1729.

30. U. Dann, 'Hanover and Great Britain 1740–60' (Oxford University, D.Phil. dissertation, 1981). 'Hanover' as a term of analysis conceals the internal rivalries and policy disputes frequent among Hanoverian ministers: Staatsarchiv Darmstadt, F23, Schulenburg-Görtz correspondence, *passim*.

31. *The Lyttelton Papers*, Southeby's catalogue for sale of 12 Dec. 1978, p. 115: Bolingbroke to George Lyttelton, 4 Nov. 1741; BL Add. MSS 32993 f. 164: ministerial memorandum, 'Heads of Business', Aug. 1741; *Common Sense*, 31 Oct. 1741.

32. Pulteney, Cobbett, vol. xi, col. 944, 10 Dec. 1740; BL Add. MSS 32697: 'now America must be fought for in Europe' (Hardwicke to Newcastle, 17 Aug. 1741).

33. D. Baugh, *British Naval Administration in the Age of Walpole* (Princeton, N.J., 1965).

34. BL Add. MSS 61467 f. 33: Earl of Stair, former envoy in Paris, to Sarah Marlborough, no date.

35. PRO SPF 91/24: the instructions for Edward Finch, sent to Russia in 1740 to negotiate an alliance, referred to an Anglo-Russian alliance as 'one of the chief securitys which seems to remain for the preservation of the Balance of Power in Europe' (29 Feb. 1740).

36. Wyndham, Walpole and Pulteney, Cobbett, vol. xi, cols 217, 228–9, 241, 21 Nov. 1739; PRO SPF 36/21 f. 217: notes in Newcastle's hand of (?)

parliamentary speech; BL Add. MSS 27981: Perceval newsletter, 21 Mar. 1730; *Flying Post; or, the Post Master*, 2 Jan. 1718, 1 Aug. 1732; *London Journal*, 24 Apr. 1725; *Mist's Weekly Journal*, 12 Mar. 1726, 27 May, 3 June, 7 Oct. 1727; *Norwich Mercury*, 7 Mar. 1730, 30 Mar. 1734; *Fog's Weekly Journal*, 16 Jan. 1731; *Hyp-Doctor*, 19 Jan. 1731, 15 July 1735, 26 Apr. 1737; *Daily Courant*, 2 Apr., 11 July 1734; *Daily Gazetteer*, 12 May 1736; *Northampton Mercury*, 8 Oct. 1739; *The Craftsman*, 2 Aug. 1740; *Champion*, 27 Oct. 1741; anon., *The False Patriot: An Epistle to Mr. Pope* (1734) p. 6; Christian Cole (ed.), *Historical and Political Memoirs* (1735) p. x.

37. G. Niedhart, *Handel und Krieg in der Britischen Weltpolitik 1738–1763* (Munich, 1979); J. R. Jones, *Britain and the World* (1980).

38. Carteret, 'Our trade is our chief support', Cobbett, vol. XI, col. 19, 15 Nov. 1739; PRO SPF 9 4/129: Keene was instructed to show Spain 'how nearly anything concerns His Majesty, that affects the trade of his subjects' (Newcastle to Keene, 4 Nov. 1737).

39. PRO SPD 36/31, SPF 99/63: representation of the merchants and sugar refiners of Bristol to George II, 29 Apr. 1734, draft to Burges, envoy in Venice, 29 Apr. 1734, Burges to Newcastle, 4, 25 June (ns) 1734; PRO SPF 75/65, 82/59: Harrington to Titley, 1, 4, Oct. 1734, Harrington to Wych, 10 Jan. 1738.

40. Chewton: Waldegrave to Horace Walpole, 16 July (ns) 1728; PRO SPF 95/131, 92/34: Board of Trade to George II, 20 Nov. 1728, Allen, envoy in Turin, to Delafaye, 17 Feb. (ns) 1731.

41. D. K. Reading, *The Anglo-Russian Commercial Treaty of 1734* (New Haven, Conn., 1938).

42. N. C. Hunt, 'The Russian Company and the Government, 1730–42', *Oxford Slavonic Papers*, 7 (1957).

43. PRO SPF 94/119: Keene to Waldegrave, 18 Jan. (ns) 1734; Merseburg, 41: Bonet to Frederick William I, 5 Apr. (ns) 1718; PRO SPF 80/78, 80/86: Robinson to Harrington, 8 Aug. (ns) 1731, 16 Mar. (ns) 1732.

44. It was claimed that mercantile pressure was stronger in Britain than elsewhere: AN Paris AM B⁷ 304: D'Aubenton, French Consul-General in Spain, to Maurepas, French Naval Minister, 3 Nov. (ns) 1730. For vociferous pressure from the Hamburg merchants see: Dresden 2676: Le Coq to Augustus II, 13 Oct. (ns) 1727; and PRO SPF 75/65: Harrington to Titley, 11 Oct. 1734.

45. 'The Turkey merchant writes against the East-India company, the Woollen Manufacturer against the callicoes' (*Evening Journal*, 9 Dec. 1727). For contrary pressures over whether sugar could be sent direct from British colonies to foreign markets see *Northampton Mercury*, 4 June 1739.

46. SRO GD 135/141/6: Dodington, envoy in Spain, to Spain, 3, 5, Oct. (ns) 1716; PRO SPF 94/218, 89/35, 94/107, 75/55, 82/56: Cayley, Consul in Cadiz, to Keene, 22 June (ns) 1728, Tyrawly, envoy in Lisbon, to Newcastle, 25 Sept. (ns) 1728, Keene to Delafaye, 10 Jan. (ns) 1731, Titley to Tilson, 10 June (ns) 1730, Wych to Harrington, 10 Aug. (ns) 1735.

47. PRO SPF 84/345: Horace Walpole to Harrington, 18 July (ns) 1735.

48. RA 190/25: 'I see no appearance of our being able to do anything for

ourselves there without foreign force' (James III, the 'Pretender', to the Jacobite Duke of Ormonde, 3 Oct. (ns) 1736).

49. AE Paris, CP Ang. 346, sup. 7: Chammorel to Morville, French Foreign Minister, 22 Nov. (ns) 1723, Morville to Chammorel, 21 Dec. (ns) 1723.

50. This was no secret. Marburg, England 184: Sparre, Swedish envoy in London, to Frederick I of Sweden, 22 May (ns) 1722.

51. PRO SPD 36/23: Minutes of the Privy Council, 30 June 1731; BL Add. MSS 32772, 33073: Newcastle to Waldegrave 26 Mar. 1731, Newcastle to his wife, 2 July 1731.

52. RA 161/32, 162/100: James III to Daniel O'Brien, Jacobite agent in Paris, 28 Apr. (ns), 16 June (ns) 1733; AE Paris, CP Ang. 380, 381: Chavigny to Chauvelin, 23 Apr. (ns), 1, 17, July (ns) 1733.

53. Chewton: Delafaye to Waldegrave, 1 Apr. 1731; BL Add. MSS 32772: Newcastle to Waldegrave, 1 Apr. 1731. This view was shared by Spain: BL Add. MSS 32798: Waldegrave to Newcastle, 16 May (ns) 1738. RO Norwich, Bradfer–Lawrence: 'our dangers from France at all times, if we are not good friends with that Crown, are immediate, and at our door, especially as long as there is a Pretender' (Horace Walpole to Townshend, 1 July (ns) 1728).

54. James III thought he would receive no French support until Britain declared war, whilst British diplomats, such as Villettes at Turin, argued that he would receive no support because the French feared it would lead to a British declaration. RA 172/85, 179/56: James to O'Brien, 11 Aug. (ns) 1734, 27 Apr. (ns) 1735; PRO SPF 92/37: Villettes to Newcastle, 16 Jan. (ns) 1734.

55. HHStA, Vienna, England Noten 2: memoranda presented to Austrian government by Duke of Wharton, 23 Aug. (ns) 1725, Sir John Graham, 17 May (ns) 1726.

56. HHStA, Vienna, England Varia 8: O'Rourke, Jacobite envoy in Vienna, to Graham, 29 Oct. (ns) 1727. Fleury told Waldegrave that a Jacobite invasion would unite the nation round George II (Chewton: Waldegrave to Walpole, 3 Nov. (ns) 1736). Perceptive Jacobites rapidly became disillusioned about the prospect of foreign assistance (HHStA, Vienna, England Varia 8: O'Rourke to James III, 23 Oct. (ns) 1728).

57. J. Black, 'British Travellers in Europe in the Early Eighteenth Century', *Dalhousie Review*, 61 (1981–2) 655–67; J. Black, 'The Grand Tour and Savoy–Piedmont in the Eighteenth Century', *Studi Piemontesi*, 13 (1984); J. Black, 'France and the Grand Tour in the Early Eighteenth Century', *Francia*, 12 (1984).

58. *Universal Journal*, 13 June 1724; *Weekly Register*, 3 Apr. 1731; *Comedian or Philosophical Enquirer*, Aug. 1732.

59. BL Add. MSS 27734: Pelham to Earl of Essex, envoy at Turin, 21 July 1735; BL Add. MSS 23788: 'In England they talk no more of the affairs of Poland, than if there were no such place in the world', Weston to Robinson, 3 July 1733.

60. For details of the Folkestone fishermen, see RO Maidstone, Sackville of Knole MSS U269 C148/4: John Jordan to Sackville Bale, 3 Sept. 1733. RO Bedford L30/9/113/16: Yorke, 9 July 1747.

61. Argyle, Cobbett, vol. XI, col. 78, 15 Nov. 1739; CUL Add. MSS 6851, p. 123: Edward Harley, parliamentary notes.

62. AE Paris, CP Ang. 376, 380: Chavigny to Chauvelin, 3 Mar. (ns) 1732, 28 Apr. (ns) 1733.

63. PRO SPF 90/34: 'To hear some of them talk, England was in a flame from the Orkney to the Scilly Islands . . . they speak as they wish' (Dickens to Weston, 12 May (ns) 1733).

64. PRO SPF 107/1B: Gyllenborg, Swedish envoy in London, to Swedish minister Görtz, 23 Oct. (ns) 1716, 7 Jan. (ns) 1717; Chewton: Tilson to Waldegrave, 6 Jan. 1730, Horace Walpole to Waldegrave, 11 Feb. 1734.

65. BL Add. MSS 48982: Townshend to Poyntz, envoy in Paris, 3 Mar. 1728; PRO SPF 84/301: Townshend to Chesterfield, 9 July 1728; BL Add. MSS 32755: with reference to Gibraltar, Fleury told Pentenriedter, Austrian envoy in Paris, 'how impossible it was either for His Majesty or his ministry, considering the nature of the English constitution, to take the least step in opposition to the bent of the whole nation' (Horace Walpole, Poyntz and William Stanhope to Newcastle, 18 May (ns) 1728).

66. 'Our natural foes', *Freeholders Journal*, 11 July 1722; *The Craftsman*, 30 Aug. 1729; BL Add. MSS 22227: Peter Wentworth to Earl of Stratford, 1 July 1731.

67. Chewton: Horace Walpole to Waldegrave, 13 Mar. 1730.

68. M. Gordon, *The True Crisis*, p. 7; anon., *The Remembrancer: Caleb's Sensible Exhortation*, p. 4.

69. PRO SPF 90/22: 'it is inconceivable what odd impressions . . . Monsr. Shippen's last speech has made here' (Du Bourgay to Townshend, 29 July (ns) 1727); UL Hull DDHO 313: Grumbkow, Prussian minister, to Reichenbach, Prussian envoy in London, 7 Mar. (ns) 1730.

70. PRO SPF 80/71: Harrington to Robinson, 28 Jan. 1731.

71. Walpole and Horace Walpole, Cobbett, vol. IX, col. 222, 229, 25 Jan. 1734; Harwicke, Cobbett, vol. XI, cols 675–6, 18 Nov. 1740; *Daily Courant*, 13 July 1734.

72. Bodl., Rawl. 120: Zamboni, Saxon agent in London, to Manteuffel, Saxon minister, 29 Mar. (ns) 1729; PRO SPF 80/67: Waldegrave to Tilson, 15 Mar. (ns) 1730.

73. RA 93/29, 84/105; Graham to Hay, Jacobite Secretary of State, 27 Apr. (ns) 1726, Wharton to James Hamilton, July (ns) 1725; PRO SPF 80/69: Robinson to Harrington, 18 Nov. (ns) 1730; PRO SPF 78/190; Poyntz to Delafaye, 29 Jan. (ns) 1729.

74. PRO SPF 80/69: Harrington to Robinson, 4 Dec. 1730; BL Add. MSS 32753: expelling James III from Avignon before the 1728 session was regarded as essential.

75. AE Paris, CP Ang. 350, 369, 376: Chammorel to Morville, 30 Apr. (ns) 1725, Broglie to Chauvelin, 9 Feb. (ns) 1730, Chavigny to Chauvelin, 11 Feb. (ns) 1732; CUL, C(H) correspondence 1379: Palm, Austrian envoy in London, to the Emperor Charles VI; HHStA, Vienna, Fonseca 21: Pentenriedter to Fonseca, 22 Mar. (ns) 1727; Pulteney, HMC Egmont Diary, III 338, 11 Feb. 1729.

76. HMC, *Egmont Diary* III 338, 11 Feb. 1729.

77. BL Add. MSS 32687: Walpole to Newcastle, 3 July 1730.

78. For George II's concern about the parliamentary implications of foreign policy see George II to Townshend, n.d., in W. Coxe, *Memoirs of the Life and Administration of Sir Robert Walpole*, vol. II, p. 528.

79. C. Roberts, 'Party and Patronage in Late Stuart England', in S. Baxter (ed.), *England's Rise to Greatness* (1983) pp. 185–212.

80. Walpole, Cobbett, vol. IX, col. 472, 13 Mar. 1734.

81. BL Add. MSS 32687: Newcastle to Townshend, 30 June 1725; CUL, C(H) correspondence 1290: Sinzendorf to Palm, 23 Mar. (ns) 1726; HHStA, Vienna, Grosse Korrespondenz 94(b): Kinsky to Eugene, Austrian minister, 8 Feb. (ns) 1729.

82. Particular concern was aroused in late 1727 when George II sought advice from St Saphorin, former envoy in Vienna. See BL Add. MSS 48928: Horace Walpole to Tilson, 3, 21 Oct. (ns) 1727; HHStA, Vienna, Noten 2: St Saphorin to Sinzendorf, 11 Dec. (ns) 1733. George II used his conversations with British and foreign envoys to suggest and receive information. See Chewton, Marburg England 202: Thomas Pelham, envoy in Paris, to Waldegrave, 7 Jan. 1732; Diemar, Hesse–Cassel envoy in London, to William VIII of Hesse–Cassel, 20, 29 Nov. (ns) 1733.

83. William Stanhope in 1728 and Hyndford in 1744 were serious instances.

84. RO Norwich, Bradfer–Lawrence: Townshend to Horace Walpole, 31 July 1728.

85. BL Add. MSS 34465: Liston to the Foreign Secretary, Carmarthen, 16 Apr. (ns) 1787. Fleury excused his policies by reference to the force of public opinion, though he could not always be believed. Nancy, Archives de Meurthe-et-Moselle 3F87: Choiseul-Stainville, Lorraine envoy in Paris, to Francis III of Lorraine, 15 Oct. (ns) 1733; BL Add. MSS 32782: Waldegrave to Newcastle, 14 Oct. (ns) 1733.

7. WALPOLE, 'THE POET'S FOE' *J. A. Downie*

1. *The Beggar's Opera and other Eighteenth-Century Plays* (1974) pp. 114, 147, 145.

2. Swift's phrase: see P. Rogers (ed.) *Jonathan Swift: The Complete Poems* (1983) p. 466.

3. I. Kramnick, *Bolingbroke and his Circle* (1968) p. 17.

4. H. Williams (ed.), *The Correspondence of Jonathan Swift* (1963–5) vol. IV, p. 504.

5. B. McCrea, *Henry Fielding and the Politics of Mid-Eighteenth-Century England* (1981) pp. 15–16.

6. J. Butt (ed.), *The Poems of Alexander Pope* (1963) pp. 421, 423–4.

7. B. A. Goldgar, *Walpole and the Wits* (1977) p. 135.

8. Ibid., p. 20.

9. D. H. Stevens, *Party Politics and English Journalism 1702–1742* (1916) p. 114.

10. Williams (ed.), *Correspondence of Swift*, vol. III, p. 265.

11. Butt (ed.), *Poems of Pope*, p. 349.

12. Ibid., p. 317.

13. Ibid., pp. 749, 608.

14. R. Halsband, *Lord Hervey* (1973) pp. 67–8.

15. Ibid., pp. 96–7, 145–8, 167–8, 171.

16. Rogers (ed.), *Jonathan Swift: Poems*, p. 911.

17. Butt (ed.), *Poems of Pope*, p. 720.

18. Williams (ed.), *Correspondence of Swift*, vol. III, pp. 415, 421.

19. Rogers (ed.), *Jonathan Swift: Poems*, p. 447.

20. Ibid., p. 532.

21. L. Hanson, *Government and the Press 1695–1763* (1936) p. 111.

22. Butt (ed.), *Poems of Pope*, pp. 410, 380–1, 393–4.

23. L. Colley, *In Defiance of Oligarchy* (1982) p. 222.

24. *Grub Street Journal*, no. 86, 26 Aug. 1731; *The Craftsman*, no. 211, 5 Sept. 1730.

25. *DNB*; Hanson, *Government and the Press*, pp. 113–14.

26. Ralph, quoted ibid., pp. 112–13; CUL, C(H) MSS 2306: Arnall to Walpole, 10 Aug. 1734. I should like to thank the Marquess of Cholmondeley for permission to quote from the Cholmondeley (Houghton) MSS.

27. Stevens, *Party Politics and English Journalism*, p. 120; Hanson, *Government and the Press*, p. 113; T. Horne, 'Politics in a Corrupt Society: William Arnall's Defense of Robert Walpole', *JHI*, XLI (1980) 602.

28. CUL, C(H) MSS 1703, 1931, 2306: Arnall to Walpole, 26 Mar. 1730; 6 Dec. 1732; 10 Aug. 1734. Cf. J. H. Plumb, *Walpole* (1960) vol. II, p. 315.

29. CUL, C(H) MSS 2306: Arnall to Walpole, 10 Aug. 1734.

30. Williams (ed.), *Correspondence of Swift*, vol. III, pp. 131, 196, 219, 421.

31. E. P. Thompson, *Whigs and Hunters* (1977) p. 287.

32. For Pope and the Poet Laureateship, see the forthcoming work of Professor Roger Lund.

33. Williams (ed.), *Correspondence of Swift*, vol. III, pp. 260, 246, 267.

34. See Martin C. Battestin, 'Four New Fielding Attributions: His Earliest Satires of Walpole', *Studies in Bibliography*, XXXVI (1983) 69–109.

35. P. Rogers, *Henry Fielding* (1979) p. 54.

36. McCrea, *Henry Fielding and Politics*, p. 16; Rogers, *Fielding*, pp. 112–13.

37. Williams (ed.), *Correspondence of Swift*, vol. III, p. 378; IV, p. 100, 230, 303.

38. See Q. Skinner, 'The Principles and Practice of Opposition: the Case of Bolingbroke versus Walpole', in N. McKendrick (ed.), *Historical Perspectives* (1974) pp. 93–128.

39. See M. Schonhorn, 'Defoe, the Language of Politics, and the Past', *Studies in the Literary Imagination*, XV (1982) 75–83.

40. *State Tracts* (1706) vol. II, p. 565.

41. Williams (ed.), *Correspondence of Swift*, vol. IV, pp. 333–4.

42. Quoted by I. Kramnick, *Bolingbroke*, p. 137.

43. Quoted by P. Langford, *The Excise Crisis* (1975) p. 18.

44. J. G. A. Pocock, *Politics, Language and Time* (1972) p. 120.

45. Williams (ed.), *Correspondence of Swift*, vol. II, p. 372.

46. Ibid., vol. IV, p. 336.

47. H. Davis (ed.), *The Prose Writings of Jonathan Swift* (1939–75) vol. xi, pp. 201–2.

48. Quoted in W. A. Speck, *Stability and Strife* (1977) p. 224.

49. Butt (ed.), *Poems of Pope*, pp. 721, 763.

50. Speck, *Stability and Strife*, p. 225.

51. Davis (ed.), *Prose Writings of Swift*, vol. iii, p. 12.

52. Ibid., vol. x, p. 87.

53. P. Rogers (ed.), *The Eighteenth Century* (1978) pp. 37–9.

54. R. Sedgwick (ed.), *John, Lord Hervey, Some Materials towards Memoirs of the Reign of King George II* (1931) pp. 263, 260–1.

8. PRINT AND POLITICS IN THE AGE OF WALPOLE   *Michael Harris*

1. Cyprian Blagden, 'The Distribution of Almanacks in the Second Half of the Seventeenth Century', *Studies in Bibliography*, 11 (1958).

2. Raymond Astbury, 'The Renewal of the Licensing Act in 1693 and its Lapse in 1695', *Library*, 5th series, xxxiii (1978).

3. *Penny Post*, Tuesday, 19 July 1715.

4. *British Mercury*, Saturday, 12 Feb. 1715.

5. *Westminster Journal*, Saturday, 16 Aug. 1746.

6. The process of newspaper distribution in London is described in Michael Harris, 'The London Newspaper Press, 1725–1746', (London University, Ph.D. dissertation, 1973) pp. 40–6.

7. For an account of the Post Office development under Allen see H. Robinson, *The British Post Office* (Princeton, N.J., 1948), and K. Ellis, *The Post Office in the Eighteenth Century* (1958).

8. An analysis of this document appears in Michael Harris, 'Newspaper Distribution during Queen Anne's Reign', *Studies in the Book Trade* (Oxford, 1975).

9. *Craftsman*, Saturday, 30 Nov. 1728.

10. *CJ*, xxix (1761–4) p. 1000.

11. Modern studies of the development of the provincial book-trade have invariably stressed the importance of newspaper publication. See, for example, Ian Maxted, ' "4 rotten cornbags and some old books": the Impact of the Printed Word in Devon', in Robin Myers and Michael Harris (eds), *Sale and Distribution of Books from 1700* (Oxford, 1982), and Alan Sterenberg, 'The Spread of Printing in Suffolk in the Eighteenth Century', in Michael Crump and Michael Harris (eds), *Searching the Eighteenth Century* (1983).

12. G. A. Cranfield, *The Development of the Provincial Newspaper, 1700–1760* (Oxford, 1962) pp. 20–1.

13. Ibid, p. 204.

14. William Maitland, *The History and Survey of London*, 2 vols (1756) vol. 2, p. 735.

15. *The Case of the Coffee-Man of London and Westminster* (n.d. but c.1728) p. 15.

16. John Brewer, *Party Ideology and Popular Politics at the Accession of George III* (Cambridge, 1976) p. 7.

17. *Daily Gazetteer*, Monday, 4 July 1737; Black, 'Political Allusions in Fielding's Coffee-House Politician', *British Journal for Eighteenth-Century Studies* (forthcoming).

18. Michael Harris, 'The Management of the London Newspaper Press during the Eighteenth Century', *Publishing History*, IV (1978).

19. Linda J. Colley, 'The Loyal Brotherhood and the Cocoa Tree: the London Organisation of the Tory Party, 1727–1760', *HJ*, xx (1977).

20. The Cocoa Tree address is advertised in the third issue and cancelled in no. 16, *Craftsman*, Monday, 23 Jan. 1727.

21. BL Add. MSS 32689: writing from Lewes in Sussex Thomas Pelham, in a letter of 20 July 1734 to the Duke of Newcastle, emphasised the need for a coffee-house as a meeting point for political supporters.

22. Brewer, *Political Ideology*, pp. 157–8.

23. *The D'Anverian History of the Affairs of Europe, for the Remarkable Year 1731* (1732) p. 81.

24. The only attempt to cater specifically for a lower level audience was made in London by commercial entrepreneurs whose activities were checked in the 1740s by a combination of political and financial pressure.

25. Support for the revenue-raising interpretation appears in Alan Downie, 'The Growth of Government Tolerance of the Press to 1790', in Robin Myers and Michael Harris (eds), *Development of the English Book Trade, 1700–1899* (Oxford, 1981).

26. For a general assessment of the use of the law of libel see Lawrence Hanson, *Government and the Press 1695–1763* (Oxford, rprt 1967).

27. Harris 'London Newspapers', pp. 251–4.

28. J. A. Downie, *Robert Harley and the Press* (Cambridge, 1979).

29. Bertrand H. Goldgar, *Walpole and the Wits* (Lincoln, Nebr., 1976).

30. A series of letters from George Oswald to Walpole as Lord Orford in August and September 1742 are concerned with publication of unspecified items. CUL, C(H) MSS correspondence 3156–9.

31. *A Report from the Committee of Secrecy Appointed to Enquire into the Conduct of Robert Earl of Orford* (1742).

32. See Michael Harris, 'Journalism as a Profession or Trade in the Eighteenth Century', in Robin Myers and Michael Harris (eds), *Author/Publisher Relations during the Eighteenth and Nineteenth Centuries* (Oxford, 1983) pp. 51–2.

33. *London Evening Post*, Thursday, 3 June 1736.

34. CUL, C(H) MSS papers 75, 10/1, 10/2, 11, 12, 13. These items only represent a sample of the materials in pamphlet form distributed on behalf of the administration. Although published anonymously, the first pamphlet has been attributed to Arnall and the fourth and fifth to Horatio Walpole.

35. The Report of the Committee of Secrecy showed that in August 1739 Buckley received £786 17s. 6d., 'for printing and delivering several Pamphlets for his Majesty's Service', and this may have been connected with items (4) and (5).

36. Harris, 'London Newspapers', pp. 204–7.

37. The State Papers (Domestic) in the Public Record Office contain a number of examinations of witnesses in libel actions taken by Buckley, for example, PRO SPD 36/44, 87.

38. *Craftsman*, XI, p. 224. The text of the pamphlet was included as an appendix to a volume of the collected edition published in fourteen volumes in 1731 and 1737.

39. CUL, C(H) correspondence 1515: John Hill to Robert Walpole, 8 Mar. 1728.

40. Harris, 'London Newspapers', pp. 197–8. The number of copies distributed of individual issues of newspaper could fluctuate widely and a single account for Arnalls's *Free Briton* in 1731 showed a variation of between 1500 and 5000 copies (see Hanson, *Government and the Press*, frontispiece).

41. Harris, 'London Newspapers', p. 206.

42. CUL, C(H), MSS Papers 74, 72.

43. *Hyp-Doctor*, Tuesday, 15 Dec. 1730.

44. Linda Colley, *In Defence of Oligarchy: The Tory Party 1714–60* (Cambridge, 1982).

45. The best analysis of the political content of the London newspapers appears in Isaac Kramnick, *Bolingbroke and his Circle* (Cambridge, Mass., 1968).

46. A good selection of such items appears in Milton Perceval (ed.), *Political Ballads Illustrating the Administration of Sir Robert Walpole* (Oxford, 1916).

47. The ownership patterns of the commercial papers supporting the Opposition are complex and obscure as are the relationships between the politicians and such publications. For an attempt to sort out some of the issues see Harris, 'London Newspapers', pp. 188–222.

48. *D'Anverian History*, p. 5.

49. On account of the notorious 'Hague Letter'.

50. *Craftsman*, Saturday, 30 Oct. 1731.

51. Cranfield, *Provincial Newspaper*, pp. 158–9.

52. For example, *Fog's Weekly Journal*, Saturday, 27 Apr. 1734.

53. *Champion*, Thursday, 13 May 1741.

54. *Craftsman*, Saturday, 23 June 1733.

55. *Fog's Weekly Journal*, Saturday, 7 and 14 July 1733.

56. *Craftsman*, Saturday, 27 Apr. 1734.

57. Lists published by Henry Goreham and John Purser. *Daily Gazetteer*, Saturday, 23 June 1739. For publication of this material in the provincial press see Cranfield, *Provincial Newspaper*, p. 102.

58. *Craftsman*, Saturday, 25 July 1741. A notice of reprinting in pamphlet form appears in *Craftsman*, Saturday, 28 Nov. 1741. For an attack on this list see *Daily Gazetteer*, Thursday, 30 July 1741.

59. See also the long lists of names of Opposition supporters meeting at the Fountain Tavern in 1742, for example *London Evening Post*, Saturday, 6 Feb. 1742.

60. *Craftsman*, Saturday, 30 Dec. 1732.

61. For example, *Great Britain's Memorial* containing anti-Walpole instructions sent up between June 1740 and June 1742.

62. *Craftsman*, Saturday, 30 Dec. 1742.

63. In particular in the *London Evening Post* and *Daily Post*.

64. Colley, *In Defence of Oligarchy*, p. 80.

65. Colley, 'Loyal Brotherhood', p. 78, n. 7. Among many references to ministerial circulars in the Opposition press is one in *London Evening Post*, Saturday, 9 Feb. 1740.

66. *Craftsman*, Saturday, 29 Nov. 1729.

67. Advertisements in the *Daily Journal*, Tuesday, 19 Jan. 1731 and *Craftsman*, Saturday, 31 Oct. 1741.

68. *Champion*, Saturday, 23 June 1741.

69. *London Evening Post*, Thursday, 3 Jan. 1745.

70. For example, *Daily Gazetteer*, Thursday, 12 May 1737.

Notes on Contributors

JEREMY BLACK is a lecturer in the Durham University History Department. Graduating from Queens' College, Cambridge, with a starred first he did research at St John's College, Oxford, and held a Harmsworth Senior scholarship at Merton College, Oxford. His doctorate was on British foreign policy, 1727–31. He has contributed essays to various books and learned journals.

EVELINE CRUICKSHANKS worked for some years on the volumes of the *History of Parliament: The House of Commons 1715–54*, ed. R. Sedgwick (1970). She is editing *The House of Commons 1690–1715* in the same series at present. Since 1981 she has been Editor of *Parliamentary History*, a yearbook covering British parliamentary institutions from the Middle Ages to the present century. She published *Political Untouchables: The Tories and the '45* in 1979 and (as editor) *Ideology and Conspiracy: Aspects of Jacobitism 1689–1759* in 1982.

H. T. DICKINSON is Richard Lodge Professor of British History at the University of Edinburgh. A graduate of Durham University, he gained his doctorate at Newcastle University where he held the Earl Grey Fellowship from 1964 to 1966. He is the author of *Bolingbroke* (1970), *Walpole and the Whig Supremacy* (1973) and *Liberty and Property: Political Ideology in 18th-Century Britain* (1977); the editor of *The Correspondence of Sir James Clavering* (1967), *Politics and Literature in the Eighteenth Century* (1974) and *The Political Works of Thomas Spence* (1982); and a contributor of essays to various books and learned journals.

J. A. DOWNIE is Senior Lecturer in English, University of London, Goldsmiths' College. He was formerly Lecturer in English Literature at Leeds University (1977–8) and University of Wales Stott Fellow at Bangor (1975–7). He is a graduate of Newcastle University. He is co-editor of *The Scriblerians* and author of *Robert Harley and the Press: Propaganda and Public Opinion in the Age of Swift and Defoe* (1979) and *Jonathan Swift, Political Writer* (1984).

MICHAEL HARRIS is Lecturer in History at the University of London Extra-mural Department. He has written widely on the eighteenth-century London press and contributed essays and articles to a variety of bibliographical publications. He is joint-editor of a series of volumes on booktrade history and is currently working on an edition of Henry Fielding's early journalism and a general study of English newspapers.

DAVID HAYTON is Research Assistant on *The History of Parliament*. He is a graduate of Manchester University, and formerly a Research Fellow at Queen's University, Belfast. He is the author of a doctoral thesis on the government of Ireland in the early eighteenth century (Oxford, 1975) and of articles in the *Bulletin of the Institute of Historical Research, Irish Historical Studies* and other journals. He is co-editor (with Thomas Bartlett) of *Penal Era and Golden Age: Essays in Irish History 1690–1800* (Belfast, 1979) and (with Clyve Jones) of *A Register of Parliamentary Lists 1660–1761* (Leicester, 1979).

MICHAEL JUBB is Assistant Keeper at the Public Record Office. He was formerly a student at Jesus College, Cambridge, and Lecturer in History at Wolverhampton Polytechnic.

BRUCE P. LENMAN is Reader in Modern History in the University of St Andrews. He was formerly Lecturer in Imperial and Commonwealth History, University of Dundee, and British Academy Newberry Fellow in Chicago. His publications include *From Esk to Tweed* (1975), *An Economic History of Modern Scotland* (1977), *The Jacobite Risings in Britain 1689–1746* (1980) and *Integration, Enlightenment and Industrialisation: Scotland 1746–1832* (1981).

Index